The Praeger Handbook on Contemporary Issues in Native America

The Praeger Handbook on Contemporary Issues in Native America

Volume 1
Linguistic, Ethnic, and Economic Revival

Bruce E. Johansen

Foreword by Philip J. Deloria

NATIVE AMERICA: YESTERDAY AND TODAY
Bruce E. Johansen, Series Editor

Westport, Connecticut
London

Library of Congress Cataloging-in-Publication Data

Johansen, Bruce E. (Bruce Elliott), 1950-
   The Praeger handbook on contemporary issues in Native America / Bruce E. Johansen ;
foreword by Philip J. Deloria.
      p. cm. — (Native America : yesterday and today, ISSN 1552–8022)
   Includes bibliographical references and index.
   ISBN–13: 978–0–275–99138–8 (set : alk. paper)
   ISBN–13: 978–0–275–99139–5 (v. 1 : alk. paper)
   ISBN–13: 978–0–275–99140–1 (v. 2 : alk. paper)
   ISBN–10: 0–275–99138–5 (set : alk. paper)
   [etc.]
   1. Indians of North America—Social conditions.   2. Indians of North
America—Government relations.   3. Indians of North America—Politics
and government.   4. Self-determination, National—United States.   I. Title.
   E98.S67J65 2007
   973.04'97—dc22   2006100439

British Library Cataloguing in Publication Data is available.

Library of Congress Catalog Card Number: 2006100439

ISBN–10:   ISBN–13:
0–275–99138–5 (set)   978–0–275–99138–8 (set)
0–275–99139–3 (vol. 1)   978–0–275–99139–5 (vol. 1)
0–275–99140–7 (vol. 2)   978–0–275–99140–1 (vol. 2)
ISSN:1552–8022

First published in 2007

Praeger Publishers, 88 Post Road West, Westport, CT 06881
An imprint of Greenwood Publishing Group, Inc.
www.praeger.com

Printed in the United States of America

The paper used in this book complies with the
Permanent Paper Standard issued by the National
Information Standards Organization (Z39.48-1984).

10   9   8   7   6   5   4   3   2   1

Contents

Foreword

Casinos. And more casinos. And yet still more casinos.

I refer not to a building boom in American Indian gaming establishments but to the single-note theme sounded by most Americans when the subject is the state of contemporary Native America. "How come 'they' are 'allowed' to have casinos? Why do 'they' get such special treatment? How much 'Indian' do I have to be in order to get my share?" And so on. Such conversations happen on airplanes, on the sidelines of soccer games, at dinner gatherings, and in a hundred other venues—all settings that tend to foreclose the detailed discussion of issues and histories that would answer such questions. It is not easy to convince a casual questioner to explore topics such as the unique constitutional status of tribal entities, the political relation between state and federal governments, the long history of treaty-making, the shorter history of federal program development, the budget cuts of the Reagan era and the concretizing of sovereignty practices, legislation concerning gaming and the resulting regulatory apparatus, and the ways tribes determine their membership—all of which make up only a few of the necessary information points for the discussion of casinos that Americans claim to crave. In the end, one often simply observes that the situation is far more complicated than the questioner could ever imagine, a highly unsatisfactory response for all concerned, and one that actually fails to advance, even in a small way, the goal of educating non-Indians to the challenges and creativities characteristic of Indian country, past and present.

Bruce Johansen's *Handbook of Contemporary Issues in Native America* offers answers to that one-note question, but it goes far beyond. Johansen insists not only on the complexity of this single issue, for example, but of its place within the broader and more complicated panorama that is Native America today. Gaming, in his treatment, fits within the larger practices of cultural, economic, political, legal, linguistic, and even nutritional revival. Fitting these pieces together, Johansen shows Indian people engaged across a dauntingly broad front in a struggle for survival and autonomy. Like all broad fronts, a certain amount of unevenness haunts the struggle: A political success is qualified by a legal setback; an effort at rethinking food is crossed by the challenges of poverty and environmental change. And yet Johansen's treatments—informed by decades of personal and intellectual observation and experience—suggest that despite the challenges, along that broad front, Native American people and societies are indeed resurgent.

This book fits logically into Bruce Johansen's own journey as a writer and scholar and reveals him to be a gift-giver of the first order. What do I mean by that? Here is a favorite example: My son's high school civics teacher asks students for five influences on U.S. democracy. The supposedly right answers from the textbook are (in mildly simplified form): English common law (visible, for instance, in the Bill of Rights); natural law, as expressed by John Locke; classical republicanism, translated from ancient Rome by Jefferson and others; Montesquieu's concern with territorial expansion and the separation of powers; and (most vaguely) the general sense of religiosity found in early America.

"Are there only five?" I ask.

"Well, that's all that are on the test."

Grumbling about the mind-killing nature of contemporary education and yet smiling at the possibility of an important educational moment, I pull down from the shelf Bruce Johansen's and Donald Grinde's *Exemplar of Liberty: Native America and the Evolution of Democracy*. "Take a look at this," I tell him, "and go back and ask your teacher about the Iroquois Confederacy."

Exemplar of Liberty and Johansen's earlier sole-authored book *Forgotten Founders: Benjamin Franklin, the Iroquois, and the Rationale for the American Revolution* (which is on the shelf in my office rather than at home) stand as signal contributions to our understanding of the early republic. As if it were somehow outrageous to add one more element to the standard list of five European influences, however, white scholars of the Iroquois and conservative pundits viciously attacked these books following their publication. And here one is able to make clear the distinction between so-called scholarly contributions and the giving of gifts. Johansen's great gift was his willingness to stand and fight, sharpen his arguments, intensify his research, and push his assertions, all in the face of a withering assault from a number of quarters. If it no longer seems a particularly outrageous assertion that perhaps the Iroquois Confederacy offered both model and advice to Franklin and other founders (and it should not), we have Bruce Johansen (as well as Grinde and a number of their other comrades) to thank for that. If a sixth influence on U.S. democratic government— an aboriginal influence—has not yet made its way into high school civics textbooks, Johansen and others have nonetheless given us the tools to continue to question the master narrative. Alterations in that narrative require repeated challenges, but we can be confident that time, quite literally, will tell. Our entire national culture, in this sense, owes a debt of gratitude for this gift—and for the others that emerge from Johansen's substantial body of writings.

My father, Vine Deloria Jr., was a longtime supporter of Bruce Johansen and his work and wrote forewords to a number of Johansen's books. With these volumes, Professor Johansen returns the favor, offering an extensive and heartfelt dedication to my father. I feel fortunate—and honored—to be able to send my appreciation, and that of my family, caroming back again in his direction. For us, this dedication comes as yet one more gift from Bruce Johansen. For you, the reader, these volumes make up another kind of gift, for they offer the stories and the tools to think richly about the state of contemporary Native America. Here one can move beyond the single-note concerns surrounding public perceptions of Indian gaming into a complicated series of issues, treated with the complexity and insight they deserve. I imagine my father looking across from the other side, smiling with his own approval at yet one more educational moment, courtesy of Bruce Johansen.

Philip J. Deloria

Preface

Studying history, I can use my imagination to draw famous figures from the past into our time to comment on what has become of their life's work. I would, for example, like to walk with Jesus Christ down any one of our shopping malls in mid-December and ask his opinion on what mercantile capitalism made of his birthday and the old custom of gift-giving. I would, similarly, like the Prophet Muhammad's thoughts on an age in which some people who profess serious devotion to his ideas express their idea of religious nationalism by ramming loaded passenger aircraft into tall buildings.

The unifying theme of this two-volume set is Native American revival of Native American traditions. To juxtapose history in this case, I would call upon Gen. Richard Henry Pratt, the founder, roughly 130 years ago, of so-called American Indian industrial schools, by which he meant to "Kill the Indian and save the man." His phrase was an advertising slogan for the schools, not (in Pratt's view, at any rate) the genocidal confession some people in our time make of it. Pratt, arguing that American Indian traditions had no place in his modern world, thought he was doing young Indians a favor by disabusing them of their parents' lifeways: cut that hair, do not speak Native languages, and learn to take their places in the grand factory assembly line of Manifest Destiny's melting pot.

Pratt's thinking carried some heavy ethnocentric baggage, and he was hardly alone in his time, or afterward. Consider, for example, the so-called white man's burden borne by Winston Churchill. He stood up to Hitler's eugenics but also supported Britain's imperial mission:

> I do not admit ... that a great wrong has been done to the Red Indians of America, or the black people of Australia. I do not admit that a wrong has been done to these people by the fact that a stronger race,

or a higher race, or a more worldly-wise race, to put it that way, has come in and taken their place. (Wheatcroft, 2006, 92)

Visiting our time, Pratt might be amazed (and perhaps a bit distraught) at the degree to which his iron-clad assumptions have been turned on their heads. Many Native Americans today speak English, to be sure, but many also are relearning their own languages, considering traditional forms of justice, growing the foods of their great-grandparents, and (in Canada) demanding financial justice from the government that maintained a nationwide system of schools that followed Pratt's model. Native American influences on society at large are recognized and celebrated. Ways of life and technologies mesh as Pratt might never have foreseen. In our self-identified census, Native Americans are the fastest-growing group of people in the United States in the twenty-first century.

This two-volume set seeks to provide a guide to Native American revival in our time. It is not comprehensive; such an errand would require a small library. It is, instead, a collection of essays and stories, some of them quite personal, drawn from my 35 years growing up in a time of Native renewal.

MATTERS OF LANGUAGE

Language has meaning, although we often speak as a matter of assumption without forethought. Consciously or not, our words frame our beliefs. Some of these words justify the taking of a continent, but they are used so easily and so often that they roll off our tongues with very little forethought.

Observant readers will find some words generally absent from this work. Except in direct quotations, for example, I avoid using the word *settler,* as a generic term for peoples who arrived from afar (usually, but not always, from Europe) to occupy land that had been utilized, sometimes for many thousands of years, by Native peoples. I find the word connotatively loaded not for what it says but for what it implies. Left unspoken is an assumption that the Native peoples whom the so-called settlers replaced themselves had no established homelands and that, by the lights of Anglo-American real estate law (of eminent domain and highest and best use), the new residents were making better use of the land and its resources. In the law, as anyone who has owned property that has been subject to eminent domain realizes, such use makes replacement legally defensible.

In matter of historical fact, most Native nations had identifiable territorial limits, even if individuals often did not own real estate in the European fashion. Their land often was utilized as well (even if not generally with the same population density) as it was following usurpation by the so-called settlers.

I may use the national affiliation (British, say) of the new residents, or the word *immigrants.* If I am in a postcolonial mood and do not mind drawing some right-wing flak, I may use—even if I try to avoid—*invaders,* which places the connotative shoe on the other foot. The shoe often fits, however, and I use the term under those conditions.

The terms of occupation frame the immigrants' entire relationship with the land's first inhabitants. Most present-day controversies involving Native Americans have roots in questions of land and resource ownership and use. This is no less true today than during the Indian wars. (Vine Deloria Jr. asked during a speech in Omaha during 1993 if non-Indians had a right to live in North America, said, "If your ancestors are buried here, you have a right to the land.")

Another word that I try to avoid is *tribal* when it is used as a generic reference to Native Americans. My first objection to this word in such a context is that many other peoples worldwide have organized as tribes at various times in the past; some still do. More fundamentally, the use of this term freezes all Native American polities at a certain level of political organization: a small scale, by which assumption once again connotatively justifies replacement by the larger, state-level organs of non-Indian so-called civilization. Once again, Anglo-American real-estate law is being invoked, often without thinking. The most engrained assumptions are the ones that we invoke without forethought. Many Native polities were (and are) organized at the nation-state or confederacy level.

FURTHER READINGS

Wheatcroft, Geoffrey. "A Man So Various: The Misappropriated Winston Churchill." *Harper's,* May 2006: 86–94.

Acknowledgments

Appreciation, as always, is due my wife, Patricia E. Keiffer, whose wisdom often laces my writing. Hopefully, our children and grandchildren (Shannon, Samantha, and Madison) will enjoy a sustainable Earth long after we have passed on, having benefited from her selfless devotion. My mother, Hazel E. Johansen, gave me the work habits necessary for the endurance-contest aspects of book authorship.

Also, I owe thanks to the director of the University of Nebraska at Omaha (UNO) School of Communication, Jeremy Lipschultz, the deans of the College of Communication, Fine Arts, and Media, Bob Welk, and Gail F. Baker, as the administrative principals who maintain an atmosphere at UNO that nourishes scholarly research, reading, and writing. The staff of the UNO library, as always, has been crucial to this work as well. Praeger editor Hilary Claggett also played a crucial role in the birthing of this set. She suggested I write it; that's basic.

This two-volume set's unifying theme is Native American revival, or (as some have phrased it) the recovery of nationhood, following many decades of suffocating colonialism by the United States government so intense that it dictated most Native Americans' every personal and collective decision No one person was more responsible for Native America's revival and sense of recovering nationhood than Vine Deloria Jr., who passed away on November 13, 2005, as these books were being written. This set, therefore, is dedicated to him, in a humble, personal tribute to a person who did so very much to shape my own life (one among many thousands of others). University of Colorado professor Charles Wilkinson, an expert in American Indian law, called Deloria "probably the most influential American Indian of the past century" (Dahl, 2005). "He was also a wonderful human being, brilliant, bitingly funny and profoundly warm and compassionate, always willing to lend a hand or lift a spirit," Wilkinson added (Dahl, 2005).

University of Minnesota American Indian Studies Professor David Wilkins, who is Lumbee, wrote in *Indian Country Today* that Deloria "was never quite comfortable with the notion that he was, in fact, the principal champion of tribal nations since he wanted—no, demanded—that each Native nation express confidence in its own national identity, develop its own unique talents and together wield their collective sovereignty, that is, their dignity and integrity, in a way that enriches them and the nations around them as well" (Wilkins, 2005). Deloria, a Standing Rock Sioux, first became nationally known during 1969, following publication of his book *Custer Died for Your Sins*. Like no other single work, this book framed the modern Native American self-determination movement. Reacting to his own influence, Deloria tried as best he could to spread his intellectual wealth around. Thus, many lives were shaped by him. This sketch of Native American revival walks in Deloria's very large footsteps.

FURTHER READINGS

Dahl, Corey. "Indian Activist and Popular Author Dies; Vine Deloria Jr. was a Retired C.U. Professor." *Boulder* (Colorado) *Daily Camera,* November 15, 2005, n.p.

Wilkins, David. "Native Visionary Spoke for All Disadvantaged Americans." *Indian Country Today,* December 1, 2005. <http://www.indiancountry.com/content.cfm?id=1096412026>.

Introduction

*A*s the idea was formalized in academia as the Sapir-Whorf hypothesis, Gen. Richard Henry Pratt, founder of the Carlisle Indian Industrial School in 1879, understood implicitly that language is the vessel, the intellectual framework, of culture. He therefore set out to pull up Native cultures by their roots by preventing children (by force if necessary) from speaking the languages of their ancestors. (Edward Sapir was a student of the ethnologist Franz Boas, whose study of Native American languages during the late nineteenth century taught him how influential they could be in shaping cultures.)

How surprised General Pratt might be if he could return today to see Native American languages blossoming the length and breadth of North America. The many people who are now reclaiming Native American languages understand their vital role just as Pratt did: Nations, by their essence, have culture, and culture, of necessity, dies without language.

This survey of Native American revival begins in chapter 1, "Back from the (Nearly) Dead: Reviving Indigenous Languages across North America." At this late date, many Native languages are being rescued nearly from the grave. The people of the Cochiti Pueblo, for example, were moved to revitalize their language after they conducted a survey that disclosed that all of its fluent speakers were 35 years of age or older. The few speakers under age 35 were semiliterate, said Mary Eunice Romero, a Karas (Pueblo). Romero then asked, "What is going to happen to our language in 20 years when those [who are] 35 years old become 55? In 20 more years, when they're 75?" ("Critical Moment," 1998).

Experiences at the Cochiti Pueblo mirror a trend across Turtle Island (North America). Native American languages, many of which have been verging on extinction, have enjoyed a revival in recent years largely due to many Native American nations' adoption of immersion programs, which teach a language as the major part of reservation school curricula. A century after boarding schools sought to wipe it out, study of Native languages in North America is thriving.

Native American nations also can not be rebuilt without financial infrastructure. Thus, Native Americans during the 1990s began to explore a key aspect of the Bureau of Indian Affairs' colonial system: Individual Indian Monies, bank accounts kept by the government that, in (often untested) theory, were to be used to hold proceeds from use of Native-owned lands. Beginning in the late 1880s, the federal government had established itself as Indian Country's bank. A century later, the supposed beneficiaries of this trust began to discover just how badly the government had bungled this self-appointed task. Chapter 2, "Where Has All the Money Gone?" explores what has become the lifework of Blackfeet accountant Eloise Cobell. During the 1980s, Cobell began to ask what had become of royalty payments owed Native Americans through Individual Indian Monies accounts operated, in theory, by the Bureau of Indian Affairs (BIA) and the Treasury Department. The result was an inquiry into a financial scandal that startled professional bankers that by the year 2000 had become the largest class-action suit ever filed against the United States government.

The trust accounts range in size from 35 cents to $1 million for individuals. Among Native bands and nations, the largest single account is the roughly $400 million set aside for the Sioux settlement of the Black Hills land claim, which has not been paid because the Sioux have not agreed to accept it. The Navajo Nation has an account worth more than $23 million. More than 300 Native American governments (with 2,965 accounts) and 300,000 Native American individuals who have trust accounts with the United States also have been wondering lately what has become of their money. It has been cold comfort to many of them who have learned that the BIA, their legal trustee, very possibly has no clue.

Cobell's efforts are one part of a much broader Native American effort to recover from pervasive poverty and reassert Native American economic independence. Chapter 3, "Economic Revival: Up from the Bottom on the Reservation," begins with a survey of contemporary reservation economic conditions and is a corrective for anyone who thinks that modern-day reservation gambling has made all Native Americans rich. Aside from some of the poorest counties in the United States, Native peoples also occupy some of Canada's most desolate real estate, as characterized by the village of Pikangikum, which has one of the world's highest per capita suicide rates. Alcoholism is still a plague in the cities as well as on rural reservations. Readers will become acquainted in this chapter with the hamlet of Whiteclay, Nebraska, where the major business is selling beer and other alcoholic beverages to Indians of the neighboring Pine Ridge Indian Reservation, where such sales are illegal.

Is gambling an answer to poverty—the new buffalo, as some Native Americans have called it? The largest Native American casino to date has been the Pequots' Foxwoods, near Ledyard, Connecticut. In other places, such as the New York Oneidas' lands in upstate New York, gambling has provided an enriched upper class the means to hire police to force antigambling traditionalists from their homes.

Among the Mohawks at Akwesasne, people have died over the issue. Akwesasne's position on the United States-Canada border also has made smuggling of cigarettes, liquor, other drugs, weapons, and human beings a major industry.

Amid the poverty illustrated by U.S. census statistics by the turn of the millennium were some signs of hope. Some reservation economies are booming with small businesses. One example (described in "Where Has All the Money Gone") is the Blackfeet of Browning, Montana, where Eloise Cobell is one of several college-educated Native people who have returned home with skills and energy that have energized reservation towns. Another is the Akwesasne Mohawk Reservation in upstate New York on the Canada-United States border near Massena, New York. The main highway there is flush with truck stops, smoke shops, restaurants, and gift shops selling merchandise that gets a tax break on the reservation, which is unique to the Iroquois. The local newspaper, *Indian Time,* also is flush with advertising. The next U.S. census may portray at least parts of Indian Country as working its way up from the bottom.

Chapter 4, "High-Stakes Genealogy: When Is a Pequot Not a Pequot?" describes efforts by Jeff Benedict, author of *Without Reservation* (2000), who purports to expose the builders of the world's largest casino (Foxwoods) as faux Pequots. As a salesman of ethnic chauvinism, Benedict has got something going here. Pandering to various racial prejudices is probably doing his bank balance no harm. *Without Reservation,* for a time, was rated in the top 100 of Amazon.com's sales rankings (among roughly 2 million listed titles). This chapter examines problems related to determining identity strictly in a multiethnic world as well as the big money behind such definitions. Arguing that the Pequots who started Foxwoods actually may be white—or is it black?—broaches a sticky historical swamp in which no one, strictly speaking, is purely anything. The first patriot to die in the American Revolution, for example, was half black, and half Native American. And Frederick Douglass, the famed black abolitionist? His mother, a slave, was probably partially Native American.

Members of identifiable nations exercise some degree of self-identity—an image of themselves not strictly defined by outsiders. To attain a measure of self-definition, Native Americans since the beginning of the modern-day self-determination movement during the 1960s have protested widespread caricatures, most notably as sports mascots and denigrating place-names, such as *squaw.* Chapter 5, "Names and Games: The Controversy Regarding 'Indian' Sports Mascots and Place-Names," casts a historical net over present-day efforts to challenge many of these names. "The pace is really picking up," said Cyd Crue, president of the Illinois chapter of the National Coalition on Racism in Sports and the Media, regarding the campaign against Indian sports mascots. "We're seeing more educators around the country, in middle schools and high schools and at universities, concerned about the racial climate in schools, ... dropping these symbols" (Badwin, 2000). Since the early 1970s, at least 1,250 of the nation's 3,000 elementary schools, high schools, and colleges with American Indian nicknames and mascots have dropped them, according to Suzan Shown Harjo, president of Washington, DC's Morningstar Institute.

A singular moment in the history of the Native American sports mascot controversy occurred during February 2002, when an intramural basketball team at the University of Northern Colorado composed of Native American, Latino, and European American students collectively decided to change its name from Native Pride to The Fighting Whites. The new name was a purposeful parody of North America's many Native American mascots, most notably nearby Eaton High School's Fighting Reds. It was the first time in popular memory that a multiethnic sports team had decided to adopt a European American stereotype as a mascot. A dozen college students on an intramural basketball team suddenly found themselves playing in the stereotypical big leagues, with the likes of the Washington Redskins, the Atlanta Braves, and the Cleveland Indians.

During the 1990s, Native American nationhood was being expressed in a large number of sovereignty summits around the United States. At one of them, during late spring 1995 in Washington, DC, I heard the Onondaga leader Oren Lyons reduce the elements of nationality to the basics. A people is sovereign, he said, when members of the group decide to behave in a sovereign manner. A collection of reinforcing individual actions thus defines the whole, and in Native America, during our time, we have seen such efforts in language, culture, finances, economies, and legal systems. History is full of examples, of course; no single guiding hand instructed the peoples in 13 British colonies that they were ready for independence. Teaching in Poland during 2005, I heard stories of many people who had decided, during the 1980s, that Soviet colonialism had to die. Native Americans, in our time, have set this course.

FURTHER READINGS

Badwin, Don. "Opposition to Indian Mascots Mounts." Associated Press, November 6, 2000.
"The Critical Moment: Funding the Perpetuation of Native Languages." Transcript of Proceedings, Lannan Foundation. Santa Fe, NM, January 26–28, 1998.

DEDICATION

On the Passing of Vine Deloria Jr.

Political and intellectual rhetoric in Native America is usually egalitarian. Most Native tradition shies away from the elevation of kings, princes, and popes. No one worthy of such a title would claim it. The passing of Vine Deloria Jr. on November 13, 2005, however, brought forth superlatives. If Native America had a pope—of course, it does not—it would have been Deloria. The grief witnessed upon his passing may be compared to Poland's grief upon the passing of Pope John Paul II, which I witnessed as a lecturer at Lublin Catholic University, where John Paul, as Karol Wojtyla, taught for nearly a quarter-century before he was called to Rome.

University of Colorado Professor Charles Wilkinson, an expert in American Indian law, called Deloria "probably the most influential American Indian of the past century" (Dahl, 2005). "He was also a wonderful human being, brilliant, bitingly funny and profoundly warm and compassionate, always willing to lend a hand or lift a spirit," Wilkinson added (Dahl, 2005).

Deloria died following complications of surgery for a ruptured abdominal aortic aneurysm at Exempla Lutheran Medical Center in Wheat Ridge, Colorado, according to his son Philip, a history professor at the University of Michigan and a noted author in his own right (Williams, 2005). Before the aneurysm surgery complications, Deloria had struggled with recovery problems from colon cancer surgery more than a month earlier.

For many days and weeks after his passing, the news rippled through Deloria's vast extended family in the United States and around the world, by e-mail and personal contact, hand to hand, ear to ear, to "all our relations," in a Native American sense. Even the rocks on which we walk sent their condolences, so it was said. I heard many Native people say that he lives—in his words and in our memories—and that we all go to the other side eventually. Many who knew

Deloria drew comfort from the belief that he will be in the other world when they pass over.

University of Minnesota American Indian Studies Professor David Wilkins, who is Lumbee, wrote in *Indian Country Today* that Deloria "was never quite comfortable with the notion that he was, in fact, the principal champion of tribal nations since he wanted—no, demanded—that each Native nation express confidence in its own national identity, develop its own unique talents and together wield their collective sovereignty, that is, their dignity and integrity, in a way that enriches them and the nations around them as well" (Wilkins, 2005). Reacting to his own influence, Deloria tried as best he could to spread his intellectual wealth around.

"Above all," wrote Wilkins, Deloria "fought tirelessly for human, not just indigenous, freedom and for ecological respect and common-sense approaches to heal the environment's many wounds. Deloria believed that America's national soul would never be cleansed until justice had been fully achieved by indigenous nations, blacks, Latinos, Asian-Americans, women, impoverished whites, any disempowered groups, and especially young people" (Wilkins, 2005).

The passing of Deloria was deeply personal around Indian Country because his network of friends and acquaintances was so large. Deloria's early books called me to a life of writing and advocacy with and about Native Americans before the Wounded Knee occupation in 1973. Later, in the early 1980s, after my initial work linking the Iroquois to the founding of democracy had been rejected by about fifty trade and academic publishers, Deloria suggested I send it to Gambit, a small Massachusetts publisher run as a retirement hobby by Lovell Thompson, formerly of Houghton-Mifflin. Thompson had declined one of Deloria's books, but Deloria liked Thompson's erudite rejection letter.

All along the way, Vine provided support and incisive words, advice, healing Indian humor, and prefaces for some of my books, as recently as *Enduring Legacies* in 2004. I am only *one* person who stood on Vine's shoulders. The number of people inspired by him is uncounted—do not try to estimate a number. I once told a colleague, University of Nebraska at Omaha religion professor Dale Stover, that I could no longer ask Vine for help; he had given me so much, and I had nothing to give back that he would ever need. "Have you realized," Stover replied, "that your work is his reward?"

A SIGNIFICANT VOICE

Deloria, a Standing Rock Sioux, first became nationally known during the late 1960s, following publication of his book *Custer Died for Your Sins*. Deloria also rose to national prominence as a spokesman for Native self-determination movements, becoming a widely respected professor, author, and social critic in several fields, including law, religion, and political science, as well as Native American studies. He was one of the best-known founders of Native American studies as a field of scholarly inquiry in the late twentieth century.

By the late 1990s, Deloria was described by Roger Dunsmore in the *Handbook of Native American Literature* as:

> The most significant voice in this generation regarding the presentation and analysis of contemporary Indian affairs, their history, present shape, and meaning.... No other voice, Indian or white, has as full a command of the overall data of Indian history or affairs, and no other voice has the moral force, the honesty, to admit mistakes and to redress them, or the edge to bite through the layers of soft tissue, through the stereotypes, myths, and outright lies, to the bone ... marrow of Indian affairs. (Dunsmore, 1996, 411)

"The great indigenous visionary, philosopher, author and activist Vine Deloria, Jr. passed over to join his ancestors today, November 13, 2005," said a statement from the Colorado American Indian Movement (2005). "Our thoughts and prayers go to his wife, Barbara, to his children [Philip, Daniel, and Jeanne] and his other relatives [a brother, a sister, and seven grandchildren]. The passing of Vine creates a huge intellectual and analytical void in the native and non-native worlds.... It is safe to say that without the example provided by the writing and the thinking of Vine Deloria, Jr., there likely would have been no American Indian Movement, [and] there would be no international indigenous peoples' movement as it exists today" (Colorado American Indian Movement, 2005).

"He had the courage and the vision," the statement continued, "to challenge the dominating society at its core. He was unapologetic in confronting the racism of United States law and policy, and he was prophetic in challenging young indigenous activists to hone their strategies. He was our elder statesman and mentor.... For many of us, Vine was a contemporary Crazy Horse" (Colorado American Indian Movement, 2005). A public memorial for Deloria was held on November 18 at the Mount Vernon Event Center, Golden, Colorado, west of Denver, as a scholarship fund was initiated in his name.

An obituary in *The New York Times* recalled that "While his *Custer* book, with its incendiary title, was categorized at the time as an angry young man's anthem, Mr. Deloria's real weapon, critics and admirers said, was his scathing, sardonic humor, which he was able to use on both sides of the Indian-white divide. He once called the Battle of the Little Bighorn, where Lt. Col. George Armstrong Custer and the Seventh Cavalry were defeated by a combined force of Sioux and Northern Cheyenne in 1876 in the Montana territory, 'a sensitivity-training session'" (Johnson, 2005). "'We have brought the white man a long way in 500 years,'" Deloria wrote in a *New York Times* op-ed article during 1976. "'From a childish search for mythical cities of gold and fountains of youth to the simple recognition that lands are essential for human existence'" (Johnson, 2005).

In person, Deloria was known for his sharp onstage wit. Addressing 500 students at Boise State University on February 28, 1998, he jested about nineteenth-century pseudoscientific assumptions that Europeans were the most intelligent race because they had the largest skulls. That was before "the discovery that Apaches had something like 100 cc's more cranial capacity than Harvard professors," Deloria joked (Etlinger, 1998).

A RENOWNED FAMILY

Deloria was part of a renowned Sioux family that had a significant impact on U.S. life and letters long before his birth. As a member of the faculty at Columbia University beginning in 1929, Ella Cara Deloria (1889–1971) gained notice as an outstanding anthropologist and linguist. She wrote *Dakota Texts* (1932), which is bilingual in Dakota and English, and *Speaking of Indians* (1944), a description of Native life before the arrival of Europeans.

Ella Cara Deloria was born in Wakpala, South Dakota; her Dakota name, Anbpetu Wastewin meant "Good Woman of the Day." She attended Oberlin College and Columbia University, from which she graduated in 1915 with a bachelor's degree. After working as a schoolteacher and an employee of the YMCA (in Indian education), Ella Cara Deloria returned to Columbia as a professor of anthropology, where she worked with Franz Boas on two major studies of Dakota language. She also authored a novel, *Waterlily,* during the 1940s. It was published in 1988, 17 years after her death. In her later years, Ella Cara Deloria continued to write, speak, and work with reservation mission schools as she added to her Dakota grammar, fearing that it might join other Native languages in historical oblivion before she could finish. She died of pneumonia at the Tripp Nursing Home, Vermillion, South Dakota, on February 12, 1971.

One of the first American Indians to become an Episcopal minister, Philip Deloria (Yankton Sioux, 1854–1931) is one of about ninety historical figures whose statues surround *Christ in Majesty* at the Washington, DC, National Episcopal Cathedral. As the longtime rector of St. Elizabeth Mission on the Standing Rock Reservation, Deloria was said to have converted thousands of Sioux to Christianity. He was the father of Ella Cara Deloria and grandfather of Vine Deloria Jr.

Vine Deloria Jr. was born in Martin, South Dakota, on the Pine Ridge Indian Reservation, on March 26, 1933. Educated in reservation schools during his early years, Deloria served in the Marine Corps between 1954 and 1956, before he earned a bachelor of science degree at Iowa State University (granted in 1958) and a bachelor of divinity at the Lutheran School of Theology in 1963. After that, Deloria served as executive director of the National Congress of American Indians. At the same time, Deloria was a member of the U.S. Board of Inquiry on Hunger and Malnutrition. Serving on this board, he found black children in the Mississippi Delta eating red clay to deal with hunger (Dunsmore, 1996, 412).

Early in his life as an activist, Deloria channeled his intellectual efforts into legal studies, entering the University of Colorado Law School in 1967. He took up legal studies expressly to advance Native rights. Deloria completed study for his law degree in 1970 and later, in 1990, joined the University of Colorado's faculty, teaching until his retirement in 2000. While teaching at the University of Colorado, Deloria's home department was history, but he also was affiliated with ethnic studies, religious studies, political science, and the law school, one indication of academic respect he commanded across many disciplines.

COMMON THEMES OF DELORIA'S WRITTEN WORK

Deloria's written work (including twenty books and more than a hundred major articles) stress a common theme, according to Dunsmore: that sin is a major element in U.S. history and that "the sinners are those who have stolen and desecrated the land" (Dunsmore, 1996, 413). On this subject, Deloria quoted Curley, a Crow chief, who is best known to history as one of the scouts for George Armstrong Custer at the Battle of the Little Bighorn in 1876. Curley is not known as a great Native American philosopher, but his words, spoken in 1912, evoke memories of Tecumseh, Sea'th'l, and Black Elk:

> The soil you see is not ordinary soil—it is the dust of the blood, the flesh and the bones of our ancestors. We fought and bled and died to keep other Indians from taking it, and we fought and bled and died helping the whites. You will have to dig down through the surface before you find nature's earth, as the upper portion is Crow.... The land is my blood and my dead; it is consecrated; and I do not want to give up any portion of it. (Dunsmore, 1996, 415)

As early as the 1950s, Deloria was engaging in acute criticism of the Indian Claims Commission, arguing that it was a device by which to avoid treaty issues, not address them. He pointed out that laws and regulations announced as so-called help to Indians often perpetuated colonialism. Historically, Deloria argued, the rights of Native Americans have trailed those of other social groups in the United States. For example, slavery of Alaska natives was not outlawed until 1886, two decades after the Civil War.

Deloria has won a broad audience among a wide variety of people for asserting, with a sharp wit, contradictions in the general cant of contemporary U.S. life. For example, in *We Talk, You Listen* (1970), Deloria recalled a conversation with a non-Indian who asked him, "What did you [Native Americans] *do* with the land when you had it?" Deloria said he did not understand the ecological irony of such a question until later, when he discovered that the Cuyahoga River running through Cleveland was flammable. So many combustible pollutants were dumped into the river that the inhabitants had to take special precautions during summer to avoid accidentally setting it on fire. "After reviewing the argument of my non-Indian friend," wrote Deloria, "I decided that he was probably correct. Whites had made better use of the land. How many Indians could have thought of creating a flammable river?" (Deloria, 1970, 9)

Deloria defined the differences between European and Native American views of the land this way:

> The tribal-communal way of life, devoid of economic competition, views land as the most vital part of man's existence. It is THEIRS. It supports them, tells them

where they live, and defines HOW they live. Land does not have the simple sentimentality of purple mountains majesty…. Rather it provides a center of the universe for the group that lives on it. As such, the people who hold land in this way always have a home to go to. Their identity is secure. They live with it and do not abstract themselves from it and live off it. (Deloria, 1970, 175)

Jousting with missionaries, Deloria in his many speeches sometimes condensed half a millennium of history in North America into one sentence: When the missionaries came, they had the book (the Bible), and Indians had the land. Now, Deloria said, they have the land, and Indians have the book.

Deloria called for adaptation of Native American land ethics to a general non-Indian society that finds itself faced with the environmental damage pursuant to 2,000 years' experience exercising the biblical commandment to multiply and subdue the earth.

American society could save itself by listening to tribal people. While this would take a radical reorientation of concepts and values, it would be well worth the effort. The land-use philosophy of Indians is so utterly simple that it seems stupid to repeat it: man must live with other forms of life on the land and not destroy it. The implications of this philosophy are very far-reaching for the contemporary political and economic system. Reorientation would mean that public interest, indeed the interest in the survival of humanity as a species, must take precedent over special economic interests. Now the laugh is ours. After four centuries of gleeful rape, the white man stands a mere generation away from extinguishing life on this planet. (Deloria, 1970, 189, 195)

Throughout his life, Deloria continued to write a number of books and articles that often took issue with Eurocentric interpretations of reality. His early books, such as *Custer Died for Your Sins* (1969), *We Talk, You Listen* (1970), and *Of Utmost Good Faith* (1971), continued to spread to new, younger audiences. In all of his works, Deloria has asserted Native American rights of occupancy to the land. Under international law, according to Deloria, Native American nations possess an equitable title of occupancy over lands upon which they lived, "and this occupancy was not to be disturbed except by voluntary and lawful sales of lands to the European country claiming the legal title to the area in question" (Lyons, 1992, 283).

Deloria's writings also compare the metaphysics of Native American and European points of view, especially in legal and religious matters. In *God Is Red* (1973), Deloria argued that American Indian spiritual traditions, far from being out-of-date, are more congruent with the needs of the modern world than is Christianity, which Deloria said fostered imperialism and disregard for the planet's ecology (Johnson, 2005). In *God Is Red,* he also contrasts Native American religion's melding of life with a concept of sacred place to the artificial of Old World doctrines.

Deloria compared the nature of sacredness in each perceptual realm. His discussion of sacredness also examines ecological themes in Native American religions. Deloria also compares the ways in which each culture perceives reality: Europeans seeing time as linear and history as a progressive sequence of events; most Native cultures as neither of these. Christianity usually portrays God as a humanlike being, often meddlesome and vengeful, whereas many Native religions place supreme authority in a great mystery symbolizing the life forces of nature.

To Deloria, the great mystery of Sioux theology becomes an ecological metaphor, as he explains ways in which Native American theologies weave a concept of cycles into life, reinforcing reverence for the land and the remains of ancestors buried in it, contrasted to Europeans' ability to move from place to place without regard for location, until the reality of the American land and its often unwritten history begin to absorb them. Deloria's beliefs are not his alone; they may be read in a historical context provided by Luther Standing Bear, Chief Sea'th'l, and other Native American leaders.

Deloria points out that many Native Americans and non-Indians have trouble communicating because, even today, their perceptual realms are different.

> The fundamental factor that keeps Indians and non-Indians from communicating is that they are speaking about two entirely different perceptions of the world. Growing up on an Indian reservation makes one acutely aware of the mysteries of the universe. Medicine men practicing their ancient ceremonies perform feats that amaze and puzzle the rational mind. The sense of contentment enjoyed by older Indians in the face of a lifetime's experience of betrayal, humiliation and paternalism stuns the outside observer. It often appears that Indians are immune to the values which foreign institutions have forced them to confront. Their minds remain fixed on other realities. (Deloria, 1979, vii)

Ernest Cassirer, who is cited approvingly by Deloria, wrote that for Native American peoples, "Nature becomes one great society, the society of life. Man is not endowed with an outstanding rank in this society. He is part of it, but he is in no respect higher than any other member" (Cassirer, 1944, 83). Commented Deloria, "All species, all forms of life, have equal status before the presence of the universal power to which they are subject. The religious requirement for all life-forms is thus harmony, and this requirement holds for every species, ours included" (Deloria, 1979, 153–54).

Deloria's work often provides a trenchant critique of progress and civilization, two connotatively loaded words that have propelled the expansion of European lifeways around the earth, two words that are usually invested by Europeandescended thinkers with connotations of uncontested goodness, or— if not goodness—at least of inevitability.

> In recent years, we have come to understand what progress is. It is the total replacement of nature by an artificial technology. Progress is the absolute destruction of the real world in favor of a technology that creates a comfortable way of life for a few fortunately situated people. Within our lifetime the difference between the Indian use of land and the white use of land will become crystal clear. The Indian lived with his land. *The white destroyed his* land. He *destroyed the planet earth.* (Hughes, 1983, 136; emphasis in original)

Entering his late sixties by the year 2000, Deloria often walked with a cane. When people asked him about it, he was prone to say he had "been bitten by a rabid Republican and got a staph infection" (Wilitz, 1997). Complaining about the left-leaning nature of the professoriat, Vincent Carroll, editorial page editor of Denver's *Rocky Mountain News,* pointed out with a straight face that Deloria was the only registered Republican among faculty of the History Department at the University of Colorado at Boulder. Carroll seemed to have missed what most people who knew Deloria knew as obvious: He had signed up as a Republican as a joke.

A consummate observer of academic rituals, Deloria was a critic of research methods often employed by scholars investigating Native American peoples:

> My original complaint against researchers is that they seem to derive all the benefits and bear no responsibility for the ways in which their findings are used. In making this accusation, I said that scholars should be required to put something back into the Indian community, preferably some form of financial support, so the community can do some things it wants to do. (Deloria, 1991, 457)

Throughout his life, Deloria was a sharp critic of many theories that often had assumed the status of revealed truth among many non-Indian academics. One of these is the assumption that Native Americans populated the Western Hemisphere solely by crossing a land bridge from Siberia, the Bering Strait theory.

> Scientists, and I use the word as loosely as possible, are committed to the view that Indians migrated to this country over an imaginary Bering Straits bridge, which comes and goes at the convenience of the scholar requiring it to complete his or her theory. Initially, at least, Indians are [said to be] homogenous. But there are also eight major language families within the Western Hemisphere, indicating to some scholars that if Indians followed the trend that can be identified in other continents, then the migration went from east to west; tourists along the Bering straits were going *to* Asia, not migrating *from* it. (Deloria, 1996))

Although some scholars debate whether Native Americans really had a religious ethic that viewed the earth as mother, contemporary Native American religious and intellectual leaders continue to use the image with a frequency that evokes the rhetoric of Tecumseh and Black Elk. Deloria, who is arguably the father of the late twentieth century's intellectual renaissance in Native America, has been arguing ecological views of history for more than three decades with a rising sense of urgency as environmental crises intensify around the world. The stakes, in Deloria's analysis, include the future of humanity (as well as other animals) as viable species on an increasingly sullied earth.

"It will take a continuing protest from an increasingly large chorus," wrote Deloria, "to reprogram the psychology of American society so that we will not irreversibly destroy the land we live on" (Deloria, 1992, 2). His sense of urgency at the speed of environmental deterioration during the last years of the twentieth century was palatable: "Only a radical reversal of our attitudes toward nature can help us," he said (Deloria, 1992, 2). "Nor do I look forward to paying the penalties that Mother Earth must now levy against us in order for Her to survive" (Deloria, 1992, 3). He continued:

> It remains for us now to learn once again that we are part of nature, not a transcendent species with no responsibilities to the natural world. As we face the twenty-first century, the next decade will be the testing ground for this proposition. We may well become one of the few species in this vast universe that has permanently ruined our home. (Deloria, 1992, 3)

REMEMBERING DELORIA

Inside the Mount Vernon Event Center in Golden, Colorado, Deloria was remembered during the late afternoon of November 18, 2005, by a standing-room-only crowd as an activist who, with biting satire and wit, provided intellectual muscle for the Native American civil rights revolution that began in the late 1960s, propelling Native peoples away from cradle-to-grave government supervision into a new era of self-determination and active pursuit of sovereignty and exercise of treaty-defined economic rights.

Deloria was eulogized not only as an American activist but also as a more general figure who challenged mainstream religious assumptions as well as the industrial state's relationship with the earth. Doug George-Kanentiio, Mohawk activist and close friend of Deloria, recalled his "laser-light ability to zero in on the contradictions, deceptions, and lies which defined so-called 'western civilization'" (George-Kanentiio, 2005, 2).

Floyd Westerman and Joanne Shennandoah sang, after which George Tinker gave a blessing. A slide show provided glimpses of Deloria and his family. He was buried in Golden, Colorado, in the Mount Vernon Cemetery. According to an account provided by Heidi McCann, who attended the service, Philip Deloria said that, in the Lakota way, those who cross over stay here for four days, that he (Vine) visited with everyone he met (McCann, 2005).

Deloria was remembered as a family man and a lover of country music who treasured a note from Gene Audrey, dogs, professional football, and old movies, who fondly recalled his days as a Marine. The program handed out at the service called him "always a warrior, who fought the good fight until the very end [who is] even now exploring the spirit world that captivated his intellect during the course of his life" ("Celebration of the Life," 2005).

At the memorial service, Norbert Hill, a close friend of Deloria's, noted that with his passing "the training wheels had been taken off." It was now time, said Hill, for each of us to continue the struggle that Deloria had led for so long, relying now on our own individual and collective knowledge and talents. It is unquestionably true that over the last four decades we in Indian Country were overly dependent on Deloria's penetrating knowledge; his exquisite wit; his cunning and hugely effective political, legal, and cultural strategies; and his delicious and biting humor (Wilkins, 2005).

The same day that Deloria was remembered and put to rest, Vincent Carroll, editorial page editor of the *Rocky Mountain News,* still seemed to be seething over Deloria's playful response to his relentless effort to portray the University of Colorado faculty as a hotbed of political liberalism. In a column on the newspaper's editorial page, Carroll coldly recalled Deloria as "wacky" (Carroll, 2005). Carroll condemned Deloria as antiscientific and for maintaining, in *Red Earth, White Lies* (1995), that American Indians "existed here 'at the beginning,' probably as contemporaries of dinosaurs, and this bizarre claim only hints at his contempt for much science" (Carroll, 2005).

The dinosaur quip is Carroll's invention, a gigantic stretch of Deloria's argument in the book. No humans existed *anywhere* for millions of years after the era of the dinosaurs, and Deloria knew that. One can only imagine the letter to the editor Deloria might have written had he been able to reply to Carroll.

Deloria's son Philip did reply:

Vine Deloria Jr.… was open to any number of ideas that might be called "wacky." He was willing to step outside the boundaries of acceptable knowledge…. Of course, this isn't the first time the *News* has felt compelled to make light of his intellectual openness and curiosity. Who could forget the complaint a couple of years ago that the Center of the American West's Wallace Stegner Award was being given, not to a legitimate figure of some import, but to a "crank"?

It might interest Mr. Carroll to know that the current thought regarding the peopling of the Americas is trending away from the simplicities of the Bering Straits theory—which, as you know, my father vehemently criticized—to a far more nuanced account, one open to multiple possibilities of multiple migrations. What looked wacky 10 years ago might well look quite plausible 10 years from now. Vine Deloria Jr. took seriously the possibility of an American Indian creationism, a position not so far removed from similar debates unfolding today. I trust that the *News* will be as zealous in patrolling the power and status of "science" when the subject is Christian creationism cloaked as "intelligent design." To do otherwise would be intellectually dishonest, if not also casually racist…. Perhaps Carroll might have waited a day? It seems unworthy of the *News*—and egregiously so—to offer such a nasty little comment on the day when Indian people from around the country were arriving *en masse* to grieve his loss and to celebrate his life. Is this the paper's general practice when a complicated thinker and public figure passes on? It seems to me ill-mannered and indecent.(Deloria, 2005)

Beating Indian drums, and demanding a meeting with editors (which was not forthcoming), the Colorado American Indian Movement (AIM) picketed the *Rocky Mountain News* the Monday after Deloria was buried. AIM's spokesman, Glenn Morris, said that Carroll had slurred a man who was "the equivalent of Thurgood Marshall, Frederick Douglass and Martin Luther King rolled into one in the eyes of the Indian world" ("AIM Fire," 2005).

The pickets at "the Rocky" recalled that little seemed to have changed since 1863, when the paper described the Ute people as "a dissolute, vagabondish, brutal and ungrateful race" that "ought to be wiped from the face of the earth" ("AIM Fire," 2005). The protesters also demanded that *Rocky Mountain News* issue an apology (which also was not forthcoming) "for its role in inciting and celebrating the Sand Creek Massacre," an 1864 assault on a peaceful Cheyenne camp in which at least 163 men women and children were murdered and mutilated ("AIM Fire," 2005).

Carroll later apologized by e-mail to Philip Deloria and then complained that he had not known Vine Deloria was being buried the day he published his derogatory column. For a man who postured as an expert news authority and who calls his own opinion column "On Point," it was a rather lame excuse. The date of Deloria's service and burial in a suburb of Denver hardly had been a state secret.

Although editors at the *Rocky Mountain News* recalled Vine Deloria Jr. as a "crank" and a "wacko," *Indian Country Today's* editors described the affection for him that poured from Native America at the same time:

> We remember the beloved teacher for his generosity of spirit. As a professor, Deloria mentored and touched many people across all ethnic and religious persuasions while always managing to teach and guide the work of scores of Native graduate students and young activists, many of whom went on to gain success and prominence on their own. He wrote prefaces and introductions and recommendations by the dozens in careful assessments of the work at hand, but was always ready to add his considerable gravity to the work of newer hands. He would not tolerate fuzzy thinking, however, and could and would hold his students to task.... In every generation, to paraphrase the late Creek Medicine Man Phillip Deere, there is one who hits the click-stone just right, and sparks the fire. In his generation, Vine Deloria Jr. sparked the intellectual fire of political, legal, historical and spiritual illumination. He lighted the path to the fountainhead of knowledge, which points the way ahead. ("In Memoriam," 2005)

FURTHER READING

"AIM Fire: The American Indian Movement Targets the Rocky." *Denver Westword,* December 15, 2005, n.p. (in Lexis).

Carroll, Vincent. "On Point: Vine Deloria's Other Side." *Rocky Mountain News,* November 18, 2005, n.p.

Cassirer, Ernest. *An Essay on Man.* New Haven, CT: Yale University Press, 1944.

"Celebration of the Life of Vine Deloria, Jr., A" Program distributed at public memorial service, Mount Vernon Event Center, Golden, CO, November 18, 2005.

Colorado American Indian Movement. "In Honor of Vine Deloria, Jr. (1933–2005)." Statement. November 14, 2005.

Dahl, Corey. "Indian Activist and Popular Author Dies; Vine Deloria Jr. Was a Retired C.U. Professor." *Boulder* (Colorado) *Daily Camera,* November 15, 2005, n.p.

Deloria, Philip J. "Deloria Reveled in Thinking Outside the Box." Letter. *Rocky Mountain News,* November 23, 2005, n.p.

Deloria, Vine, Jr. "Commentary: Research, Redskins, and Reality." *American Indian Quarterly* 15, no. 4 (Fall 1991): 457–68.

Deloria, Vine, Jr. *Custer Died for Your Sins: An Indian Manifesto.* Norman: University of Oklahoma Press, [1969]1988.

Deloria, Vine, Jr. E-mail to Bruce E. Johansen, May 15, 1996.

Deloria, Vine, Jr. *God Is Red: A Native View of Religion.* 2nd ed. Golden, CO: North American Press/Fulcrum, 1992.

Deloria, Vine, Jr. *The Metaphysics of Modern Existence.* San Francisco: Harper and Row, 1979.

Deloria, Vine, Jr. *Of Utmost Good Faith.* San Francisco: Straight Arrow Books, 1971.

Deloria, Vine, Jr. *Red Earth, White Lies: Native Americans and the Myth of Scientific Fact.* New York: Scribner, 1995.

Deloria, Vine, Jr. *We Talk, You Listen: New Tribes, New Turf.* New York: Macmillan, 1970.

Dunsmore, Roger. "Vine Deloria, Jr." *Handbook of Native American Literature.* Ed. Andrew Wiget. New York: Garland, 1996. 411–15.

Etlinger, Charles. "Indian Scholar Blows Holes in Theories: Deloria Says Lazy Scientists Adjust Facts to Fit Ideas." *Idaho Statesman,* February 28, 1998: 1-B.

George-Kanentiio, Doug. "Deloria as I Knew Him." *Indian Time* 23, no. 46 (November 17, 2005): 2–3.

Hughes, J. Donald. *American Indian Ecology.* El Paso: University of Texas Press, 1983.

"In Memoriam: Vine Deloria Jr." *Indian Country Today.* November 17, 2005. <http://www.indiancountry.com/content.cfm?id=1096411939>.

Johnson, Kirk. "Vine Deloria Jr., Champion of Indian Rights, Dies at 72." *The New York Times,* November 15, 2005. <http://www.nytimes.com/2005/11/15/national/15deloria.html

Lyons, Oren, John Mohawk, Vine Deloria Jr., Laurence Hauptman, Howard Berman, Donald A. Grinde Jr., Curtis Berkey, and Robert Venables. *Exiled in the Land of the Free: Democracy, Indian Nations, and the Constitution.* Santa Fe, NM: Clear Light, 1992.

McCann, Heidi. Personal communication with the author. November 19, 2005.

Wilitz, Teresa. "An Anniversary Celebration: Native American Author Exults in Gadfly Role at Newberry Conference." *Chicago Tribune,* September 15, 1997: Tempo 1.

Wilkins, David. "Native Visionary Spoke for All Disadvantaged Americans." *Indian Country Today.* December 1, 2005. <http://www.indiancountry.com/content.cfm?id=1096412026>.

Williams, Matt. "Renowned Native American Scholar Dies." *Colorado Daily,* November 14, 2005. <http://www.coloradodaily.com/articles/2005/11/14/news/c_u_and_boulder/news2.txt>.

Volume 1
Linguistic, Ethnic,
and Economic Revival

CHAPTER 1

⁓

Back from the (Nearly) Dead: Reviving Indigenous Languages across North America

Roughly 1,200 languages were spoken in North and South America in 1491, in perhaps 180 linguistic families; 86 languages in 5 to 15 families were spoken in the area now called California, making it comparable to all of Europe, where people speak languages in only 4 families (Mann, 2005, 164). Juxtaposing language diversity with assertions that Native Americans have been resident in the Western Hemisphere only about 10,000 years, Charles C. Mann asks how so many languages could have evolved in so short a time.

This is a good question, and hardly a new one. Thomas Jefferson, who was a student of America's indigenous languages, asked the same question before 1800. Jefferson collected information on Native American languages all his adult life; after his second term as president ended in 1809, he was ready to write about it. His source material was being shipped from the White House to Monticello when thieves set upon the boat carrying them on the Potomac River. Unhappy that they found only paper, the thieves threw Jefferson's priceless notes, which were worth no money, into the river.

Roughly 360,000 people within today's United States speak an indigenous language. A list of speakers by language has been compiled and is available (Estes, 1999). According to this list, the most widely diffused language by far is Navajo, with nearly 150,000 speakers. After that, Western Ojibwa (35,000) and Dakota (20,000) are most widely spoken.

This list is subject to interpretation, however. For example, "Mohawk" does not appear on the list, although the author of this book knows several speakers of that language personally. Mohawk immersion classes are offered at Kanatsiohareke, a Mohawk traditionals' settlement near Fonda, New York. An article in *Indian Time,* a newspaper at Akwesasne, has said that about 5,000 Mohawks speak their language in some measure, compared to 12 Tuscarora, 50 Seneca, 60 Cayuga, 14 Onondaga, and 160 Oneida (Graef, 2005). A Mohawk Immersion Program conducted by the Ahkwesahsne Mohawk Board of Education has developed to the point at which it occupies two rooms: one outfitted as a classroom, the other as a living room. By 2005, the program was planning "to have weekly guest speakers in various professions, [such as] firefighting, police service, [and] construction work, from individuals who are fluent in Mohawk." The maintenance and custodial staff at Tsi Snaihne School, where the classes are held, speak fluent Mohawk, "and their casual use of the language around the students could greatly benefit them" (Burns, September 1, 2005). Shannon Burns, writing in Akwesasne's *Indian Time,* described a Mohawk-immersion class for six- to nine-year-olds who "conversed with one another in their traditional language, discussing anything from who was going to sing the next song to how much money they had for snack time" (Burns, September 1, 2005).

The teaching of Mohawk has, in fact, developed quite a bit. The Akwesasne Freedom School conducts a Mohawk language-immersion curriculum that includes recitation of the Thanksgiving Address in Mohawk as a centerpiece of the introduction and study of the language there. In nearby public schools with a large proportion of Mohawk students, the Thanksgiving Address also has been recited in both English and Mohawk. At one point in 2005, the address was banned at Salmon River High School (near the reservation) as a prayer (violating the separation of church and state, so school officials alleged). This ban provoked protests by several hundred Mohawk students. (For more information on the revival of Mohawk, see the section "Revival of Mohawk and Oneida.")

Immersion, today's preferred method of teaching Native American languages, can start very early in life. The Flathead Reservation in western Montana operates Nkwusm, a Salish immersion school for preschoolers at Arlee in a former bowling alley that also houses a casino. More than thirty years ago. Loddie Ayaprun pioneered a bilingual Yup'ik immersion kindergarten program in Bethel, Alaska, for tundra villages across the Yukon-Kuskokwim Delta. Today, the school, still the only one of its kind, bears her name. More than half the children in the area now speak the language ("In the Language," 2004; Barton, 2004).

Some immersion programs have a large geographic reach. Kenneth Funmaker of the Ho-chunk nation (Winnebago), for example, has taken part in a program that draws students from a reservation that is spread, in pieces, across 14 counties, about 200 miles from one end to the other. The program, with 20 to 32 teachers at any given time, also provides immersion language education in some urban areas with large numbers of Ho-chunk people, including Chicago; Minneapolis and St. Paul, Minnesota; and Madison, Wisconsin.

LANGUAGE AS THE BASIS OF SOVEREIGNTY

Why teach language? Richard Littlebear, who is Cheyenne, said that "language is the basis of sovereignty" (Reyhner, Cantoni, St. Clair, and Yazzie, 1999, 1–2) as well as the vessel of culture. During the nineteenth century, said Littlebear, the

United States showed its respect for Native American languages' essential role in culture by trying to eliminate them. "We have all those attributes that comprise sovereign nations: a governance structure, law and order, jurisprudence, a literature, a land base, spiritual and sacred practice, and that one attribute that holds all of these ... together: our languages. So once our languages disappear, each one of these attributes begins to fall apart until they are all gone" (Reyhner et al., 1999, 2). Littlebear said that, for the Cheyenne, the transition to a written language occurred about a century ago. As more and more communication took place in English, "Those in my generation who speak the Cheyenne language are quite possibly the last generation able to joke in our own language" (Reyhner et al., 1999, 1–2).

The prestige of a language and the self-esteem of its speakers may play a pivotal role in its revitalization. Navajo, for instance, was in steep decline until the 1940s, when the language, once deemed worthless by many Anglo-Americans, was used by the Navajo code talkers to confuse the Germans and Japanese during World War II. With Navajo's validity as a real, complex, and useful language suddenly nationally acknowledged, its usage increased, and today this language is spoken widely (Redish, 2001). Today, for example, bilingual calendars are printed in Navajo and English. On November 20, 2005, the Oakland Raiders–Denver Broncos National Football League game was broadcast in Navajo on KTNN, a 50,000-watt AM station owned and operated by the Navajo Nation.

WHAT IS LOST WITH LOSS OF A LANGUAGE

Many immersion programs were initiated after parents became concerned about (in the words of author Joshua Fishman) "What you lose when you lose your language." Wrote Fishman:

> The most important relationship between language and culture ... is that most of the culture is expressed in the language. Take language away from the culture and you take away its greetings, its curses, its praises, its laws, its literature, its songs, riddles, proverbs, and prayers. The culture could not be expressed and handled in any other way. You are losing all those things that essentially are the way of life, the way of thought, the way of valuing the land upon which you live and the human reality that you're talking about. ("Critical Moment," 1998)

Fishman, a pioneer in the revitalization of indigenous languages worldwide, has provided a theoretical structure for the revivals that are being carried out on reservations. His works, and others inspired by what he has written (Assembly of First Nations, 1990; Cantoni, 1996; Fishman, 1991, 1996), often are cited at conferences at which revival of indigenous languages are a major subject.

Today, about 190 indigenous languages survive, but a great many of them are in imminent danger of being lost. Michael Krauss, former president of the Society for the Study of Indigenous Languages, has written that only 20 of 175 surviving Native American languages in the United States still are being learned by children as a first language from their parents (Krauss, 1992, 6).

Many immersion programs started after middle-aged or elderly members of Native nations discovered that the use of their languages had become restricted to a few elders and would vanish as collective cultural knowledge upon their deaths. This knowledge has provided motivation in case after case for efforts to teach Native languages to young people. Littlebear said that families must retrieve their rightful position as the first teachers of native languages. "They must talk our languages every day, everywhere, with anyone," he said (Johansen, 2000, 57).

Darryl Kipp, codirector of the Piegen Institute, a language-immersion program on Montana's Blackfeet Reservation, estimated that without programs to teach young people Native languages, 70 percent of those spoken today in North America will die with the next few generations of elders. As on many other reservations, the Blackfeet Confederacy (totaling about 40,000 people) started language immersion as a response to the failure of education provided them by outside governments and agencies: "Out of the 17,000 that belong to my band, less than 1 percent have a college education. Sixty-five percent of the students in our schools never finish the tenth grade," said Kipp ("Critical Moment," 1998).

He continued:

> These are damming statistics about a Western form of education that fails to educate us. The promise that we would give up our language, move forth as English-speaking people and become successful in the world, has not come true. This may never become present unless we use our Native language. When it is reintroduced to a child, this can be used as a very powerful force and source of healing. When we look at the beautiful, happy faces of the children re-immersed in their language, we begin to realize again that Native Americans have potential and possibilities. ("Critical Moment," 1998)

Kipp said that language is too often taken for granted, like the rugged Rocky Mountains with which the Blackfeet live. "Many a day we get up and forget they are even there," said Kipp. "In America, we tend to treat language as a strictly political issue. We never talk about the aesthetics, beauty, or many attributes that come through a diversity of languages." When he is asked why the Blackfeet want to preserve their language, Kipp is tempted to answer "Why do we wish to breathe air?" or "Why do we wish to continue walking on this earth?" ("Critical Moment," 1998). Language-immersion instruction on Kipp's reserve is now provided to 500 children a year. "We have a goal," said Piegen cofounder Dorothy Still Smoking, "that ... 100 per cent of our Blackfeet children leaving Head Start will have proficient Blackfeet speaking skills" (Johansen, 2000, 57).

Kipp was one of several speakers at the Santa Fe conference who urged that Native languages be conceived as living, evolving communities of speech: "We look at Native languages as part of the future. We cannot relegate them to the dusty bins of history of the artifact shelf of a museum, but as a living presence with ourselves" ("Critical Moment," 1998). Kauanoe Kamana, a leader in Hawaiian language revitalization, said, "We are really aggressive, especially in the area of Hawaiian word development. If a language is to be living, it has to change and move. You cannot have a language that is stuck in another century" (Johansen, 2000, 58).

Kipp committed himself to a revival of his Native language after discovering that the last elder speakers of it might take the language to the grave with them. Kipp came to the language after having been an English professor and a writer.

> The first time I understood our language was in peril was in 1985, when we did a research project. We went to homes in our reserve and asked people if they spoke the language and what they did that reflected our tribalism. We found that almost all the speakers in our community were over the age of 50, and that there were no children, teenagers, 30- or 40-year-olds who could speak our language. It didn't take a mathematician or prophet to determine how long our language would last. (Johansen, 2000, 58)

After that study, a group of Blackfeet, including Kipp, spent five years developing ways to teach the language. They encountered some opposition from Blackfeet who asserted that knowledge of the language was of little practical use. One woman asked him, "Can you make soup of your language?" Kipp replied, "I struggled and had a hard time with that one. While I can't necessarily make soup, we can make healthy children, and healthy children can make all kinds of soups" ("Critical Moment," 1998).

Among the Comanche, a language-immersion program has been started that utilizes master speakers who teach entire families (who then use the language at home) at once. Several Pueblo communities, including Cochiti, Acoma, and Laguna, maintain immersion programs that take place in a ceremonial context. Hawaiian Native people have established immersion programs that span several islands. "If our language dies, if our culture dies," Kipp said, "We die as a people to the world.... We cannot let that happen" ("Critical Moment," 1998).

Commented Ernestine Hayes, an assistant professor of English at the University of Alaska Southeast and a member of the Wolf House of the Kaagwaantaan clan:

> Language does not only express a thought, it contributes to formation of that thought. Measurement of time is a clear example of this principle. In many indigenous cultures, time is fluid and divided into relatively unstructured components. In European-based cultures, however, time is divided into countable sections, and when the natural reality cannot be dismissed, adjustments such as leap year are made as though they are a reasonable step in a rational process. As far as concepts of time are concerned, members of indigenous cultures traditionally rise in the morning, eat when they feel hunger, and go to bed when they feel the need for sleep. On the other hand, members of minute-counting cultures traditionally rise at the hour the alarm is set to go off, eat at noon and at six o'clock, and go to bed after the 11 P.M. news. This seemingly superficial lifestyle inconsistency expresses a difference in perception that begins when children are learning to talk and are taught the words for time. (Hayes, 2005)

USING LANGUAGE TO RECOVER CULTURE

Language immersion sometimes is taught as part of broader culture reclamation. For example, during July 2005, the Arapahos' Wind River College hosted a three-day immersion-language camp for adults that taught language as well as elements of religion and culture. "We teach on the protocol of the religion, the history of the tribe, wellness and health the way it used to be compared to now," said Eugene Ridgely, bilingual education coordinator for the college. "We get into traditional games, then some social dancing" (Dillon, 2005).

Many of the participants pick up only a few words of Arapaho at the camp, but they also buy English-Arapaho dictionaries and at-home tutorials. The camp also spurs demand for language classes offered at the college and other cultural-renewal activities on the reservation. The idea is to preserve culture as well as language. "If we had retained the language like we should have, the family structure would still be strong," said Zona Moss, Ridgely's secretary at the college. "It lies within the language, within the culture." Ardeline Spotted Elk, a great-grandmother who has spent her life on the reservation, spent the three days teaching about kinship, or *neito'eino'*, traditions in the tribe.

At the camp, *Jackson Hole Star-Tribune* staff writer Jenni Dillon described how:

> Two lines of women sit facing each other, hidden from the afternoon sun under a tent canopy behind the Wind River Tribal College. The hands of four of the women swing back and forth in time with beating drums, fists closed. Each woman hides a small stick on one of her hands. It is up to a player from the opposing team to guess where the sticks are hidden, earning points for her team in a traditional Arapaho hand game called *koxouhtiit*. About 100 yards away, under another canopy, Arapaho adults step in a circle as drums echo off the stone of the old mission building nearby. They are learning traditional social dances, or *nii'eihii ho'eii*. (Dillon, 2005)

The recovery of culture among the Arapahos at Wind River also addresses decay of family structures among assimilated families. Some children are being raised by their grandparents because of drug and alcohol abuse by parents. Residents of the reservation say alcoholism remains a chronic problem, and methamphetamine use has been rising. Brian and Margo Williams, a couple raising seven children, described family members, friends, and acquaintances who have become addicted to the drug, abandoning their children or stealing from friends and neighbors to support their habits. "Meth around here is getting crazy," Margo said. Brian's uncle and aunt, Darrell and Billy Hanway, are raising their three-year-old granddaughter, whose father was killed while impaired in a driving accident. They also have a one-month-old grandchild who was born in a treatment facility due to his mother's drug addiction (Dillon, 2005).

NATIVE LANGUAGE AS AN AID TO LEARNING ENGLISH

Bill Wilson of the Punana Leo school said that the word *immersion* does not entirely cover the activities of these new language schools. "We are not talking just about immersion. We are talking about going to school in a Native language, if you're a Native speaker or not. In Hawaii, we have one community that has all Native speakers" (Johansen, 2000, 59).

Wilson said that children who are immersed in their Native languages also tend to do well at learning English when it is introduced. "One of our immersion children won the state English-language award. He'd only had one hour of English a day starting in the fifth grade." Learning English is not difficult for immersion students, said Wilson, because they are submerged in it as soon as they leave school. At school, instruction is half in Hawaiian and half in English. Students in immersion school "reach parity with non-immersion students in reading comprehension, vocabulary, and grammatical knowledge," said Wilson. "They have not lost anything, and they have gained a language" (Johansen, 2000, 59). Hawaiian immersion teachers told a U.S. Senate hearing in 2003 that their students have an 85 percent acceptance rate at colleges and universities (Wittmeyer, 2003).

A PLETHORA OF CONFERENCES

Language revival has spawned many conferences, of which the following is a sampling:

Second Annual Sahaptian Conference, sponsored by the Northwest Indian Language Institute and Heritage University, Toppenish, Washington, February 24–26, 2006.

Georgetown University Round Table on Languages and Linguistics 2006 Endangered and Minority Languages and Language Varieties: Defining, Documenting, and Developing, Washington, DC., March 3–5, 2006.

2006 Yuman Family Language Summit, Yuma, Arizona, March 10–12, 2006.

Seventh Biennial Language Is Life Conference for California Indian Languages, Marin Headlands Institute, Sausalito, California, March 24–26, 2006.

Conference on Endangered Languages and Cultures of Native America, University of Utah, Salt Lake City, Utah, March 31–April 2, 2006.

12th Annual Anishinaabemowin Teg Language Conference, Sault Ste. Marie, Michigan, March 30–April 2, 2006.

Third Oxford-Kobe Linguistics Seminar on "The Linguistics of Endangered Languages," Kobe, Japan, April 2–5, 2006.

Global Convention on Language Issues and Bilingual Education, Singapore, April 8–9, 2006.

American Indian Education Conference, Full Circle: Embracing Our Traditions and Values in Education, Fresno, California, April 13–15, 2006.

Giving the Gift of Language II: A Symposia and Teacher Training Workshop for Native Language Instruction and Acquisition, Missoula, Montana, April 24–27, 2006.

Indigenous Issues and Voices in Educational Research and Assessment (RACE 2006), Tempe, Arizona, April 27–29, 2006.

Celebrating the Circles of Knowledge: Mind, Body, Spirit, and Emotions of Research, Aboriginal Education Research Forum, Winnipeg, Manitoba, May 31–June 2, 2006.

2006 Stabilizing Indigenous Languages Conference, Buffalo, New York, May 18–21, 2006.

A Symposium of the 52nd International Congress of Americanists: The Languages of Central America Caribbean Coast: Articulating Society, Culture in the Present, Past and Future, Seville, Spain, July 17–21, 2006.

2007 Conference of the International Society for Language Studies, Honolulu, Hawaii, April 2–4, 2007.

The "Breath of Life" conference, held annually at the University of California–Berkeley, brings together many people to speak languages once thought to be dead or dying. At UC Berkeley, a companion conference, "Stabilizing Indigenous Languages," drew several hundred indigenous people and linguists from around the country and the world to learn how to rescue their own endangered languages.

A newspaper account in the *Contra Costa Times* described Bill Combs speaking his first words of Wintun:

> In front of hundreds of indigenous people and linguists from around the world, California Indian Bill Combs held a sheet of paper in front of him Friday and nervously spoke the lost language of his ancestors. While his cousin Norma Yeager translated, he read the Wintun words for frog, deer and other animals, complete with the glottal stops, or deep-throated clicking sounds, that he had practiced all week. The 34-year-old man wearing a T-shirt and shorts finished his presentation by looking up at the audience gathered in Pauley Ballroom and telling them in Wintun what he had recently learned to do after being denied the opportunity all his life. "I am speaking my language." (Chang, 2004)

The "Breath of Life" conference helped about fifty California Indians learn to read, write, and speak their languages. Many of these languages had been regarded as dead, retrieved in pieces through the university's archive of language recordings. Some of the participants have found recordings of grandparents and other family members speaking their languages decades ago with aid of UC Berkeley anthropologists (Chang, 2004).

Mamie Elsie Powell, a 72-year-old resident of the Grindstone Indian Rancheria in Glenn County, said she grew up without speaking Nomelaki, her native tongue, although she remembered hearing her father and other relatives speak it while growing up. Her father, who died at age 101 in 1987, was aware of the importance of his language and made hours of recordings of himself speaking it. "I am one of the few people around who remembers what my language sounds like," Powell said. "I have my father's tapes" (Chang, 2004).

Darlene Franco of the Native Californian Action Network said that her grandmother and grandfather were the last in her family to use Native language as a living tool in their daily lives.

The language started breaking down in my mother's generation. She didn't speak English until she was eight years old, and was forced to go to boarding school where the language was beaten out of her. She was far away from home. As a result, when I was growing up, my parents wanted me to speak English. They wanted me to survive in this world, but, in doing so, they didn't let us forget who we were. Ceremonies were still carried on. (Johansen, 2000, 59)

Franco teaches at an immersion pre-school, where "We have two- to six-year-old kids who are learning and speaking the language every day" (Johansen, 2000, 59).

AMERICAN INDIAN LANGUAGE DEVELOPMENT RESOURCES

The American Indian Language Development Institute (AILDI) at the University of Arizona Department of Language, Reading, and Culture, College of Education in Tucson hosts an annual summer institute, a residential program, offering six credit hours. The institute primarily trains teachers how to instruct Native languages and integrate them into school curricula.

Ofelia Zepeda (a Tohono O'odham), a cofounder and director of the institute, told *Indian Country Today* that half of his 22,000-member nation speak a native language of hushed, lilting sounds, "perfect for making songs about rain and corn or writing poems about desert clouds" (Burnham, 2006). The Tohono O'odham were formerly called the Papago (a word derived by Spanish speakers from the O'odham phrase for "bean eaters"). Tohono O'odham means "desert people." A linguist at the University of Arizona, Zepeda sharpens her language skills as a working poet. Her poems, often about women, range from an elegy to an aging centenarian with floor-length white hair to a fond recollection of the poet's mother, whom the family knew as the "best tortilla maker west of the Mississippi" (Burnham, 2006).

Even with such a large proportion of speakers, young people are not learning the Tohono O'odham language at home, said Zepeda. In school, O'odham classes often are isolated from the rest of the curriculum. Zepeda explained that she is still waiting for leaders to do something decisive about language loss. A practical writing system for O'odham, devised in the 1960s, has official status. Aside from Zepeda's books and an occasional article in the Tohono O'odham newspaper, however, use of the language is confined to scholarly efforts (Burnham, 2006).

According to the program's Web site, Students in the program attend classes taught by University of Arizona and visiting faculty. Participants acquire skills and learn methods for incorporating appropriate linguistic and cultural knowledge into their school's curriculum, learn general linguistic investigation skills applicable at the community level, and have an opportunity to learn new and innovative language teaching strategies through "micro-teaching" activities. The theme for 2006 was "Gathering Talk: Documenting, Describing and Revitalizing Our Languages" (American Indian Language Development Institute, 2005).

AILDI was founded in 1978 with support from the National Endowment for the Humanities. Begun by Lucille Watahomigie (Hualapai), director of the nationally recognized Hualapai Bilingual/Bicultural Program, and linguist Leanne Hinton, of San Diego State University, the institute trained 18 Native speakers of the five Yuman languages. The only program requirement was for participants to be Native speakers who were interested in working with their respective languages. The focus of the first institute was "Historical/Comparative Linguistics: Syntax and Orthography of Yuman Languages." By 1996, the institute was enrolling 116 participants representing language groups throughout the United States and Canada and from Venezuela and Brazil (McCarty, Watahomigie, Yamamoto, and Zapeda, 2006).

The Society for the Study of the Indigenous Languages of the Americas (SSILA, on the Internet at http://www.ssila.org/) was founded in December 1981 as an international scholarly organization representing American Indian linguistics. The society has approximately 900 members, more than a third of them residing outside the United States. The society maintains a comprehensive listing of articles on American Indian languages in more than a hundred academic journals (1988 to the present). The group also maintains an index of abstracts for more than two hundred dissertations and theses on American Indian languages and related topics, also dated 1988 to the present.

The revival of indigenous languages—immersion training has become one of the hottest educational tickets in Indian Country—is in stark contrast to the somber purge of Native languages and cultures that was delivered more than a century ago with the federal government's historical emphasis on assimilation into English-speaking mainstream culture. That assimilation program was encapsulated in the slogan "Kill the Indian, save the man," which was used by Gen. Richard Henry Pratt, who founded the Carlisle Indian Industrial School in 1879. Julia Kushner, who has worked with the Arikara, cites studies indicating that 90 percent of the 175 Native languages that survived General Pratt's cultural gauntlet today have no child speakers (Reyhner et al., 1999, 81). That figure dates from the mid-1990s.

"NATIVE NATIONS, NATIVE VOICES"

The language revival movement has become strong enough to sustain a festival called "Native Nations, Native Voices," which honors contemporary Native language writers in their own languages. Native language writers were invited to participate during July 2005 in a three-day festival sponsored by the Indian Pueblo Cultural Center of Albuquerque, New Mexico.

The conference was organized by Gordon Bronitsky of Bronitsky and Associates in Albuquerque. Participants included:

1. Greenland—Jokum Nielsen (Kalaallisut [Greenlandic]).
2. Canada—Floyd Favel (Cree) and Peter Irniq (Inuktitut).
3. United States—Eveline Battiest Steele (Choctaw), Nia Francisco and Nora Yazzie (Navajo), Dominik Tsosie (Navajo), Virgil Reeder (Kawaikagamedzene [Laguna Pueblo]), and Frances Washburn (Lakota).

4. Hawaii—Kainani Kahaunaele and Larry Kimura (Hawaiian).

5. Saipan—Frances Sablan (Chamorro).

6. Guam—Peter Onedera (Chamorro).

7. Mexico—Jesus Salinas Pedraza (Nyahnyu [Otomi]), Diego Mèndez Guzmán (Tzeltal Maya), Ruperta Bautista Vazquez (Tzotzil Maya), and Jun Tiburcio (Totonac).

8. Peru—Martin Castillo (Quechua) and Felix Julca (Quechua).

9. Brazil—Nanblá Grakan (Xokleng).

A CONFERENCE IN SANTA FE

Immersion programs had become popular enough by 1998 to sustain a wide-ranging conference, "The Critical Moment: Funding the Perpetuation of Native Languages." The conference, held January 26–28, 1998, in Santa Fe, New Mexico, was sponsored by the Lannan Foundation, which has made Native language reclamation one of its funding priorities.

Language-immersion programs are part of a growing commitment to traditional Native education, often initiated by parents and educational professionals seeking an alternative to students' alienation and high dropout rates in federal or local public schools. Mary Eunice Romero said that her people came to language revival as they sought "to understand why our children were not being referred to gifted programs. Our children are just as gifted as any other child" (Johansen, 2000, 56).

This quest brought Romero and her associates to a realization that the Karas concept of giftedness was quite different from the dominant standard in most non-Indian schools. These schools tended to define giftedness in terms of tests and grades, whereas, said Romero, to the Karas, "gifts and talents ... are expressed in traditional terms" and directed not toward the fame and fortune of an intelligent individual, but to the well-being of the community as a whole (Johansen, 2000, 56). To many immersion educators, the revival of Native languages constitutes an exercise of community-based intellect. "When we talk about trying to revitalize our language," said Romero, "it is survival of how we think, who we are, and what we truly believe our children should be. We want to pass this information down to our children in the right way, the appropriate way" (Johansen, 2000, 56).

The Santa Fe conference allowed participants from across the continent to share the histories and curricula of immersion programs while also coaching participants in ways to raise funds for their programs, many of which rely on a combination of federal funds (such as Head Start) and private donations. The Lannan Foundation also sought, through this conference, to raise the salience of Native American language revitalization for other funding organizations.

Janet Voorhees, executive director of the Lannan Foundation, said that Native language revitalization benefits everyone, not just the Native peoples who are maintaining and enhancing languages that serve as vehicles for traditional cultures.

For non-Indians, said Voorhees, Native language revival "will result in a world that is more deeply compassionate, wise, more caring and protective of the Earth, and more beautiful for it songs, ceremonies, and prayers" (Johansen, 2000, 56–57).

Voorhees quoted Dorothy Lazore, a teacher of immersion Mohawk at Akwesasne, describing a basic paradigm shift in how Native children view schooling: "For Native people, after so much pain and tragedy connected with their experience of school, we finally now see Native children, their teachers and their families, happy and engaged in the joy of learning and growing and being themselves in the immersion setting" (Johansen, 2000, 56–57).

BARELY IN TIME

The emphasis on language revival is arriving barely in time for some Native American languages, those that have reached stage eight of Joshua A. Fishman's eight stages of language loss, when only a few elders speak the tongue that once served an entire people at home and in their working lives (Fishman, 1991).

Only two elders spoke the Osage language in 2004 when Carolyn Quintero prepared to publish *Osage Grammar* (Lincoln: University of Nebraska Press, 2005). *Osage Grammar* was the first documentation of how the language works, including its phonology, morphology, and syntax. The book includes more than 2,000 sentences from Osage speakers, verb conjugations, derivations and suffixes, kinship terms, as well as the nominal system. Author Quintero, who is president of Inter Lingua, Inc., documented the language for more than twenty years, transcribing hundreds of hours of interviews from elderly speakers before they passed away. Even for the large Yakama Nation, Mavis Kindness, language program manager, estimated there might be only 100 elders left out of the 9,700 Yakamas who understand and speak their language (Lacitis, 2005).

Two books have been developed from a series of symposia on teaching indigenous languages that have been held annually since 1994 (Reyhner, 1997; Reyhner et al., 1999). The symposia have gathered roughly 300 people a year at several venues around the United States. Several were held at Northern Arizona University, where they were sponsored by its Multicultural Education Program, a subdivision of the university's Center for Excellence in Education. These two books celebrate the rediscovery of language with a sense of joy. Reyhner's books present concrete, tested strategies for preserving Native languages as living tools of culture in daily life, not as museum pieces of a presumably also-dead culture. Fishman's landmark book, *Reversing Language Shift: Theoretical and Empirical Foundations of Assistance to Threatened Languages,* published in the United Kingdom in 1991, is cited throughout these two volumes.

The reach of language revivals described in these books is worldwide; lessons and examples are freely borrowed from the Maori of New Zealand, who have had an active language-revival program for several decades. The New Zealand government has maintained a Maori Language Commission since 1987. These two books also describe Native peoples' efforts to revive their languages in Australia and Northern Africa.

"Repatriated Bones, Unrepatriated Spirits," a poem by Richard Littlebear, which appears at the beginning of *Revitalizing Native Languages* (Reyhner et al., 1999), reveals a sense that revival of Native American languages closes a historical and cultural circle:

> We were brought back here
> to a place we don't know.
>   ...
>
> We were brought back here
> and yet we are lost.
>   ...
>
> But now we are starting to sing our songs.
> We are singing our songs
> that will help us find our way.
>   ...
>
> We came back to a people who
> look like us but whose language
> we do not understand anymore.
>
> Yet we know in our hearts
> they are feeling good too, to have
> us back here among them

—Reyhner et al., 1999, iv

In *Revitalizing Indigenous Languages,* editor Jon Reyhner and colleagues stress the need to use a revitalized language as a living tool to teach academic subjects, not as a second language. The language must be restored to its place in everyday life of a people, he believes. This belief is widely shared.

FEDERAL FUNDING FOR LANGUAGE IMMERSION?

One wonders what General Pratt would think of the joy with which Native peoples across North America are recovering their languages a century after his boarding schools prohibited the speaking of them and did it, so he said, for Native peoples' own good. Pratt and other reformers of that era thought they were doing Native peoples a favor, that their policies were a humane alternative to outright extermination. Left unconsidered a century ago was a third option: that a rich quilt of diverse Native languages would be preserved and cultivated. Barely in time, as many of them were losing their last speakers, that is what we are seeing today.

A measure that might have General Pratt turning over in his grave has been advanced by advocates of language-immersion schools: federal funding, just as the boarding schools were funded a century and more ago.

Late in September 2006, the U.S. House of Representatives approved The Esther Martinez Native Languages Preservation Act to establish grants for governments, colleges, and other educational organizations working to preserve native cultures and languages. Martinez was a Tewa storyteller and linguist who died in September 2006. If passed by the Senate and signed into law, the bill would authorize competitive grants through the U.S. Department of Health and Human Services to establish native-language programs for students under the age of seven and their families. The bill also would increase support for language-immersion programs.

University of California–Berkeley Linguistics Professor Leanne Hinton, who has advanced the idea, testified before the U.S. Senate Committee on Indian Affairs during May 2003 in support of S 575, a bill that would give long-term funding to Native American language survival schools, another name for immersion programs. "These are languages that exist no place else in the world," Hinton said. "They're a part of what makes America America" (Wittmeyer, 2003). Of 85 indigenous languages in California, 35 have no speakers, and the remaining 50 are spoken by only a few elders. "We've found that teaching the kids everything in their native language is the most effective way of doing it," Hinton said. "If people aren't learning the language at home, they've got to learn somewhere, and school is the next best thing" (Wittmeyer, 2003).

Native communities that have too few speakers remaining to staff an entire immersion program may establish a master-apprentice learning program in which a single teacher is assigned to a student. Through such a program, enough young adults may learn a given language to eventually form the core of an immersion program. Hinton hosts the biennial "Breath of Life" conference at the University of California–Berkeley (described previously), which helps revive Native American languages that have no living speakers. Languages with no living speakers sometimes can be revived, at least in part, from documents. "We have sound archives and paper archives on campus," Hinton said. "We invite California Indians to come learn how to use their languages" (Wittmeyer, 2003).

FEDERAL GRANTS FOR DOCUMENTING ENDANGERED LANGUAGES

In an effort to rescue some threatened languages, the National Endowment for the Humanities and the National Science Foundation in May 2005 announced a $4.4 million program of grants and fellowships designed to preserve both written and spoken elements of more than seventy threatened languages, including more than a dozen Native American languages, before they become extinct. The project, called Documenting Endangered Languages, awarded 13 fellowships and 26 institutional grants for projects ranging from digitizing Cherokee writings in North Carolina to documenting the Kaw language in Oklahoma (Nugent, 2005).

"These languages are the DNA of our human culture, and if we lose them, we will be losing a unique and irreplaceable part of our experience," said Bruce Cole, chairman of the National Endowment for the Humanities. "The scholars tell us there are almost 7,000 languages in the world, and that half of them will probably be lost in the next century" (Nugent, 2005). Cole said that about 400 of the world's languages now have fewer than 100 fluent speakers each, and that 74 of them are Native American languages in the United States (Nugent, 2005).

"I'm not happy about this, because when we lose a language, we also lose a culture," said Anthony Aristar, a Wayne State University linguistics researcher who directs a $2 million archival project aimed in part at preserving in a large database dying Indian languages. . "But the research shows that there probably won't be any Native American languages left around the Great Lakes by the middle of this century. There are now only 10 or 12 fluent speakers of Potawatomi left in the entire Midwest, for example, and most are elderly. When they die in a few years, they'll probably take the language with them. Losing a language like Potawatomi is a major setback for all of us because in most cases, you also lose the poetry and the songs and the entire oral tradition" (Nugent, 2005).

SHOULD NATIVE LANGUAGE BE WRITTEN OR SOLELY ORAL?

Reyhner's and colleagues two books (1997, 1999) present a balanced summary of a subject that causes controversy in Native language revitalization studies: Should the revived language be written or solely oral? Some language activists point out that many Native languages were first committed to writing by missionaries seeking, as Reyhner writes, "to translate their Bible and convert Natives from their traditional religions" (Reyhner et al., 1999, xviii). These two volumes present a wide range of programs that have evolved locally, some in opposition to earlier efforts at written languages by church-affiliated programs and others that have grown out of the same type of programs. Although some of the programs strive to maintain an emphasis on spoken language to the exclusion of written communication, others emphasize production of written bilingual sources in the Native language to be revived, as well as in English. Some of the programs use computers extensively, whereas others avoid them as a culturally inappropriate intrusion.

Fishman himself comes down squarely on the side of literacy: "Unless they are entirely withdrawn from the modern world, minority ethnolinguistic groups need to be literate in their mother tongue (as well as in some language of wider communication)," he asserts (Reyhner et al., 1999, 38).

The often disputed distinction between oral and literate language may be culturally artificial because many Native American cultures possessed forms of written communication, even if many European immigrants did not recognize them as such. From the wampum belts of the Haudenosaunee (Iroquois) to the illustrated codices of the Aztecs and Maya to the winter counts of the Plains, written communication was used in America long before Columbus arrived. Reyhner quotes H. Russell Bernard as he urges Native Americans to establish publishing houses (Reyhner et al., 1999, xiii).

LANGUAGE REVIVAL, MUSIC, DANCE, AND OTHER METHODS

Language revival also has been used in some cases to encourage the expression of Native oral histories, in written and spoken forms, as well as to enhance and preserve musical expression. Some teachers of language are finding that music is an amazingly effective way to introduce young students to languages and cultural heritage. "Why music?" asks Amar Almasude, who writes about language revival in Northern Africa:

It is perhaps the best vehicle for becoming acquainted with humans. It is the expression that is the most pervasive. In songs, human society is portrayed and everyday experiences are reflected. Their themes are usually social issues and historical events, including national and religious feasts and holidays.... Thus, music is a fundamental element in human life. (Reyhner et al., 1999, 121)

Reyhner's books present precise descriptions and examples from teachers who have been involved in a wide variety of language-revival programs, from several Native bands in British Columbia to the Cheyenne, Yaqui, Arapaho, and Navajo. While describing individual programs, these books also sketch the common pedagogical essentials basic to all language-revitalization efforts.

Reyhner suggests use of the so-called three Ms of language revitalization: methods, materials, and motivation.

Methods deal with what teaching techniques will be used at what age levels and stages of language loss. Materials deal with what things will be available for teachers and learners to use, including audiotapes, videotapes, storybooks, dictionaries, grammars, textbooks, and computer software. Motivation deals with increasing the prestige (including giving recognition and awards to individuals and groups who make special efforts) and usefulness of the indigenous language in the community, and using teaching methods that learners enjoy, so they will come back for more indigenous language instruction." (Reyhner et al., 1999, xviii)

Language must become a familiar part of a student's life; immersion specialists believe that 600 to 700 hours of such contact is necessary to acquire the kind of fluency that allows for transmission of culture from generation to generation.

These two books are a treasure trove of linguistic innovation, describing how Native languages are being revitalized in some ways that are very old and in other ways that use modern technology to extend the reach of oral cultures. In Mexico, traditional Aztec Danza (dance) is being used to teach classical Nahuatl. The dances are part of an 18-ceremony ecological calendar, so, while learning the language, students also absorb some knowledge of Aztec history and culture. These ceremonies deal with rain, germination, ripening of corn, war victory, hunting, and the tribal dead, according to authors of a study on "revenacularizing" classical Nahuatl through Aztec dance. The authors list the intertwined benefits of this approach, by which students acquire not only knowledge of language, but also, "Nahua [Aztec] history from an indigenous perspective, a deeper understanding of Danza steps, creation myths, [and the] making and playing of indigenous [musical] instruments" (Reyhner, 1997, 71).

RADIO AND TELEPHONE AS VEHICLES OF LANGUAGE REVIVAL

The *eyepaha* of a traditional Lakota Sioux community circulated through a camp sharing information about the day's plans and events. This oral tradition is reflected today through the operation of community radio stations owned and operated by American Indians (Smith and Cornette, 2004).

Michael Krauss, director of the Alaska Native Language Program at the University of Alaska–Fairbanks, once compared mainstream media to cultural nerve gas because they destroy the cultural identities and languages of indigenous communities. For several generations, powerful AM radio stations from distant communities were the only broadcast voice that reached the rural areas where many Natives lived. They transmitted English-language programming together with Western culture and values into Indian homes; little was related to Native culture or Native concerns (Smith and Cornette, 2004).

The first Native-owned radio stations began operating in 1971. By 2004, more than two dozen Native American stations were broadcasting in the United States, with new stations being launched each year. In the Dakotas alone, six community radio stations now broadcast from Indian reservations. KINI, KILI, and KLND-FM all speak to the Lakota Sioux, and KSWS-FM serves a Dakota Sioux reservation. KMHA-FM represents the three affiliated tribes of the Mandan, Arikara, and Hidatsa nations, and KEYA-FM serves a Chippewa reservation (Smith and Cornette, 2004).

Beginning in 1983, KILI-FM broadcast to the Lakota people on the Pine Ridge Reservation. "The Voice of the Lakota Nation" is the slogan that motivates KILI's small paid staff and several volunteers. The station covers major events on the reservation, including tribal council meetings, powwows, government hearings, and sporting events.

KILI offers several hours of programming each day in the Lakota language. Sometimes both Lakota and English are broadcast together, as during the "Morning Wakalyapi [coffee] Show," which uses Lakota more than half the time and English the rest of the time but offers an entirely Native American programming blend of music and information (Smith and Cornette, 2004). Leonard Bruguier, director of the Institute of American Indian Studies at the University of South Dakota, said that Indian radio ties people into an extended family. It not only informs people but also helps maintain and validate Indian languages and cultures, he said (Smith and Cornette, 2004).

In Alaska, a growing number of Deg Hit'an (Ingalik Athabascan) people have been teaching each other their language, Deg Xinag, over the telephone, using conference calls. Telephone technology allows widely dispersed speakers of the language to create a channel to practice their skills and to teach each other new phrases and words. Phone conferences are hardly immersive (because the calls last only an hour a week), but language is being taught. Callers have joined the conversations from as far away as Seattle.

In a similar vein, 660 KTNN-AM, the Navajo Nation's official radio station, offers instruction in the Navajo language over the air in an attempt to follow Joshua Fishman's advice that revitalized languages, to be successful, must be shared by a people via the communications media of their communities. "The Voice of the Navajo Nation," as KTNN is called, has a signal that reaches from Albuquerque, New Mexico, to Phoenix, Arizona. In 2005, New Mexico State University student Cuyler Frank did play-by-play in Navajo of a September 23 football game between his school and the University of California–Berkeley. The game, in which Frank was joined by Lanell Pahe of Crownpoint, New Mexico, was broadcast on New Mexico State's Web site ("NMSU Student," 2005).

ALASKA: "TLINGIT CAN FLOURISH"

Sealaska Heritage Institute (SHI) of Juneau, Alaska, during summer 2004 offered Tlingit immersion retreats in Hoonah and near Sitka to revitalize the endangered language. Tlingit speakers and students of the language lived in a Tlingit-speaking world 24 hours a day from August 9 to August 19 during an immersion retreat at Icy Strait Lodge in Hoonah. A second retreat was held August 11–21 near Sitka at Dog Point Fish Camp, called in Tlingit Waashdaanx'.

"The program gives both speakers and learners a habitat where Tlingit can flourish," said SHI President Rosita Worl. "The immersion approach appears to accelerate the rate at which learners acquire the Tlingit language" ("Sealaska," 2004). Daily activities included gathering and processing Native foods as fluent speakers gave directions in Tlingit. Participants also sang, drummed, danced, and told stories in Tlingit.

A grant from the Alaska state Administration for Native Americans funded two language-immersion retreats per year in 2003, 2004, and 2005 in Sitka and the Glacier Bay-Hoonah area. About 74 percent of the project, or $148,000, was funded through federal money, and 26 percent through nongovernmental sources.

According to Ernestine Hayes, an assistant professor of English at the University of Alaska Southeast and a member of the Wolf House of the Kaagwaantaan clan, the Native languages of southeastern Alaska are among the world's most endangered. The grandparents of Alaska Natives who are college-aged today were punished for speaking their Native languages. Few young people speak their Native languages today, and the languages are not generally being taught in the home as a child's mother tongue. The situation is desperate, she said, "and little time is left in which to save these beautiful languages that express an extraordinary way to see our world" (Hayes, 2005).

Additional Alaska Native language programs have been offered by the Goldbelt Corporation and Sealaska Corporation. Elementary, intermediate, and advanced Tlingit, as well as elementary Haida, have been taught at the University of Alaska Southeast by Native speakers who are fluent and also understand the worldview expressed by the languages, as reflected in their syntax and grammar and their cultural references. According to Hayes, the languages are being taught with a sense of community and respect for the language's ceremonial significance, valuing "both tradition and transformation" (Hayes, 2005).

Richard Dauenhauer of Juneau was appointed as the University of Alaska President's Professor of Alaska Native Languages, a three-year position at the University of Alaska Southeast. Dauenhauer said this is a critical time to focus on Tlingit, Haida, and Tsimshian languages because the fluent speakers are growing older and many already have died. "The difference is with the Native languages in Alaska, this is the homeland, and if the language dies out here it dies out forever," he said (Morrison, 2005).

University of Alaska Southeast anthropology professor Daniel Monteith said that the Tlingit culture is alive and well, but the language is in need of some attention. "Linguists have kind of predicted, unless we get younger speakers learning the language, that we probably have ballpark 20 to 30 years more before Tlingit will no longer be a living language," said Monteith. "For Haida, we have our work cut out for us even more. The time is shorter" (Morrison, 2005).

Dauenhauer began teaching upper-division Tlingit courses at the University of Alaska Southeast during the fall semester of 2005, including a distance-education class with audio hookups between Sitka, Klukwan, Hoonah, and Juneau. He said that his wife, Nora, whose first language is Tlingit, has been helping teach in and out of the classroom (Morrison, 2005). Dauenhauer said that his courses use teams consisting of elders and younger speakers who teach together. He also stressed the importance of encouraging younger speakers. Dauenhauer also intends to aid students as they assemble a body of Tlingit literature by transcribing recordings of oral histories and traditions. "It's very important at this stage to be able to write the names down correctly so the next generation will know what they are and how to pronounce them," he said. "It's extremely important to do this while there are still speakers alive who have that full range, because some of the younger speakers don't have that full range that the elderly have" (Morrison, 2005).

Dauenhauer said that he believes Native students who learn their traditional language and take pride in their culture will do better in other academic courses. "The schools have traditionally been pretty much the enemies of Native language and culture, historically," he said. "I think with the revival and doing the languages in the school and getting them in the academic canon in a meaningful way ... you do get a psychological boost" (Morrison, 2005).

SEEKING A NEW CURRICULUM ON THE KENAI PENINSULA

As recently as the mid-1960s, students in Nanwalek, Alaska, near Homer, on the Kenai Peninsula, were ordered to lick the floor of a school in Homer whenever they spoke their parents' Sugt'stun language. In 2006, with fluent speakers down to fewer than a hundred, Nanwalek's elders enlisted the school's aid to help save their dying language. Nanwalek parents and elders asked the Kenai Peninsula Borough School District to include Sugt'stun in the high school's core curriculum (Kizzia, 2006).

School officials demurred at the request, arguing that budget cuts, new federal rules, and Nanwalek's low achievement-test scores forced them to emphasize basic English and mathematics required by the Bush administration's No Child Left Behind law. The native parents were not happy with the administration's suggestion that children who wanted to learn a second language take a computer course in Spanish. In the meantime, a village resident who had returned from Fairbanks with a master's degree in education and a Native language specialty was working as an aide with younger students, and covertly teaching Sugt'stun to high school students during an elective period set aside for art.

"The kids are using it at home, they're so eager and anxious to show off," said a parent, Nancy Yeaton (Kizzia, 2006). Teaching the language is a political issue to the parents and elders, some of whom "recalled being mocked or smacked by teachers for speaking Sugt'stun. One told how he was forced to go outdoors and hold the school flag pole for an hour in a snowstorm" (Kizzia, 2006). Use of the same school to revitalize language has thus become a richly relished historical irony.

"O COME, ALL YE FAITHFUL" IN INUPIAQ

A Methodist Church in Nome, Alaska, has adapted Christmas carols to the Inupiaq language. Among the standards sung by the choir is "O Come, All Ye Faithful." "To young people it's a very difficult language now," said Esther Bourdon, age 77, a Native Alaskan who grew up speaking Inupiaq in Wales, an Inupiat village on the westernmost point of Alaska's Seward Peninsula. On a clear day, Russia's easternmost shore is visible from Wales (Marigza, 2005).

The intricate nature of the Inupiaq language has hindered its survival. When the oral culture of family and nature-centered storytelling and singing waned, the language began to die. The Bureau of Indian Affairs also hindered retention of the language by prohibiting its use in boarding schools. The worldwide influenza pandemic of 1918 and 1919 also killed many elders who spoke the language, taking parts of the culture with them.

Bourdon said that during her 50 years at the Nome Community United Methodist Church, three of its pastors have learned to speak the language and have encouraged its use among the congregation of about 35 people, about two-thirds of whom are native. The number of people working to revive the language through the church by 2005 was twice the size of its congregation (Marigza, 2005). When the Revs. John and Debbie Pitney were assigned to the Community United Methodist Church in 1981, they decided to learn as much of the language as they could. They acquired enough vocabulary and syntax to translate several hymns, compiling a book that is used today by the church choir.

Rev. Lucile Barton, pastor of the church in 2005, said, "We sing the Doxology in Inupiaq most of the time, and ... translate a portion of the Gospel reading each Sunday as well" (Marigza, 2005). Barton, who is learning the language herself, is the only non-Native in the 10-person choir. Translating hymns into Inupiaq has not been easy because it is mainly a spoken language that does not adapt easily to printed text. "It has sounds that we don't use in English and you have to listen carefully and learn to repeat those sounds, and also when it's written the words get very, very long," Barton said (Marigza, 2005).

The Inupiaq choir is known far beyond the walls of the church and often is asked to sing at funerals and other traditional ceremonies for Native Alaskans, keeping the culture alive.

ATHABASCAN LANGUAGE DEVELOPMENT IN ALASKA

The Athabascan Language Development Institute, part of the Alaska Native Language Center, initiated at the University of Alaska–Fairbanks campus in 1998, brought together Athabascan speakers from around the state to teach and learn their languages, recapture history, preserve it, and make it a part of modern native cultures. "The language has very few speakers," said Gary Holton, assistant professor with the language center and an organizer of the institute. "Basically the people don't have enough opportunity to speak it" (Neyman, 2004).

Holton said that Dena'ina, like many Athabascan languages, has been disappearing because, in many cases, the only people who know it are elderly. As they die, the knowledge of the language dies with them. Gladys Evanoff traveled from Nondalton, where she has lived since 1950, to attend the class. She grew up in Pedro Bay hearing her grandmother speak Dena'ina and said her husband was fluent in the language, but they did not use it." No one really speaks it in Nondalton," she said. "They don't even understand it. My own kids don't speak it. And whose fault is that? It's the parents' fault.... We never taught it to our kids because when [my husband] went to school, he was kept from speaking it.... That's why so many people don't want to speak it now, because they were held back from their own language and culture" (Neyman, 2004).

Three people in Alaska's Chickaloon Village are hoping that CD-ROMs will help draw back the Ahtna Athabascan language (used between Upper Cook Inlet and the Copper River region) from the brink of extinction. Dimi Macheras, Kari Johns, and Daniel Harrison, among others, are working to preserve their traditional Athabascan culture by preserving the Ahtna Athabascan language with help from the Chickaloon Village tribal government. On Joshua Fishman's eight-step language-revitalization scale, the Ahtna Athabascan language has been rated at stage eight, closest to extinction (Martinson, 2005).

In 1972, about 200 fluent Ahtna Athabascan speakers lived in the region, according to the University of Alaska–Fairbanks' Alaska Native Language Center. In 1988, there were 100 fluent speakers. In 1994, there were fewer than eighty, and by 2004 fewer than fifty remained. Between October 2003 and February 2004, five fluent speakers of the language died, leaving descendents who did not learn and can not speak the language. Shortly after 2000, the Chickaloon Village Traditional Council conducted a language survey that indicated only 1 percent of its citizens spoke the Ahtna Athabascan language fluently (Martinson, 2005).

"It all started back in 1992, when my grandma decided that we needed to preserve our culture, and especially the language," Macheras said (Martinson, 2005). His grandmother is Katherine Wade, a village elder, one of the last of the elders to speak their native tongue fluently. She also founded of the village's Ya Ne Dah Ah School. "So she started teaching it and documenting it," Macheras said. "Her and Daniel went through and recorded a bunch of language and wrote down the words and phrases and eventually, we were out of school and we were hired back at the village and that was where Kari and Daniel began documenting it. Grandma wanted to see some CD-ROMs made eventually, and that was her idea" (Martinson, 2005).

Macheras is an artist who has been designing artwork for covers of an eight-CD set used to teach the language. The illustrations depict scenes of different tales and legends from their culture, images meant to help younger children understand their history. "There were generational gaps in the language," said Macheras's cousin, Kari Johns. "We had some people who were forbidden to speak it and then other pockets of people who were able to speak it, so some people still exist who know it, but they are very few. There are a lot of our people who couldn't learn it, because it had been forgotten by many" (Martinson, 2005).

LINGUISTIC RIGHTS IN CANADA

In mid-2005, the Canadian federal government apologized to the First Nations for government complicity in the linguistic and cultural genocide of the original inhabitants, agreeing to negotiate a global proposal meant to heal and reconcile the damage. Frank Iacobucci, a Canadian judge charged with crafting the details of the proposal, said he would address one essential human right: the full and equitable restoration of First Nations' linguistic rights.

Aboriginal linguistic rights have been a major part of Canada's attempt to undo the damage of residential schools, which aimed to eradicate children's knowledge of their native languages. The schools took children from their homes and punished them for speaking the languages in a determined attempt "to sever normal intergenerational cultural transmission between the children and their families and communities, and to forcibly deny them access to the rich spiritual resources, humor and story-telling that had been part of community life since time immemorial" (Martin, 2005).

Canada's apology could lead to several attempts to revitalize aboriginal languages there, including the teaching of Native languages in many schools, both as a subject of study and as a language of instruction, according to Ian Martin, an associate professor of English at Glendon College, York University. The apology creates, according to Martin, "A right to aboriginal-language immersion programs in communities where the language is seriously endangered" (Martin, 2005). Martin also advocates enactment of an Aboriginal Languages Revitalization and Affirmation Act as part of the social-renewal package. "One component," wrote Martin in the *Toronto Star,* "should be the establishment of an Aboriginal Languages Commissioner's office to report annually on the linguistic situation within aboriginal communities (both on and off reserve), and to evaluate steps taken and steps needed to further the goals of the act" (Martin, 2005).

Although the Canadian federal government set aside $172 million in 2002 in response to pressure from First Nations to revitalize their First Nations' languages, only a small amount was disbursed during the next three years. The government said it was waiting to establish a national corporation to distribute the funds, though many Native people said that such an entity, the First Nations Confederacy of Cultural Education Centers (FNCCEC) had existed for 35 years. "First Nations languages—Canada's national treasures—are dwindling away daily while Ottawa dithers," said Gilbert W. Whiteduck, president of FNCCEC (First Nations Confederacy of Cultural Education Centers, 2005). The FNCCEC represents 87 First Nations cultural-education centers in Canada that work with more than 400 First Nations communities. It distributes $5 million in operational funds annually to its member centers. The funds originate from the Federal Cultural Centers Program administered by the Department of Indian Affairs.

The Canadian Federal Task Force on Aboriginal Cultures and Languages late in 2005 released a report calling on the Canadian government to immediately begin funding Aboriginal language projects before it is too late. "Canada's past assimilative actions, particularly the residential school system, cannot be ignored. Canada's failure to protect First Nation, Inuit and Metis languages and cultures means it must now provide the resources necessary to restore them. All federal departments share this responsibility. However, First Nation, Inuit and Metis peoples must also take their rightful place as the first and foremost teachers of their own languages and cultures," the report said (Wiwcha, 2005).

The report asserted, "Forcibly removing language and culture from individual First Nation, Inuit and Metis people is tantamount to a breach of Aboriginal and treaty rights, as well as a breach of the Crown's [federal government's] fiduciary duty, and should therefore be compensable. It is also our view that Canada's refusal to compensate individuals who continue to suffer the devastating effects of their loss of connection to their communities and their languages, cultures and spiritual beliefs fails to uphold the honour of the Crown. Further, this refusal has the effect of appearing to relegate First Nation, Inuit and Metis languages to the position of subjugated languages that can be forcibly removed from the memories of the people who spoke them, with impunity" (Wiwcha, 2005).

The exact number of languages and dialects in Canada is unknown, but approximately 61 are spoken today. First Nations of Canada speak 51 languages. Inuit speak various dialects of Inuktitut, and Métis speak Michif as well as some First Nation languages (Wiwcha, 2005).

Most First Nation languages in Canada are listed as endangered because Interior Salish languages—along with the languages in the Tsimshian family, Kwakw'ala, Nuu-chah-nulth, and several of the smaller Dene languages in northern British Columbia, the Northwest Territories, and the Yukon—fell within a range of more than 300, but fewer than 1,000, speakers (Wiwcha, 2005).

RECLAMATION OF NUUCHAHNULTH ON VANCOUVER ISLAND

Roughly 300 people, fewer than 10 percent of descendants of a Native American people on Vancouver Island, still speak Nuuchahnulth, but very few young people in the community on Vancouver Island know the language. A dictionary has been compiled to help teach it. The dictionary, which has 7,500 entries, is the result of 15 years of research into the language. It is based on both work with current speakers and notes from linguist Edward Sapir, taken almost a century ago ("Bid to Save," 2005).

John Stonham of Newcastle University, who has compiled the dictionary, said that linguists find the language fascinating because of its complexity. "Entire sentences can be built up into a single word, ... [b]ut there are also some concepts that can be encapsulated in a single syllable. A single sound describes the state of remaining in seclusion when the husband goes out to hunt, for example," Stonham said that *hina?aluk* means "I look out for what I know is to happen," and *Simaacyin?ahinnaanuhsim?aki* means, "Their whaling spears were poised in the bow" ("Bid to Save," 2005). Stonham hopes providing a dictionary will encourage teachers to use the language in the classroom and that older people, too, will be spurred into passing on their language to the next generation.

SAVING SAANICH ON VANCOUVER ISLAND

Saving indigenous languages often involves the sum total of many individual efforts in widely dispersed places. Such is the case for John Elliott, who has been carrying on his father's work to preserve Sencoten, an indigenous language spoken by Coast Salish First Nations on both sides of the Strait of Juan de Fuca, with the Saanich Peninsula at its heart (Clarke, 2006). Elliott, who teaches at the Lau'Welnew Native school, has dedicated thirty years to the language. His father, Dave Elliott, a fisherman, worked as a janitor for the Saanich Indian School Board when he decided to create a phonetic alphabet for Sencoten, a difficult task because the language includes many letters that are difficult to reproduce in English.

"My father used to say the language was dying and people were losing the whole value system," Elliott recalled. "I'm taking his work one step further" (Clarke, 2006). The language, which had about 7,000 fluent speakers when the first speakers of English arrived on Vancouver Island a century-and-a-half ago, was down to two dozen elders when the Elliotts began their work. The residential school system prevented most children from learning the language.

Today, about 200 of the tribal schools' students study the language, and the program has been around long enough that former students are now parents who speak the language around their children. "The fluency's coming, but it's slow. It took 50 years to take it out of us through the boarding schools," Elliott said (Clarke, 2006). They are using First Voices (http://www.firstvoices.ca), a Web site and cooperative venture between the Saanich Indian School Board and the provincially funded First People's Heritage Language and Culture Council, which "contains still pictures, video clips, recorded voices, games and other features to pique the interest of young learners" (Clarke, 2006).

KLAMATH LANGUAGE CLOSE TO EXTINCTION

Mabie "Neva" Eggsman, one of the last living keepers of the Klamath language, died in 2003 at age 95. Eggsman was the Klamath Tribes' master language teacher, and her death left a void the Klamaths have been struggling to fill ever since. Klamath and Modoc, which is a closely related language, are near extinction, with no known living Native speakers. Today, in an attempt to reclaim the language, Randee Sheppard, one of two part-time language teachers for the tribes, takes the language into the classrooms of Mills and Chiloquin elementary schools and helps teach at the Culture Camp for children every year. It is hard because she herself is not fluent and has been left without anyone with whom she can converse ("Preserving the Klamath Tongue," 2005).

Klamath Tribes Council Member Bobby David, age 70, grew up hearing his grandparents speak Klamath early in the morning as they cooked breakfast. In David's estimation, by the 1940s the language had nearly died out on the reservation. The English-only educations of boarding schools were a major factor, an experience that left many people bitter and unwilling to speak their languages. "We were not allowed to even speak with each other," said Marni Morrow, one of the organizers of the Culture Camp ("Preserving the Klamath Tongue," 2005).

Oregon passed a law in 2001 that allows Native American languages to be taught by people who pass a proficiency test but may not have a teacher's license. David, who can speak some of the language (but is not fluent), is one of the certified teachers. He said learning the language is important to connect people to their past. "I think there's a connection," he said. "I know what I'm doing now, but what did I do? Where do I come from? Where is my past?" he said ("Preserving the Klamath Tongue," 2005).

The Klamath have two dictionaries of the language that were compiled by linguists—one in the late 1800s and another in the 1950s when about 300 people could speak the language. Tapes, based on recordings of Native speakers, and instructional books have been made for people trying to learn the language.

THINKING IN YUROK

From the Little River and the Klamath River on the Pacific coast, inland up the Klamath River to Weitchpec, Yurok people, many of them young, are reclaiming a language that had all but died by 1950, along with Hupa, Wiyot, Tolowa, Karuk, Mattole and Chilula, and others. At that time, Yurok children were being taken from their families and sent to boarding schools, where they were beaten with words of shame for speaking the languages of their ancestors. Elderly speakers aged and passed away (Sims, 2006).

Late in 2005, the language was being reclaimed with the help of the few surviving elders who still speak it, such as Archie Thompson and Jimmie James, both in their nineties. Meetings were being held at Potawot Village, where several dozen people discussed the language and its future in a mixture of Yurok and English, as part of the Yurok Elder Wisdom Preservation Project. Language preservation is now aimed at the grandchildren and great-grandchildren of people Thompson's and James's age.

"All of us here, we know how to talk, and we know what it sounds like," Thompson said, including elders such as Aileen Figueroa and Georgiana Trull. "I hope I'm not discouraging you, but what you need to get hold of is the real word, and what the language really means.... You got to speak it good and strong," James continued (Sims, 2006).

Kathleen Vigil, age 62 in 2005, a resident of Westhaven, founded the Yurok Elder Wisdom Preservation Project because she knew that time was running short. Vigil, daughter of Aileen Figueroa, is one of the oldest members of the Yurok Tribe and a master speaker of the language. "There was a gathering in Klamath for the Yurok language, and a cry came out," Vigil said. "My mother was 91 or 92 at that time, and we really needed to do some documentation on her" (Sims, 2006).

Figueroa has been one of the Yurok people's treasure troves of information, including old stories and history, related in the traditional language. Yurok had been offered once weekly at Hoopa High School as a so-called foreign language for 20 years, but existing classes were not covering the need to impart tradition along with lists of words. Soon, daily classes in culture and language were being offered at the American Indian Academy charter school in McKinleyville, with Figueroa and Vigil teaching.

One of Georgiana Trull's grandsons, 25-year-old Frankie Joe Myers, said that one of the positive things about living in this day and age is the wider U.S. culture no longer pressures people to give up their roots, as it did in the past. "In my father's generation, it wasn't looked on as positive to be Indian," he said. "In a way, it's become popular. It's become cool to be Indian." Learning the language went along with the rebirth of traditional dances—the Brush Dance, the World Renewal Ceremony—over the past few decades, and these ceremonies, together with the language, strengthened his identity as a Yurok, he said (Sims, 2006).

Students of the language realized that they were thinking in English and translating into Yurok. They also needed to recapture the rhythm of their elders' speech. Carole Lewis, age 54, who had been studying Yurok for about 20 years, apologized to the elders: "I can see the sorrow they have for their language, because in a way we're murdering it" (Sims, 2006). She asked students to listen more closely to the audio recordings made by the elders.

The Preservation Project plans to compose a standard lesson plan for new students, to increase attendance at community-college classes in the language, and to begin an annual summer immersion camp as they continue to record speech and stories of the elders.

MUCKLESHOOT: DOWN TO THE LAST SPEAKER

In Auburn, Washington, near Seattle, on the Muckleshoot Reservation, Ellen Williams, age 81 in 2005, is the last person living who is still fluent in a native language that, "with its clicking and consonants with popping sounds, is so vastly different from English" (Lacitis, 2005). She has helped teach Whulshootseed, the Muckleshoot language, at the tribal college with aid from Donna Starr, one of its two language instructors. Starr learned the language from her mother and then took classes in the language, rating her fluency as intermediate. Williams helps Starr with correct pronunciations and meanings (Lacitis, 2005). It was transmitted entirely orally until the 1960s.

Thom Hess, a retired linguistics professor at the University of Victoria in British Columbia, with two others compiled a Lushootseed dictionary that includes language that once was spoken from Olympia to the Skagit River Valley. Whulshootseed is one of dialects. "The language is the best mirror of the culture. Each of our words encapsulates our view of the world," said Hess (Lacitis, 2005).

These languages have more than a dozen words for salmon and trout, reflecting the importance of the fish to them. "They would refer to the different species, sex, degree of maturity, times of the year they returned, whether they came back on schedule or out of schedule," said Hess (Lacitis, 2005).

The language has evolved over the decades, even when it had many more fluent speakers, to incorporate new words. *Refrigerator* is translated as "by means of making things cold." *Stove* is translated as "making things with fire" (Lacitis, 2005). During 2003, Washington's Board of Education initiated a three-year pilot program awarding a First Peoples teacher certification for individuals fluent in a native language. By early 2005, 13 certificates had been awarded.

LANGUAGE IMMERSION IN HAWAII

Kauanoe Kamana, a leader in Hawaiian language revitalization, outlined the steps that led to language-immersion schools in Hawaii. First, he said, a group of people must decide to put forward the effort required to maintain a living language. Kamana was not a speaker of his Native language when he committed himself to its preservation. "Most of the teachers had to learn it as a second language," he said (Johansen, 2000, 58).

Once a commitment to the language was made, a small group of people began to develop plans for organized instruction in it. "When we began, it was a belief," said Kamana. "We didn't begin with money.... We didn't all live in the same community. We are university-level secondary-school teachers in the Hawaiian language from different islands. We decided one day that what had been happening at the university system was not enough" (Johansen, 2000, 58). "We began in 1983 with the idea," said Kamana. "We were eating dinner one night and I said, 'Yeah, let's do it.' We got a non-profit licensed business and started opening schools. You can't do it alone. You have to do it in a group" (Johansen, 2000, 58).

Kamana and others in Hawaii studied as many other examples of indigenous-language revival as they could find, including the Maoris of New Zealand, who have been using elders to teach their language to young children, even babies. The Hawaiians decided to name their school Punana Leo, which means "the Hawaiian language lives, shall live, [and] will live" ("Critical Moment," 1998).

Having assembled a core of committed people, Kamana and others then built support for language revitalization in their communities. "Our first stage was to find people ... like parents who wanted it," said Kamana ("Critical Moment," 1998). Soon they had a schoolroom and a teacher. Next, they researched the best ways to teach the Native Hawaiian language to their children. The curriculum was created locally; Kamana said that he developed the curriculum for grades 7 through 11.

Attention to financial resources became a concern for Punana Leo's language revivalists only after public support was evident. Money comes because they are doing a good job, Kamana believes. Once popular demand enhanced prospects for funding, the Punana Leo school became a physical reality, with buildings, materials, teachers, and curricula. Once a school is established, said Kamana, the stress must be placed on producing people who utilize the language in their daily lives.

Kamana's experiences were shared to some degree by Edna Viak McClean, an Inupiag instructor at Ilishavilk College in Bear, Alaska. Any immersion program may fail if it lacks a core of committed people, she said. The second biggest hurdle, she said, is the lack of educated Native language speakers who can serve as translators, curriculum developers, teachers, advocates, and people versed in the fundamentals of an immersion program who can advocate for it with the school board and funding agencies. McClean said that another common concern is the need to ensure Native cultural transmission in the language schools.

An eight-disk CD-ROM course in Hawaiian, "Instant Hawaiian Immersion" (Seattle, Washington: Topics Entertainment, $29.95), was being sold by 2004 in Costco and Borders bookstores on the islands. By 2004, the audio CD series was selling 25,000 sets per month (Gee, 2004). Hawaiian sovereignty advocates are aiming to make the islands' society bilingual, to place the Hawaiian language on a par with English. Kaliko Beamer-Trapp, a Hawaiian language teacher who developed the audio CD series, is among those who think Hawaiian should be spoken all the time at work and play and used more commonly in legal documents.

Kiele Akana-Gooch, who translates historic Hawaiian documents into English for Alu Like (an education-oriented Hawaiian nonprofit agency), said that many people do not know that Hawaiian is an official language of the state, along with English, and that Hawaii is the only state with two official languages. So much has changed since a time when speaking Hawaiian "used to be forbidden"—when Hawaii was subjugated to rule of the United States in 1898, she said. "People can write checks in Hawaiian, testify before the Legislature in Hawaiian (with an interpreter), and write land deeds—all the major functions…. I'm really proud that the Hawaiian language is being embraced. It's about time," she added. "I'd like to see Hawaii become more of a bilingual state, like in Canada [where, on all store merchandise] one side is written in French and the other side in English," she said (Gee, 2004).

Ulukau: The Hawaiian Electronic Library, an online digital library, has been placing Hawaiian vocabulary and some literature a click away from anyone in the world (Viotti, 2004). The Bible, two Hawaiian-English dictionaries, a journal of archival Hawaiian texts, a collection of Hawaiian-language newspapers, and a book about Kamehameha (a Hawaiian king whose statue stands in the U.S. Capitol) have been posted at Ulukau (http://ulukau.olelo.hawaii.edu/english.php).

The dictionaries on the newly launched e-library, which beginning in 2004 were receiving more than 10,000 hits per day, are by far its most popular element, the creators said. The site is posted in mirror-image Hawaiian and English-language versions: You switch back and forth from a link at the top of every page. It is the brainchild of two parent organizations: the Native Hawaiian Library, a program of Alu Like, Inc., and the Hale Kuamo'o Center for Hawaiian Language at the University of Hawai'i–Hilo (Viotti, 2004).

In 1999, a team at the University of Waikato in New Zealand developed the free digital program Greenstone, the software that underlies the university's Maori Language Newspaper Project as well as Ulukau. Stefan Boddie, one of the team members in New Zealand, remains on call as a consultant for Ulukau. He helps the Hawaii staffers make their own enhancements work with the base program, which Boddie said is kept very simple so that less-developed nations can use it on the kind of computer systems they have. "One of the main goals was that it would be free and easy to run on old computers," Boddie said in a telephone interview, adding that digital libraries can be saved on CDs for use in places where the Internet is not available (Viotti, 2004).

Keola Donaghy, technology coordinator at the University of Hawai'i–Hilo language center, said that an add-on keypad on the page enables users of the online dictionary to tap out Hawaiian diacritical marks—the *'okina* and the *kahako*—regardless of their own computer gear. And, he said, the search mechanism will hunt for words that appear as stand-alone entries as well as parts of other words—a boon for those researching compound Hawaiian personal or place names, he said. "It does an inclusive search," Donaghy said. "Say you were looking for the word *ali'i*. It could give you that and any word that contains the word *ali'i*" (Viotti, 2004).

REVIVAL OF DAKOTA AND OJIBWEMOWIN IN MINNESOTA AND WISCONSIN

Minnesota's state name comes from a Dakota word meaning "sky-tinted waters," but by 2004 fewer than 30 fully fluent Dakota speakers remained in the state, according to the Minneapolis-St. Paul–based Dakota Ojibwe Language Revitalization Alliance. A 1995 survey of reservations in Minnesota, Wisconsin, and Michigan found only 418 fluent Ojibwemowin speakers, none younger than 45 years of age. "We really need our language and culture," alliance member Jennifer Bendickson said. "If children don't know their culture and their language, then they become lost because they are missing that part of themselves" (Kuchera, 2004). The alliance, comprised of elders, fluent Dakota and Ojibwemowin speakers, educators, and others, formed in June 2003 at the Fond du Lac Reservation.

"The Mille Lacs Band, for example, has spent an incredible amount on language," said Rosemary Christensen, a Mole Lake Ojibwe who teaches American Indian studies at the University of Wisconsin–Green Bay. "Even before they had a casino, they were spending money to preserve and strengthen their language" (Kuchera, 2004). At the band's Nay Ah Shing Schools in Onamia, Minnesota, courses in Ojibwe language, history, and culture are part of the curriculum. In 2000, the band opened the Ojibwe Language and Cultural Awareness Grounds near Rutledge. The University of Wisconsin–Stevens Point Native American Center has held a summer language-immersion camp each summer since 2002 at Red Cliff. Lac Courte Oreilles sponsors a similar camp. The Fond du Lac Band offers regular language instruction at centers in Cloquet, Old Sawyer, and Brookston. "If you put together all those little groups of people, then you have a really large group of people trying to revitalize their language," Bendickson said. "That is very encouraging" (Kuchera, 2004).

Language revival has taken some interesting turns in the Dakotas. For example, teams from Sioux reservation schools in North Dakota, South Dakota, and Manitoba competed in Dakota-language Scrabble on March 24, 2006, at the Sisseton-Wahpeton tribe's Dakota Magic Casino pavilion near Hankinson, North Dakota.

As part of the effort, students and elders compiled a 207-page *Official Dakotah Scrabble Dictionary*. The Dakota Scrabble initiative was authorized by Hasbro, the makers of Scrabble, and supported financially by the company's chairman, Alan Hassenfeld. Hasbro also provided permission for an educational version of the game. Each set was handcrafted by Dakota. The tiles were made of stone mined from a quarry near Milbank, South Dakota ("U.S.-Canadian," 2006).

OJIBWE AND DAKOTA LANGUAGE REVITALIZATION IN MINNESOTA

With fewer than 30 fully fluent Dakota speakers living in Minnesota and few fully fluent speakers left on each of the seven Ojibwe reservations there, the need to work together to revitalize languages has become an imperative. Jennifer Bendickson, coordinator for the American Indian Early Childhood Leaders Circle, which organized the Language Revitalization Alliance, says, "If someone lost his or her German or Irish or Swedish language over the past generations, you can go back to Germany or Sweden and learn it. If we lose our Dakota or Ojibwe languages, there will be no place to learn this. This is the home of the Dakota and Ojibwe languages" (LaFortune, 2004).

The Language Revitalization Alliance is a gathering of elders, fluent Dakota and Ojibwe speakers, early childhood and child-care providers, members from all 11 native groups in Minnesota, and educators, school achievement, education advocates, and community members. This alliance has been meeting since June 2003 to examine the existing barriers and opportunities to language revitalization, gathering people who are concerned about the loss of language, supporting each other's work, and building awareness at the state and local levels of language revitalization and immersion programs.

DAKOTA LANGUAGE IN RAP MUSIC

The first rap song recorded in the Dakota language was produced in a joint effort by the Sisseton Wahpeton College and the Association on American Indian Affairs. The rap song, titled "Wicozani Mitawa," or "My Life," was recorded at a studio on the Sisseton Wahpeton College campus in Sisseton, South Dakota, on the Lake Traverse Reservation. The Sisseton Wahpeton College president, William Harjo Lone Fight, who has worked in Native American language restoration, said, "For a language to flourish it has to be used. That is the bottom line. This son helps bring Dakota into the 21st century as a living language with relevance to our youth" (Leiste, 2005).

Tammy DeCoteau has devised many ways to coax children into speaking their native Dakota language, one of them being rap music. She has been a driving force behind a series of efforts to expose young people on the Lake Traverse Reservation to their ancestral language with efforts that include recording popular children's songs and publishing illustrated phrase books and nursery rhymes in Dakota Sioux. "We're just branching out in another genre," said DeCoteau, who is director of American Indian language programs for the Association of American

Indian Affairs (Springer, 2005). More than 250 compact discs containing "Wico-zani Mitawa," recorded in late August 2005, have been distributed free of charge to young people on the reservation, with its tribal headquarters at Agency Village near Sisseton.

The recording project was initiated by a conversation DeCoteau had with one of her nephews, Tristan Eastman, who writes and performs rap songs. "She asked me if I could write a rap song for kids," Eastman said. "I asked her if she meant nursery school kids. She said no, people your age." Eastman, who was 20 in 2005, estimates that 97 percent of kids on the reservation listen to rap or hip-hop music. "A lot of kids want to live in the hip-hop culture and do what they see on TV," he said. "It's breaking us from who we are." One of the song's messages, from the point of view of a young man who fights despair, is to embrace native pride and stand up for traditional culture (Springer, 2005).

Rap music was like a foreign language to the elders who helped with the translation into Dakota. "The elders didn't have much experience with rap," DeCoteau said. She had them listen to an English version, with a piano accompaniment and pulsing drumbeat. "They figured rap wasn't all that bad." Orsen and Edwina Bernard were the lead translators of Eastman's lyrics. To capture the spirit, Orsen Bernard crossed the generational divide. "I had to think where this young fellow was coming from," he said. It was not all that difficult; all he had to do was remember his own struggles as a young man (Springer, 2005).

Dakota language instruction is part of the curriculum of both kindergarten through 12th grade and the tribal college. The tribal council is considering making Dakota its official language and has channeled about $100,000 of its casino revenues into language restoration in recent years, said Harjo Lone Fight. "The sense of urgency has increased since the language-speaking population has decreased," he said. "Thirty years ago, there seemed to be an endless supply." The 2000 U.S. census found that only 3 percent of the tribe's 11,000 members speak Dakota, DeCoteau said. Most fluent speakers are elderly (Springer, 2005).

THE LAKOTA LANGUAGE CONSORTIUM

The Lakota language is being taught through efforts of the nonprofit Lakota Language Consortium (http://www.lakhota.org), which develops the Lakota-language teaching materials used in 23 schools. The consortium also trains language teachers.

Tribal elders and traditional leaders have kept the language alive for future generations. Eighty-one-year-old Clarence Wolf Guts, the last surviving Lakota code talker from World War II, said, "Our people need to know that Lakota had an important position and to learn to be proud to speak Lakota. It is good that the kids are now learning Lakota in the schools." Oglala Sioux Tribe Vice President Alex White Plume explained that through the group's efforts, "We are finally making some progress in teaching the language to the children" ("Lakota on Path," 2006).

The consortium received a prestigious language revitalization award, the Ken Hale Prize, from the Society for the Study of the Indigenous Languages of the Americas. The award was given in part for the consortium's community-language work and deep commitment to the promotion and revitalization of Lakota. The group's linguistic director, Jan Ullrich, said, "Revitalizing a language is no easy task and much more needs to be done to educate the public about the state of endangered languages and the needs of indigenous peoples" ("Lakota on Path," 2006).

The consortium also advocates use of the Lakota language within the community by providing incentives for young people, developing Lakota-language television programming, and expanding the literature available in the language. The Washington Redskins Charitable Foundation and Sioux Tools have donated to the cause.

A LAKOTA LANGUAGE CAMP

A summer Lakota language- and culture-immersion camp near Cherry Creek on the Cheyenne River Indian Reservation combines ceremonies with language instruction. Sponsored by the Cheyenne River Indian Reservation's governing authority, Si Tanka University, the reservation's Takini School, and Waonspekiye Oyasin (a teacher-training organization), the camp hosts each year about 40 people interested in learning the Lakota way. Karen Little Wounded awoke in her tent at dawn to take part in a traditional morning star ceremony. Every night during the camp, she sang, danced, and learned to interpret dreams ("Lakota Immersion," 2005).

During 2005, the camp was held from June 12 through 17 on the reservation. Carole Rave, one of its organizers, said the camp is free for tribal members and costs about $500 per day for others. That money, along with funding from Waonspekiye Oyasin, pays for the camp, Rave said, adding that non-Indians are welcome.

In addition to participation in traditional ceremonies, the camp offers training in Lakota by language teachers from the reservation's various schools and colleges. Those instructors often become students because they are working toward certification as Lakota teachers, Rave said ("Lakota Immersion," 2005). Besides basic Lakota for nonspeakers, the classes teach Lakota history, culture, and philosophy. She said tribal elders play an important role in the camp, both as teachers and as participants. In 2004, elders offered instruction in traditional practices such as drying meat and erecting tepees and were honored with a dance, Rave said.

Lakota has been used in community politics as well. Ron His Horse Is Thunder (who is a descendent of Sitting Bull), who was elected leader of the Standing Rock Lakota in 2005, pledged to learn his native language before his term ends in 2009. If he has not learned it (his ambition is to hold meetings in the language), His Horse Is Thunder said he will not run for a second term. "Most tribal governments meet and talk in English. In schools, English is the primary language," he said. "In Indian schools there are classes in Indian language—Lakota language here—but that is the only place in the whole school where Indian language is spoken. Street signs are written in English. Almost everything is in English. If we are going to save our languages, we need to show our children that it has value." As of 2005, 25 percent to 30 percent of the Standing Rock Sioux can speak at least some of the language (Logue, 2005).

WHITE CLAY IMMERSION SCHOOL: ASSINIBOINE AND GROS VENTRE LANGUAGE REVIVAL

Following a naming ceremony and a community feast, Fort Belknap Native peoples dedicated a new cultural learning center on June 1, 2005. The 7,000-square-foot building on the Fort Belknap College campus is dedicated to preserving the heritage and native languages of the reservation's Assiniboine and Gros Ventre peoples (Ogden, 2005). The new building provides a home for the college's White Clay Immersion School, an effort to pass the language on to new generations. Pupils will receive a contemporary education supplemented with White Clay language whenever possible, said Lynette Chandler, the school's director (Ogden, 2005).

The first students at the school included second- and third-graders who had studied in a part-time White Clay language program since they were in the Head Start program. The college was hiring three teachers for the kindergarten through eighth grade program, Chandler said. "At least two will have bachelor's degrees in elementary education and at least one will be fluent" (Ogden, 2005). "We are going to give them everything they need to become the next generation of speakers, of educators, of leaders," she said. "This is the last stand for the Gros Ventre language" (Ogden, 2005).

A COMPACT DISC OF SONGS IN HOPI

Ferrell Secakuku and Anita Poleahla produced a compact disc called "Learning through Hopi Songs" in spring 2005 that helps teach the language. "We wanted to inspire younger children, to provide a way for them to hear the words, to put themselves into the Hopi language, to bring them back to speaking Hopi," Secakuku said. "We are working uphill; it's a challenge to bring back the Hopi language.... I thought this would be a good way to inspire the younger generation along with their parents and grandparents" (Wilson, 2005).

Secakuku, a former Hopi government chairman, met Natasa Garic in a graduate-level anthropology class at Northern Arizona University (NAU). Garic, a Serbian Croatian from Slovenia, was an international student in the Anthropology Department and a 2002 graduate in cultural anthropology from NAU who was fluent in English and Croatian, and also spoke Italian and German. She said she has always been interested in ancient cultures and Native people. She originally came to Arizona to study the Navajo and has worked closely with the Hopi. A professional volleyball player, Garic is passionate about archaeology, petroglyphs, and the tracing of migration patterns (Wilson, 2005).

Garic, Secakuku, and Poleahla chose the Hopi maidenhood ceremony, deciding to bring the experience into Hopi homes and classrooms. This would allow children who might not otherwise see the ceremony to share the experience. Rather than filming video footage of the ceremony, Garic decided to use still photographs (Wilson, 2005). "I wanted children to associate the words of the song with the pictures. I wanted historic photos to represent cultural continuity," Garic said. "I tried to make it about the young woman represented in the pictures, and about her family. I hope that the experience [of viewing the presentation] will spark an interest in other cultural roles" (Wilson, 2005).

"Songs from 'Learning through Hopi Songs' has received a lot of play in northern Arizona. We hear the songs everywhere," Poleahla said. "We hear them on the radio, students are singing them" (Wilson, 2005).

LANGUAGE LESSONS AT COCHITI PUEBLO

The people of the Cochiti Pueblo were moved to revitalize their language after they conducted a survey that disclosed that all of its fluent speakers were 35 years of age or older. The few speakers younger than age 35 were semiliterate, said Mary Eunice Romero, a Karas (Pueblo). Romero then asked, "What is going to happen to our language in 20 years when those [who are] 35 years old become 55? In 20 more years, when they're 75?" ("Critical Moment," 1998)

The Cochiti immersion program began in 1996, with a summer program for 30 children, under instructions from the Tribal Council that all instruction be carried out orally, with no written texts. After that, according to Romero, the program grew quickly:

> When the kids went home, they spread the news that, "Wow, they're not using any English. They're not writing. It's just totally in Cochiti." We started out with four teachers. The next day, we got 60 kids. By the third week, we had 90 kids. By the end of the summer, the kids were starting to speak. ("Critical Moment," 1998)

Romero also watched the mode of instruction change the behavior of the children:

> The behavior change was a major miracle. These kids came in rowdy as can be. By the time they left, [they] knew the appropriate protocol of how you enter a house, greet your elder, say good-bye. The fact that they could use verbal communication for the most important piece of culture, values, and love started a chain reaction in the community. ("Critical Moment," 1998)

Experiences at the Cochiti Pueblo mirror a trend across Turtle Island (North America). Native American languages, many of which have been verging on extinction, have enjoyed a revival in recent years due largely to many Native American nations' adoption of immersion programs, which teach a language as the major part of many reservation school curricula.

PRESERVING LANGUAGE AT ACOMITA PUEBLO

At the Acomita Pueblo, six boys sat around a table with leather and metal tools piled in front of them. Across the room, five girls gathered around another table filled with sewing machines and many-colored fabrics. In this classroom at the Acoma Senior Citizens Center, the Acoma Language Retention Program convened young and old in traditional activities to preserve Acoma language and culture. The Acoma Language Retention Program started in 1997 to teach the Keresan language to non-Keresan-speaking Acoma children. Ninety youngsters enrolled (Kie, 2005).

Vina Leno, an Acoma who has directed the language program since 2001, said it began when two women, Christine Simms, from the University of New Mexico Department of Linguistics, and Donna Boynton, a certified teacher from Acoma, met with a group of elders and discussed what losing the Keresan language might mean for the future of the pueblo. "The elders agreed that if we do not teach the language to the young ones, we will eventually lose our language and then we will not have a culture," said Leno (Kie, 2005). She said the first group of students was assembled in a language-immersion camp.

In 1998, the two women submitted their first planning grant proposal to the Administration for Native Americans. The Acomita Pueblo was awarded $50,000 to survey the Acoma community about the importance of developing a language-retention program. "The results showed that a lot of our young people wanted to speak the language," she said (Kie, 2005).

The program has held an immersion camp every summer since 1998, focusing on a different age group each year. Leno said some children came back to the program and told their teachers that when they tried to speak Keresan at home, their parents did not understand the language. "Our program director at the time felt that there was also a need to teach the parents," said Leno (Kie, 2005). The program also educated the elders about new language-teaching methods that were being used to teach the Acoma students. "Our people used to learn the language by talking to their parents or grandparents, but now things are different," said Leno (Kie, 2005). She added that not all parents and grandparents could speak the language fluently enough to teach other family members.

Acoma language teachers later were certified by the pueblo and given access to the Cibola County school system, where they teach classes at Laguna-Acoma and Cubero as well as in the Sky City Community School. "We also discovered that one group that was not being helped was the high school-aged student," said Leno (Kie, 2005).

TECHNOLOGY AND HAND PUPPETS HELP
TEACH POMOS' DIALECT TO CHILDREN

Although only a few elders of the Big Valley band of Pomo Indians are still fluent in their language, younger Pomos are learning words and phrases with technological aid. For example, according to an account by Shadi Rahimi for the Pacific News Service, 18-year-old Kristin Amparo, a tribal member of the Big Valley band of Pomo Indians, lives with her parents and five siblings in a large house on their reservation in Clear Lake, about three hours by car north of San Francisco. Kristin and her 14-year-old sister Felicia speak the Pomos' Bahtssal language on the 153-acre, 470-member Big Valley reservation. Both are learning to speak the dialect as part of a newly formed language program (Rahimi, 2005).

"We tell our mom stuff in Bahtssal, like, 'I have to go,'" said Kristin Amparo, who had never heard the language spoken before she began studying it under the new initiative. "It's really fun to learn" (Rahimi, 2005). According to Pomo historians, the decline in fluency in Bahtssal stems from the U.S. Senate's refusal in 1852 to ratify a federal treaty that had promised the Big Valley tribe 72 square miles of land on the south side of Clear Lake. Within a year, the area (in which the Pomos have lived for at least 11,000 years) was being carved up as private property by immigrating European Americans. Soon, Pomos were working on the immigrants' ranches as their children learned English in nearby schools.

James Bluewolf, who directs the language program, sees it as an exercise in cultural preservation as well as in healing. "People are still suffering from post-traumatic stress after being forced to give up everything they had," he said. "But [members of] every culture [come] to a point where they are ready to make a change" (Rahimi, 2005).

In Clear Lake, according to Rahimi's account, "The epicenter of that change sits among piles of scrap metal, wood and rusty cars, in a building that looks like it has dropped from the sky. It is tiny and tidy, and painted a bright swimming-pool blue. Inside this building, which houses the tribal language program, young mothers watch their chubby-cheeked toddlers play in a preschool class held by the nonprofit Lake County Tribal Health Consortium. In a cramped office past the play area ... Bluewolf smiles at the children's squeals. A stocky, soft-spoken man who once ran a landscaping business, Bluewolf has been using technology tribal ancestors could not have imagined to preserve and promote the tribal language" (Rahimi, 2005).

Bluewolf records Bahtssal as spoken by the few elders who still are fluent, which he then edits into half-hour audio segments that air on the community radio station and gives free to interested Pomos as compact discs. He also has written a 15-week curriculum for teaching Bahtssal. With younger children, Blue-wolf sometimes uses hand puppets to teach the language. In addition, Bluewolf rehearses teenagers to perform skits that teach words and phrases such as *Chiin the'a 'eh* (How are you?) and *Q'odii* (Good). Bluewolf edits videotapes of the skits for the Lake County television station, as well as DVDs.

A MIAMI DICTIONARY

Without a single fluent speaker remaining, the Miami Tribe of Oklahoma hopes to revive its language through the publication of a dictionary. Daryl Baldwin, a co-editor of the dictionary, said its book has been drawn from records spanning three centuries, beginning with dictionaries created by French missionaries of the late seventeenth and early eighteenth centuries, including word lists and texts collected in the nineteenth and early twentieth centuries. The project, a collaborative effort with Miami University of Ohio, began in 1991 ("Miami Dictionary," 2005).

"Our language is rich and complex," said Baldwin. "The dictionary proves it is a lie that the 'savage' Indian only needed 2,000 or 3,000 words to communicate" ("Miami Dictionary," 2005). The Miami language died like many others, as part of an English-only campaign the U.S. government conducted in an assimilation policy that lasted into the 1960s. "I never learned the language," said Floyd Leonard, a 78-year-old chief of the Miamis. "It wasn't something that was done when I was a child" ("Miami Dictionary," 2005).

Baldwin, an Ohio native and Miami Tribe of Oklahoma member, said a language is part of what defines a people. "Most of us have been removed from our cultural heritage," Baldwin said. "We started asking, What is Miami? Without speakers of the language, it's hard to get a glimpse of what that means. Language is culture" ("Miami Dictionary," 2005).

The dictionary was published in June 2005. Related projects include a field guide to plant species found in the Miamis' historical lands in Ohio and Indiana, which is expected to be finished in 2007, and a mapping project that will reclaim Miami place names. An audio CD of Miami speakers that contains vocabulary, phrases, conversation, the Miami origin story, and the Lord's Prayer was completed in 2002.

THE PRAIRIE BAND OF POTAWATOMI ARRESTS DECLINE OF ITS LANGUAGE

A small group of young people on the Prairie Band Potawatomi Indian Reservation in northeastern Kansas decided to stop the decline of indigenous language on their reservation, despite scoffing by some who said they would fail ("Community Effort," 1995). Eddie Joe Mitchell, with a strong background in English and journalism at Washburn University, was one of the early organizers and often played the role of facilitator by sounding out the words and writing them on a makeshift blackboard. Potawatomi elders, who wanted the language to continue, came forward to teach. Men such as Nelson Potts and Irving Shopteese were instrumental in the early days of the class. After these two men died, Potawatomi women such as Cecilia "Meeks" Jackson and Alberta "Shaw no que" Wamego stepped forward ("Community Effort," 1995).

When the class started in 1990, fifty to sixty students attended the class. Of these original students, only three remained with the group from the beginning—Eddie Joe Mitchell, Mary Wabnum, and Mary LeClere. Since then, the students have accumulated 6,000 words of the language and developed an ability to use them in sentences. During the ensuing decade, "The influence has spread out among the community to where the usage is more prevalent today. Mostly, by every-day use by the participants, the elders and their children are now using parts of the language in daily situations" ("Community Effort," 1995).

STREET SIGNS IN CHEROKEE

The 13,000-member Eastern Band of Cherokees in 2004 began posting 400 street signs in Cherokee as well as English on its reservation. The new signs were three years in the making and cost $45,000. They standardized the reservation's emergency dispatch system, cut down response times, and offered better directions for officers in the field, said Molly Grant, director of the tribe's Emergency Management Department (Ostendorff, 2004). The street signs are part of the Eastern Band of Cherokees' efforts to make the language part of everyday life, which also includes mandatory language classes in school, a television program about the language, classes for adults on a CD-ROM that details the Cherokee syllabary, or alphabet, ceremonies, and conduct of some council meetings in Cherokee and English (Ostendorff, 2004).

REVIVAL OF MOHAWK AND ONEIDA

In some cases, language revitalization becomes part of general community life. At Akwesasne, the weekly community newspaper, *Indian Time,* carries regular Mohawk language lessons by Mary Arquette and covers everyday situations, such as weather. *Teiowerataséhne,* "It was a windstorm"; *Ionen'onkión:ne,* "It was hailing." A quarter of the Mohawks at Akwesasne speak Mohawk with some degree of fluency. Radio station 97.3 CKON-FM at Akwesasne broadcasts some of its talk shows in Mohawk and receives calls from as far away as the Kanesatake and Kahnawake Mohawk reserves in Canada. Children's books are being published in Mohawk by the Circle of Knowledge Office of the Ahkwesahsne Mohawk Board of Education.

Kanien'keha, the Mohawk language, is being studied by Mohawks at Kahnawake using a computer-based program called Rosetta Stone. The Rosetta Stone method, developed by a Virginia-based company in 1994 as an alternative to traditional language teaching, uses Native speakers and everyday language on audio as well as written text, writing, and speaking exercises. It has been used for many years to teach European and Asian languages such as Hebrew, Thai, Pashto, and Arabic as well as Latin. Mohawk will be the first American aboriginal language available in Rosetta Stone. The company also is working with the Seminoles of Florida and an Inuit community in northwestern Alaska.

Rosetta Stone is structured exclusively around the target language. "It uses no translation. That's why it's especially good for this type of undertaking. It never says that this word in Mohawk is equivalent to this word in English or French, where the language would lose some meaning," said Ilse Ackerman, head of the endangered languages program at Fairfield Language Technologies (Stastna, 2004). It uses repetition, pictures, text, and the recorded voices of aboriginal speakers to mimic the way we naturally acquire language. Students work through lessons online or on a CD-ROM (Stastna, 2004).

Kahnawake is providing the translators, editors, and aboriginal speakers to produce the content, and the company provides the template and adapts the software. It charges $240,000 to create a first-level package of 300 hours of instruction, which Fairfield claims is equivalent to one year of in-class training, and another $170,000 for the second level (Stastna, 2004). The reserve's language and cultural center received 1,000 CD-ROM copies of the first-level. It was not decided whether it will charge for the software but will reserve some copies for use in schools, said Kanatakta, the center's executive director (Stastna, 2004). Only about 10 percent of roughly 7,000 Mohawks at Kahnawake, near Montreal, speak Mohawk; thirty years ago, more than 20 percent spoke the language (Stastna, 2004). Most of the remaining speakers are elderly. The Rosetta Stone project is part of a five-year, $6.5 million commitment to revive the Mohawk language in a broader initiative by the Canadian federal government. The project also includes TV and radio programming, adult immersion courses, and workplace language training.

Kahnawake Mohawk Grand Chief Michael Delisle and other leaders of the Kahnawake reserve south of Montreal began in 2006 to require all of its 900 public employees to enroll in Mohawk language lessons that use interactive software. Hospital staff, police, firefighters, librarians, sewer plant operators and social workers, among others, started on-the-job Mohawk language studies September 1. The target is to make 30 per cent of Kahnawake's public employees fluent speakers in five years, 60 per cent in 10 years and 80 per cent in 15 years (Cornacchia, 2006). At present, about 1,000 of Kahnawake's 8,000 residents speak Mohawk. The language will be taught with the Rosetta Stone software.

"The value of what this could mean socially and politically is monumental," Delisle said, adding that "so much of who we are is in our language ... We want to re-establish it as part of our heritage" (Cornacchia, 2006).The Kanienkehaka (Mohawk) community at Kanatsiohareke (Place of the Clean Pot), in the Mohawk River Valley of New York, has made cultural revitalization its main reason for being. Tom Porter, a traditional Mohawk chief at Akwesasne before he moved to found Kanatsiohareke in 1993, explained that language is a cornerstone of cultural revival. Thus, Kanatsiohareke's major focus has been Mohawk language-immersion classes, mostly during summers. "Once a people have lost their language, they have lost as much as maybe 50 percent of their cultural connections because there is so much tied up in the language that cannot be translated," said Kay Olan, codirector of Kanatsiohareke (Matthews, 2003).

> It is not a matter of saying words, it is a matter of passing on to future generations who we are as a people, what our original instructions are that were given to us by the Creator in terms of how we are supposed to act, how we are supposed to relate to each other and to the rest of the natural world and to the universe; how we fit in and our role. For example, incorporated into the simple act of counting from one to 10 in the Mohawk language is a retelling of our Creation Story. If we lose our language we lose that. (Matthews, 2003)

Classes also are offered for people who are already fluent in Mohawk but want to learn ceremonial speeches for wakes, funerals, and marriages. Only a handful of people remain who know the language of ceremony.

Mohawk has been adapted to contemporary usage in several ways. Monigarr Legacy Corp., created by Akwesasne Mohawk Monica Peters, has created a digital system "that allows users to type in an English phrase and hear a character-on-screen say an [English] phrase back in Mohawk" (Burns, August

18, 2005). The phrase also appears on the screen in text. The system can be accessed from any equipment that uses a voice box. At her Cornwall Island home, she has a Billy Bass (a talking, wall-mounted, artificial fish) that repeats Mohawk from English phrases typed into her computer.

Oneidas in New York decided during 2003 to join with Berlitz, the language company, to teach their language, but no one in the state spoke it fluently. Two teachers were invited to visit from an Oneida settlement in Thames, Ontario. They began teaching the language to eight New York Oneidas in 40-hour-per-week classes that began in February 2004 and ended in October. They were taught to introduce the language to others. "I don't want to see it die, and it's dying," said Sheri Beglen, one of the Oneidas taking the Berlitz course. "It's a dire situation for the language, probably more than anyone realizes" (Coin, 2004). "We could teach you 10,000 words, but if you don't know how to put them in a sentence, it doesn't matter," said Ray George, one of two teachers brought in from the Oneida of the Thames Reservation in Ontario. Of the 500 Thames Oneidas who spoke the language twenty years ago, only 100 are still alive (Coin, 2004).

The New York Oneida Nation contacted Berlitz in late 2002 for help. The worldwide language company, known for its conversational approach to teaching, also has worked with Lakotas in South Dakota. The Oneida project is far more extensive, said Deniz Ghrewati, Berlitz's district director for New England. "It was everything from learning the language to teaching the techniques to providing the materials," Ghrewati said. "It's a total program" (Coin, 2004). Berlitz provided detailed course materials in English late in 2003. George and Norma Jamieson, the other teacher, then spent several months translating the material into Oneida.

JOHN PEABODY HARRINGTON'S PAPERS

For five decades, John Peabody Harrington wandered the West, listening to the last speakers of several dozen Native languages, scribbling notes into notebooks, and packing them away. Harrington was "secretive and paranoid," according to one account, "a packrat who stuffed much of his work into boxes, crates and steamer trunks" (Anton, 2004). Following his death in 1961, his papers were found stuffed into "warehouses, attics, basements, even chicken coops." During the 1960s, his papers were collected at the Smithsonian Institution, where he once worked. "Six tons of material, much of it worthless," recalled Catherine A. Callaghan, a linguist who sorted through the Harrington papers when they arrived at the Smithsonian. "There was blank paper, dirty old shirts, half-eaten sandwiches.... Mixed in with all of that were these treasures" (Anton, 2004).

Four decades after his death, however, Harrington's work is being used to revive a number of nearly dead Native languages. Researchers at the University of California–Davis, backed by a National Science Foundation grant, are transcribing Harrington's million pages of often hardly legible, scribbled writing, much of it in his own code of Spanish or phonetic script, into electronic form that can be searched word by word, a task that may take them twenty years. "I very much doubt I will see the end of it," said project codirector Victor Golla, a 65-year-old professor of linguistics at Humboldt State University. "Like Harrington's original project, you do this for the future benefit of other people." "It's impenetrable," said Martha Macri, director of the University of California–Davis Native American Language Center and codirector of the effort to computerize Harrington's papers. "It's too hard to read his handwriting. Few people can tolerate looking at it for long periods of time" (Anton, 2004).

In recent years, Harrington's work has been used by California's Native peoples who have been attempting to establish federal recognition, settle territorial claims, and protect sacred sites from development as well as revive their languages. The Muwekma Ohlone tribe in the San Francisco Bay Area, for example, is using a dictionary compiled from Harrington's research to teach its members the Chochenyo language, which had been given up as dead for more than sixty years. "They've gone from knowing nothing to being able to carry on a short conversation, sing songs and play games. Now they're starting to do some creative writing," said University of California–Berkeley linguistics professor Juliette Blevins, who works with them. "We are reconstructing a whole language using his material" (Anton, 2004).

Harrington, who was born in 1884 and raised in Santa Barbara, studied classical languages and anthropology at Stanford University, where he graduated at the top of his class in three years. Harrington refused a Rhodes scholarship but studied anthropology and linguistics at universities in Europe on his own. Some of his professors marveled at his flawless ear, which allowed Harrington to write down every word said to him (Anton, 2004).

In 1915, Harrington was hired as a field linguist with the Smithsonian's Bureau of American Ethnology, a job that allowed him to indulge his wanderlust as he traveled from California to Alaska, attempting to record all he could of Native life and languages before they were obliterated. Jack Marr, a retired Fullerton, California, engineer who worked for Harrington as an assistant, beginning as a teenager, recalled that "He'd travel into a remote area by bus and get off and walk miles by himself to a trading post and ask, 'Where can I find the Indians?'" (Anton, 2004). Sometimes, during the 1930s and 1940s, Harrington would penetrate remote locations on horseback. A recluse, Harrington dressed in rags, and did not care about money. He often slept on the dirt floors of his interviewees' homes, eating dried beef, chili, and crackers for months. Harrington also paid no attention to publishing what he found.

Harrington married once, to Carobeth Tucker, then a linguistics student. Harrington dragged her along on his travels, even late in her pregnancy with their daughter. Tucker divorced Harrington after seven years to pursue her own career as a linguist and ethnographer.

A report at the *Los Angeles Times* characterized Harrington as a contradictory character who appreciated the nuances of Native American cultures but was a fervent anti-Semite. "He was," wrote reporter Mike Anton, "a workaholic who never quite finished a project [and] a social misfit who had no close friends but could charm suspicious strangers into divulging their most profound secrets" (Anton, 2004). Marr hauled a 35-pound recording machine powered by a car battery for Harrington, who told him that Native languages would be lost forever if he did not document them.

In 1994, Joyce Stanfield Perry, a Juaneño leader in California's Orange County, searched the Smithsonian for documentation to support federal recognition for their tribe. They found, in a box of recordings by one of Harrington's assistants during the 1930s, the voice of Anastacia de Majel, who was then in her seventies, one of the last speakers of the Juaneño language. "We wept," Perry said. "It truly was like our ancestors were talking directly to us." Perry, who also runs a nonprofit Indian education and cultural foundation, estimates that 10,000 pages of Harrington's notes refer to her people. As they are entered into the database, a dictionary of her native language is emerging. So far, it contains 1,200 words (Anton, 2004).

FURTHER READING

American Indian Language Development Institute. "History." December 8, 2005. <http://www.u.arizona.edu/~aildi/About_Us/history.html>.

Anton, Mike. "A California Linguist's Mountain of Scribbled Notes Is the Key to Nearly Forgotten Native American Languages." *Los Angeles Times,* July 2, 2004, n.p.

Assembly of First Nations [Canada]. *Towards Linguistic Justice for First Nations.* Ottawa, ON: Education Secretariat, Assembly of First Nations, 1990.

Barton, Rhonda. "Charter School Keeps Native Language Alive; Determined Teachers Enhance Students' Cultural Identity." *Northwest Education Magazine* 9, no. 3 (Spring 2004). <http://www.nwrel.org/nwedu/09-03/charter.php>.

"Bid to Save Nearly-lost Language." *BBC.* May 26, 2005. <http://news.bbc.co.uk/go/pr/fr/-/2/hi/americas/4583455.stm>.

Burnham, Philip. "O'odham Linguist Comes to Washington." *Indian Country Today,* January 4, 2006., n.p., <www.ccsso.org/content/PDFs/LCENewsletterJan06.pdf>.

Burns, Shannon. "Mohawk Immersion Program Goes Full-speed Ahead." *Indian Time,* September 1, 2005: 6.

Burns, Shannon. "Mohawk Language Is Just a Mouse Click Away." *Indian Time* (Akwesasne), August 18, 2005: 1, 3.

Cantoni, G., ed. *Stabilizing Indigenous Languages.* Flagstaff: Northern Arizona University, 1996.

Chang, Jack. "State's Indians Uncover the Past." *Contra Costa Times,* June 14, 2004, n.p.

Clarke, Brennan. "Central Saanich Teacher Leading Charge to Save Local Indigenous Language from Extinction." *Victoria News,* April 21, 2006. <http://listserv.arizona.edu/cgi-bin/wa?A2=ind0604&L=ilat&P=5431>.

Coin, Glenn. "Oneida Spoken Here; Eight Taking Classes in Tribe's Language to Keep It Alive." *Syracuse Post-Standard,* October 6, 2004, n.p. <http://www.syracuse.com/news>.

"Community Effort Brings Potawatomi to a New Generation of the Prairie Band." *Topeka Capital Journal,* November 2, 1995, n.p.

Cornacchia, Cheryl. "Ancient Tongue, Modern Software: Kahnawake AIMS to Revive Mohawk Language; All Its 900 Public Employees Must Take Lessons." Montreal

Gazette, June 12, 2006. <http://www.canada.com/montrealgazette/news/story. html?id=bda326ef-1b41-4c86-b821-5ac47c5c5e4a&k=40064>.

"The Critical Moment: Funding the Perpetuation of Native Languages" Transcript of Proceedings, Lannan Foundation. Santa Fe, NM, January 26–28, 1998.

Dillon, Jenni. "It Lies within the Culture." *Jackson Hole* (Wyoming) *Star-Tribune*, August 30, 2005. <http://www.jacksonholestartrib.com/articles/2005/08/30/news/wyoming/ 8a4b695d8986c7718725706c006ef74c.txt>.

Estes, James. "How Many Indigenous Languages are Spoken in the United States? By How Many Speakers?" National Clearinghouse for Bilingual Education. Rutgers University, 1999. <http://www.rci.rutgers.edu/~jcamacho/363/nativetoday.htm>.

First Nations Confederacy of Cultural Education Centers. "First Nations Languages Funds Languish in Ottawa." Press release. September 21, 2005. <http://www.newswire. ca/en/releases/archive/September2005/21/c2181.html>.

Fishman, Joshua F. "Maintaining Languages: What Works, What Doesn't?" *Stabilizing Indigenous Languages*. Ed. G. Cantoni. Flagstaff: Northern Arizona University, 1996, 186–98.

Fishman, Joshua F. *Reversing Language Shift: Theoretical and Empirical Foundations of Assistance to Threatened Languages*. Clevedon, U.K.: Multilingual Matters, 1991.

Gee, Pat. "Native Speech: An Audio CD Package Aims to Give the Hawaiian Language the Place It Deserves in Everyday Life." *Honolulu Star-Bulletin*, May 24, 2004. <http:// starbulletin.com/2004/05/24/features/story1.html>.

Graef, Christine. "N.C.C.C. [North Country Community College] to Include Mohawk Language and Culture in Evening Course." *Indian Time* 23, no. 227 (July 7, 2005): 7.

Hayes, Ernestine. "Indigenous Languages Key to Cultural Identity." *Juneau Empire*, June 12, 2005. <http://www.juneauempire.com/stories/061205/opi_20050612023.shtml>.

"In the Language of Our Ancestors; Programs in Montana and Washington Give Voice to Disappearing Words." *Northwest Education Magazine* 9, no.3 (Spring 2004). <http:// listserv.arizona.edu/cgi-bin/wa?A2=ind0405&L=ilat&P=1316>.

Johansen, Bruce E. "Living and Breathing: Native Languages Come Alive." *Native Americas* 17, no. 1 (Spring 2000): 56–59.

Kie, Will. "Language Program Preserves Ancient Language." *Cibola Beacon*, June 28, 2005. <http://www.cibolabeacon.com/articles/2005/06/28/news/news1.txt>.

Kizzia, Tom. "Natives Want Their Dying Language Taught; Nanwalek: Village Asks Kenai School District to Make Sugt'stun Part of Curriculum." *Anchorage Daily News*, April 9, 2006. <http://www.adn.com/news/alaska/rural/story/7611812p-7522874c.html>.

Krauss, Michael. "The World's Languages in Crisis." *Language* 68 (1992): 6–10.

Kuchera, Steve. "Bands Focus on Preservation; Language Revitalization Groups Work to Save Minnesota's First Languages and Cultures." *Duluth News-Tribune*, June 28, 2004. <listserv.arizona.edu/cgi-bin/ wa?A2=ind0406&L=ilat&P=3891>.

Lacitis, Erik. "Last Few Whulshootseed Speakers Spread the Word." *Seattle Times*, February 11, 2005. <listserv.arizona.edu/cgi-bin/ wa?A2=ind0502&L=ilat&P=1530>.

LaFortune, Richard. "Ojibwe and Dakota Language Revitalization Moves Forward in Minnesota." Press release. April 20, 2004.

"Lakota Immersion Camp Teaches Tribal Language, Traditions." *Sioux City Journal*, April 29, 2005. <listserv.arizona.edu/cgi-bin/ wa?A2=ind0504&L=ilat&P=6792>.

"Lakota on Path to Recapture Language." *Ascribe Newsletter*, March 15, 2006 (from Lexis).

Leiste, Matthew. "College Uses Rap Music to Preserve a Language." Sisseton Wahpeton College. Press release. August 21, 2005. <http://news.ucwe.com/content/view/523/2/>.

Logue, Susan. "New Lakota Leader Puts Emphasis on Language." *Voice of America.* November 29, 2005. <http://www.voanews.com/english/AmericanLife/2005-11-29-voa42.cfm>.

Mann, Charles C. *1491: New Revelations of the Americas Before Columbus.* New York: Alfred A. Knopf, 2005.

Marigza, Lilla. "Nome Congregation Keeps Native Language Alive in Ministry." *Worldwide Faith News Archives.* December 21, 2005. <http://www.wfn.org/2005/12/msg00192.html>.

Martin, Ian. "Restoring Linguistic Rights for Aboriginals." *Toronto Star,* June 3, 2005. <www.caslt.org/Info2/newsenglishjuly05.htm>.

Martinson, Bob. "Using Technology to Resurrect a Near-Forgotten Language." *The Frontiersman.* February 13, 2005. <http://www.frontiersman.com/articles/2005/02/13/news/news6.txt>.

Matthews, Lisa. "More Than Words; Mohawk Language and Cultural Revitalization in New York: Interview with Kay Olan, Co-director of Kanatsiohareke." *Cultural Survival* 27, no. 4 (December 15, 2003). <www.cs.org/publications/csq/index.cfm?id=27.4>.

McCarty, Teresa L., Lucille J. Watahomigie, Akira Y. Yamamoto, and Ofelia Zepeda. "School-Community-University Collaborations: The American Indian Language Development Institute." *Teaching Indigenous Languages.* Ed. Jon Reyhner. Flagstaff: Northern Arizona University, 1997. January 6, 2006. <http://jan.ucc.nau.edu/~jar/TIL_9.html>.

"Miami Dictionary." *Associated Press.* June 29, 2005. <http://indianz.com/News/2005/007960.asp>.

Morrison, Eric. "Dauenhauer Teaches Language That's on the Edge." *Juneau Empire,* September 21, 2005. <http://www.juneauempire.com/stories/092105/loc_20050922052.shtml>.

Neyman, Jenny. "Class Helps Preserve Dena'ina Heritage." *Fairbanks News-Miner,* June 27, 2004. <listserv.arizona.edu/cgi-bin/ wa?A2=ind0406&L=ilat&P=3247>.

"NMSU Student to Do Play-by-Play in Navajo." Associated Press, September 22, 2005. *KOBTV.com.* <http://www.kobtv.com/index.cfm?viewer=storyviewer&id=21791&cat=NMSPORTS>.

Nugent, Tom. "As Tribal Speakers Dwindle, a Rush to Teach Their Words: Native American Languages at Risk." *Boston Globe,* May 31, 2005. <listserv.arizona.edu/cgi-bin/wa?A2=ind0505&L=ilat&D=1&P=7735>.

Ogden, Karen. "Tribal College Expands with Dedication of Cultural Center." *Great Falls* (Montana) *Tribune,* June 2, 2005, n.p.

Ostendorff, Jon. "Signs Spell Out Tribe's Passion to Revitalize Native Language." *Asheville Citizen-Times,* May 12, 2004. <http://cgi.citizen-times.com/cgi-bin/story/regional/54741>.

"Preserving the Klamath Tongue." *Klamath Falls Herald and News,* July 31, 2005. <http://www.heraldandnews.com/articles/2005/07/31/news/top_stories/top1.txt>.

Quintero, Carolyn. *Osage Grammar.* Lincoln: University of Nebraska Press, 2005.

Rahimi, Shadi. "American Indian Youths Preserve the Past, One Word at a Time." *Pacific News Service, Youth News Feature.* May 11, 2005.

Redish, Laura. "Native Languages of the Americas: Endangered Language Revitalization and Revival." March 2001. <http://www.native-languages.org/revive.htm>.

Reyhner, Jon, ed. *Teaching Indigenous Languages.* Flagstaff: Center for Excellence in Education, Northern Arizona University, 1997.

Reyhner, Jon, Gina Cantoni, Robert N. St. Clair, and Evangeline Parsons Yazzie. *Revitalizing Native Languages*. Flagstaff: Center for Excellence in Education, Northern Arizona University, 1999.

"Sealaska Heritage Offers Immersion Retreats." *JuneauEmpire.com*. July 30, 2004. <listserv.arizona.edu/cgi-bin/ wa?A2=ind0407&L=ilat&P=4228>.

Sims, Hank. "Speak It Good and Strong; Yurok Youth Vow to Bring Back the Language of Their Ancestors." *North Coast Journal,* January 12, 2006. Via IndigenousNewsNetwork@topica.com, no 618 (January 13, 2006).

Smith, Bruce, and M. L. Cornette. "Defining a New Oral Tradition: American Indian Radio in the Dakotas." *SANTEC Weekly Newsletter*. University of South Dakota, March 1, 2004.

Springer, Patrick. "Spreading the Word: Project Uses Translated Rap Music as Means for Younger American Indians to Learn Native Language." *Fargo Forum*, September 12, 2005. <http://www.in-forum.com/articles/index.cfm?id=102752&section=News>.

Stastna, Kazi. "There's No M for Mohawk; Language Fading, Software May Help Delay Disappearance." *Montreal Gazette,* April 27, 2004, n.p.

"U.S.-Canadian Native Students Play Scrabble Tournament in Dakota Language." *Associated Press*. March 25, 2006 (in Lexis).

Viotti, Vicki. "Native Language Goes Online." *Honolulu Advertiser,* April 4, 2004. <http://the.honoluluadvertiser.com/article/2004/Apr/04/ln/ln21a.html/?print=on>.

Wilson, S. J. "Utilizing Song and Film to Teach Hopi Language." *Navajo Hopi Observer,* April 2005. <listserv.arizona.edu/cgi-bin/ wa?A2=ind0504&L=ilat&T=0&P=1797>.

Wittmeyer, Alicia. "Linguistics Prof Revives Fight to Save Indigenous Languages; Pushes Senate Committee to Fund Immersion Schools." *The Daily Californian* (University of California–Berkeley), May 27, 2003. <http://www.dailycal.org/particle.php?id=11838>.

Wiwcha, David. "Task Force Calls for Funding of Aboriginal Language Project." *Today.* October 4, 2005, n.p.

CHAPTER 2

❧

Where Has All the Money Gone?

Beginning in 1887 through the General Allotment Act (sometimes known after its primary congressional sponsor, Senator Henry Dawes), American Indians were brought (rarely willingly) into what President George W. Bush later would call the "ownership society," the lower rungs of capitalism, with their communal lands extinguished and as much as 90 percent parceled out to immigrant non-Indians. The lands remaining under Native ownership often included natural resources (lumber and, later, oil, natural gas, and other things) that were exploited by non-Indians. In theory, like other owners of resources, the Native landowners were supposed to be paid royalties through the Bureau of Indian Affairs (BIA) and the Treasury Department, through accounts called Individual Indian Monies.

More than a century later, when Blackfeet Nation accountant Eloise Cobell filed a lawsuit to narrow the distance between that theory and a reality of mismanagement and fraud, she had only the slightest inkling of the financial monster she had discovered. First estimates of mismanaged funds ranged from $2 billion to $4 billion (Johansen, 1997, 14)—a lot of money, surely, but a pittance compared to the $176 billion that was estimated 10 years later. By 2006, the Individual Indian Monies mess had become the stuff of political and legal legend, nine years after the class-action case that became known as *Cobell v. Norton* was first filed. With 500,000 plaintiffs, the case has grown to be the largest class action ever filed against the U.S. federal government. Employing more than 100 lawyers on the payrolls of the Interior and Treasury departments, *Cobell v. Norton* (after Cobell, the lead plaintiff, and Gale Norton, then secretary of the Interior) has become the largest single employer of federal legal talent in the history of the republic.

Cobell rented a modest four-room office in Browning, Montana, and by 2005 had funded her legal challenge with about $12 million in grant money.

Characterized as "small, soft-voiced, and an energetic 59 years old [in 2005]—she refers to herself as 'kind of hyper' even six weeks after undergoing surgery to donate a kidney to her husband—Cobell seems an unlikely crusader. But she is the great-granddaughter of Mountain Chief, part of a pantheon of legendary Blackfeet warriors who battled the U.S. government as far back as its original real-estate emissaries, Lewis and Clark" (Whitty, 2005). During 2002, the Blackfeet awarded Cobell status as a warrior, rare for a woman, but hardly inappropriate at a time when robbery takes novel forms.

REDEFINING "TRUST"

Not even George Orwell, in his imaginary world where the names of government agencies described the opposite of their intentions, could have topped the wordplay at the Bureau of Indian Affairs. Try this one on Big Brother: "Trust," as in *trust responsibility* and *trust account*. Not even Orwellian Newspeak could describe what became of all varieties of trust among those Native Americans for whom the BIA became banker.

More than three hundred Native American governments (with 2,965 accounts as of 1992) and 500,000 Native American individuals who have trust accounts with the Great White Father soon were asking what had become of their money. It has been cold comfort to many of them who have learned that the BIA, their legal trustee, very possibly had not a clue. Even then the adversarial legal system dragged on as if in perpetual motion, the government unwilling to make things right as best it could. Instead, by 2006, Uncle Sam's legal talent was focused on successfully convincing a higher court to dismiss the judge it believed was biased. More on this later.

The trust accounts ranged in size from 35 cents to $1 million for individuals. Among Native bands and nations, the largest single account was the roughly $400 million set aside for the Sioux settlement of the Black Hills land claim, which has not been paid because the Sioux have not agreed to accept it. The Navajo Nation had an account worth $23 million. Three-quarters of the group trust assets were held by 8 percent of Native nations in 1992, according to a 1992 report of the House Committee on Government Operations titled *Misplaced Trust: The Bureau of Indian Affairs Mismanagement of the Indian Trust Funds.*

How much money was at stake? In 1997, the commonly accepted figure was between $2 billion and $3 billion. By late 2002, lead prosecutor Dennis Gingold placed the figure at "far north of $10 billion" (Kennedy, 2002). A report prepared for the Interior Department suggested that the federal government's total liability might reach $40 billion. Tack on a few billion more and you have Uncle Sam's annual bill for the Iraq War in 2004. A report prepared for the Interior Department in 2004 suggested that the federal government's total liability to Native Americans eventually might reach $40 billion, which would work out to about $80,000 per plaintiff. Even that paled next to the bill as calculated by the plaintiffs for a century-plus of fraud plus interest: $176 billion.

AN ACCOUNTING LESSON

Eloise Cobell has spent much of her life in and near the reservation town of Browning, Montana. She was one of eight children in a house with no electricity or running water. The major form of entertainment was old-fashioned: oral history, parents telling stories to children, sometimes describing Baker's Massacre, during which U.S. soldiers killed about two hundred Blackfeet, a majority of them women and children, following an ambush near the Marias River. As a child, Cobell also sometimes heard stories from her parents and their neighbors about small government checks they received that never seemed to bear any relationship to reality.

After high school, Cobell graduated from Great Falls Commercial College and then studied for two years at Montana State University. Her education at the university was interrupted when she returned to the reservation to take care of her terminally ill mother. During a sojourn off the reservation in her twenties, Eloise met Alvin, her husband, who is also Blackfeet, in Seattle. He was fishing off the Alaska coast, and she held a job as an accountant at a Seattle television station, KIRO.

At the age of 30, Cobell returned to Browning with Alvin to resume a life on the family ranch. As one of few Blackfeet with training in the fiscal arts, Cobell was offered a job as the reservation government's accountant. At the time, Browning had practically no Native-owned businesses; unemployment rose to more than 70 percent in winter (which can last into May) when construction employment ceased.

Cobell found the Blackfeet accounting system "in total chaos" (Kennedy, 2002). Some trust accounts were being charged negative interest. Checks were being posted against accounts without her knowledge, even though she was supposed to be the only valid signatory. Cobell served as treasurer of the Blackfeet from 1970 through 1983, 13 years putting Blackfeet accounting on a sound footing while also working her ranch with her husband.

In 1983, after the government shut down the only bank on the reservation, Cobell formed the idea of founding an Indian-owned bank. Told it would never work, she went back to school, became a banker, and in 1987 threw open the doors of the Blackfeet National Bank, the first national bank located on a reservation in the United States and the first owned by Native Americans. Within 15 years, this institution had grown into the Native American Bank, with 23 Native American nations from across the country investing as much as $1 million apiece (Whitty, 2005).

Following its creation, the bank provided loans to Native Americans to help start businesses that otherwise never would have been financed. In a few years, Cobell could point to several businesses in Browning that she had helped finance: the Glacier Restaurant, Browning Video, the Dollar Store (Kennedy, 2002). By 2005, Cobell's assay into banking had helped provide Browning with more than 200 enterprises, 80 percent of them Indian-owned (Whitty, 2005). Cobell soon was spending much of her time (apart from the many hours devoted to the court case and ranch chores with Alvin) tutoring Blackfeet and other Native peoples in ways to best start their own businesses.

RESERVATION STORIES

During her years as the Blackfeet's accountant, Cobell traveled the reservation, visiting one family after another. Cobell noticed oil wells pumping on Blackfeet land, large herds of cattle grazing, and fields of alfalfa rippling, all owned by non-Indian tenants on Blackfeet land. Many of the tenants lived in well-kept houses and drove new cars as their Blackfeet landlords lived in cold, leaky government housing, largely unemployed and undereducated, and survived on commodity food. "Why couldn't an Indian—a landholding Indian at that, get a mortgage or a bank loan to start his or her own life?" wondered Cobell (Whitty, 2005).

Cobell heard from Jim Little Bull, 82 years of age in 2005, who still was living in a tiny, nearly unfurnished home in Browning that was heated with an ancient wood stove. When Little Bull's mother, Mary Little Bull, passed away many years ago, the government taxed her estate $7,000 for the operation and management of an irrigation system on her allotment. Although ditches had been dug on the land, irrigation equipment never was installed, and no water other than rainfall ever had run through it. Initially, Little Bull was afraid to ask questions, worried his own Individual Indian Monies would be withheld to pay his mother's bill. Unable to pay the debt, he silently forfeited her land back to the government (Whitty, 2005).

James Mad Dog Kennerly occupied hereditary allotments with as many as five working oil wells at a time. From these he received a government-issued royalty check for approximately $30 per month. He lives in a house smaller than many modern walk-in closets. The drive to his oil-producing property at the eastern edge of the Blackfeet Nation passes through two worlds: Browning's bleak government housing, followed by miles of prosperous farmland. "That's my land, right here," said Kennerly, pointing to another of his allotments, leased not to an oil company but to a Hutterite farming colony, an Amish-like community that, ironically, works property communally. These farms are large and prosperous, consisting of large barns and well-tended fields. Kennerly complained that the Interior Department—which manages one-fifth of all land in the country—leases his lands for far less than the going rate (Whitty, 2005).

Cobell's education in the BIA's ways of banking began with a detailed examination of the Blackfeet's trust accounts. After Cobell discovered a number of problematic transactions, she began asking questions. She then began to ask what had become of royalty payments owed Native Americans through Individual Indian Monies accounts.

One resident of the reservation, for example, wanted to know why her family was receiving less than $1,000 per year for the 7,000 acres of family land that the government leased to non-Indians, who were using it to graze cattle and extract timber, oil, and other minerals. Other people were raising questions as well. During the mid-1980s, David Henry, an accountant and the first CPA to be employed by the BIA in Billings, Montana, found that the agency had deposited between $7.5 million and $11 million more in banks than it had dispersed to Indian account holders of Individual Indian Monies. When Henry, who was 56 years of age at the time, took his findings to his superiors at the BIA in 1986, he was fired. He appealed the firing all the way to the U.S. Supreme Court and was denied. Because he had been on the job less than a year, the BIA contended that Henry lacked rights to appeal.

Henry, who said that local Indians gave him the nickname "Whistleblower," later worked full-time as a critic of the BIA, especially of its accounting practices (or lack thereof). He also wrote a book titled *Stealing from Indians* (1995). The *Billings Gazette* characterized the book as "part autobiography, part screed, and part expose" (Johansen, 1997, 16).

People often asked Cobell what kept her going. "The stories that I tell you about are the stories that drive me," she said (Szpaller, 2005). Cobell grew up without television. Instead, neighbors and family gathered in the evenings and listened to stories. One thread tied together much of what she heard, she said, "If I could only get my money from the Indian agent" (Szpaller, 2005). Cobell's aunt once needed money to take her uncle to the hospital. The aunt took a wagon to the Indian agent's office. It was early November, and snow rose to her aunt's chest. "She said they kept them outside all day, and it was cold," Cobell said. She did not receive her check until April. "That was the treatment that the government gave individual Indian people," Cobell said (Szpaller, 2005).

COBELL'S INQUIRIES REBUFFED BY THE BUREAU OF INDIAN AFFAIRS

Cobell explained why she took on the U.S. Department of the Interior. She believes that no one should have to sue for simple access to their own money. First and foremost, Cobell said, the class-action suit that she initiated asks the government to fix its flawed accounting system. "This is not rocket science," she said. "This is fixing accounting systems" (Szpaller, 2005). The lawsuit also asks that the government give an accounting to individual Indians, and it requests restitution as needed.

Cobell did not decide to file suit lightly, but only after several rebuffs by the government that displayed an unwillingness to take the trust-accounts problem seriously. "They said, 'Oh, you don't know how to read the reports,'" Cobell recalled. "I think they were trying to embarrass me, but it did the opposite—it made me mad" (Awehali, 2003).

THE HERITAGE OF ALLOTMENT

Cobell's demand for an accounting was a challenge to more than a century of business as usual at the BIA. Beginning during the term of President Andrew Jackson and expanded and refined in the General Allotment Act (1887), trust accounts were created in the names of individual Native Americans into which the Interior Department deposited monies due them from use of land and resources. These deposits could be made for such things as the sale of timber or exploitation of mineral rights as well as leases of land for grazing and farming. Some of the funds came from tribal per capita payments and others from settlement of land or water claims.

Allotment was advanced by so-called reformers who contended that life as farmers was the only alternative to extermination for Indians as the frontier closed around them. The theory of turning Indians into farmers in the Jeffersonian yeoman image was outdated by the late nineteenth century as the United States industrialized rapidly. The rigid allotments also failed to take into account the amount of land needed to sustain a family in the arid West.

Allotments were fixed by the act at 160 acres (a quarter section) for the head of a family or 80 acres (an eighth section) for a single person older than 18 years of age. The land was to be held in trust for 25 years and then released in fee simple to the owner. The act then held that an Indian would become a U.S. citizen subject to the laws of the state in which he or she resided. The act indicated that allotment would extinguish Indian title to the land.

The introduction of private property was advanced ideologically as an aid in civilizing native peoples. In reality, allotment mainly was a government-sponsored real-estate agency for transferring land from Indians to European Americans. As a result of allotment, Indian-owned landholdings were reduced from 138 million acres in 1887 to about 50 million in 1934, according to John Collier, commissioner of Indian affairs at the end of the period. Sixty million acres were lost through the release of surplus lands to federal government ownership or sale to homesteaders. Twenty-six million acres of land were transferred to non-Indians after they were released from trust status, by purchase, fraud, mortgage foreclosures, and tax sales. Of the 48 million acres remaining in Indian hands by 1934, 20 million were too arid for productive farming, which had been the goal of allotment. By 1933, 49 percent of Indians on allotted reservations were landless. At that time, 96 percent of all reservation Indians were earning less than $200 a year.

Because allotment was based on the model of the Anglo-American nuclear family, many Indians who were subjected to its provisions were required to do more than change their property-holding customs. Native extended families were devastated by the allotment system, in which close relatives who had lived together often were given distant parcels of land. Long-established ties between grandmothers and their children were severed and a long-standing family structures destroyed. Indian men who were married to more than one wife were told to divest their extra relatives. Vine Deloria Jr. recalled the tearful response of the Kiowa chief Quanah Parker, who, when told that he must give up his extra wives, "told the [Indian] agent that, if he must give them up, he could not choose which one to surrender and that the agent must do it for him" (Deloria and Lytle, 1983, 197).

According to legal scholar Charles F. Wilkinson, "Allotment and the other assimilationist programs that complemented it devastated Indian land base, weakened

Indian culture, sapped the vitality of tribal legislative and judicial processes, and opened most Indian reservations for settlement by non-Indians (Wilkinson, 1987, 19). U.S. political leaders understood this to be the upshot of allotment at the time. President Theodore Roosevelt, for example, said, "The General Allotment Act is a mighty pulverizing engine to break up the tribal mass. It acts directly upon the family and the individual" (Johansen, 1997, 19). Over the generations, many individual allotments were subdivided into miniscule plots by inheritances, rendering many of them nearly useless for agriculture.

The breakdown of Native American estate, as well as tribal governments and family relations, was the stated aim of allotment legislation. The BIA's own publications acknowledge that the trust of U.S. Indian policy in the 1870s and 1880s was to "further minimize the functions of tribal leaders and tribal institutions and to continually strengthen the position of the government representative and his subordinates, and to improve the effectiveness of their programs to break down traditional patterns within the Indian communities" (Johansen, 1997, 21).

Other voices were raised at the time against allotment and other forms of assimilation. Ethnologist Lewis Henry Morgan, known as the founder of U.S. anthropology, predicted that a result of allotment for the Indian "would unquestionably be, that in a very short time he would divest himself of every foot of land and fall into poverty" (Johansen, 1997, 21). Morgan was echoing the minority opinion of the Congressional Committee of Indian Affairs on the Allotment Act:

> The real purpose of this bill is to get at the Indian lands and open them up to settlement. The provisions for the apparent benefit of the Indians are but the pretext to get his lands and occupy them.... If this were done in the name of greed, it would be bad enough; but to do it in the name of humanity, and under the cloak of an ardent desire to promote the Indian's welfare by making him like ourselves whether he will or not, is infinitely worse. (Johansen, 1997, 21)

Although allotment impoverished many Indians as Morgan foresaw, the Bureau of Indian Affairs prospered. By 1934, with Indian estate making up less than half the area it had before allotment began, the Indian Bureau had increased its staff (6,000 people) and its budget ($23 million per year) 400 percent.

Mismanagement of the Individual Indian Monies accounts surfaced early in the twentieth century when several full-blooded members of the Five Civilized Tribes in Oklahoma Territory were found dead of starvation despite the fact that they had Individual Indian Monies accounts worth hundreds of thousands of dollars. The BIA had been diverting their income to pay for construction of schools and churches.

WARDS PUT THE BUREAU OF INDIAN AFFAIRS ON TRIAL

Before Cobell's challenge, many Individual Indian Monies account holders had been wary of confronting the system because the BIA could (and sometimes did) declare them incompetent to handle their own money, as wards of the agency.

Trust—a word often used in banking circles—is also the legal rubric under which the BIA (or other agencies of the Interior Department) first became Indians' bankers. The so-called handlers of Indians in the War Department, Interior Department, and BIA always have had available to them two versions of reality: one is the official ideology of trust, meaning "guardianship," the kindly language of a supposedly benevolent Great White Father, of "the most exacting fiduciary standards," "due care," and "moral obligations of the highest responsibility and trust."

Consider that federal agencies that had lost, abused, and otherwise bungled the Indians' funds were empowered, by their interpretation of the law, to decide whether Native individuals were competent to handle their own money. If the BIA could find their money, and if it was not gambled away in a failed savings and loan back in the 1980s, a Native nation or Individual Indian Money account holder still might not have access to funds.

Helen Avalos, assistant attorney general for the Navajo Nation, noted that, considering the record, it should be obvious that it was the government, not the Indians, that was not competent. "I guess they thought the money would be misspent," Avalos told the *Santa Fe New Mexican*. "But it turns out that everything they suspected we would do wrong, they have done wrong" (Johansen, 1997, 14).

Wardship, in American Indian law and policy, refers to a legal doctrine, said to be based on opinions by U.S. Supreme Court Chief Justice John Marshall during the 1830s that Native Americans live in "dependent domestic nations" and are therefore wards of the federal government. The Bureau of Indian Affairs was initially established to hold Indians' land and resources in trust. Wardship status rationalized the establishment of Indian reservations and schools to assimilate Native Americans into mainstream U.S. culture.

The idea of Native sovereignty in modern times has been developed in large part in opposition to wardship doctrines. Indians reacted to a social-control system that was so tight that in many cases (e.g., if a will affected the status of allotted land) individual actions of Native American people were subject to approval by the secretary of the Interior Department.

The assertion of states rights over Native territory in the Southeast provided the legal grist for a 1832 Supreme Court decision written by Justice Marshall. In *Worcester v. Georgia,* Marshall wrote that inhabitants of Native nations had assumed a relationship of pupilage (wardship) in their relations with the United States. Using this doctrine, which has no constitutional basis, the executive branch of the U.S. government, principally through the Bureau of Indian Affairs, has created a superstructure of policies and programs that have had a vast impact on individual Native Americans and their governments. Through the use of the plenary power of Congress, such policies as allotment divested much of the Indian estate between 1854 and 1934.

A concept of wardship also has been used since the mid-nineteenth century to construct for American Indians a cradle-to-grave social-control system that was described during the mid-twentieth century by legal scholar Felix Cohen:

Under the reign of these magic words [*wardship* and *trust*] nothing Indian was safe. The Indian's hair was cut, his dances forbidden, his oil lands, timber lands, and grazing lands were disposed of by Indian agents and Indian commissioners for whom the magic word "wardship" always made up for lack of statutory authority. (Johansen, 1997, 19)

Although Marshall's opinions have been used as a legal rationale for government policies that have treated American Indians as wards, "There is nothing," according to Robert T. Coulter, executive director of the Indian Law Resource Center, "in the rulings of the Marshall Court [that] even remotely suggested that the United States could unilaterally impose a guardian-ward relationship on Indians, that it held trust title to Indian lands, or that, as trustee, it could dispose of lands without Indian consent" (Coulter and Tullberg, 1984, 199).

Wardship as historically practiced by the Bureau of Indian Affairs differs markedly from the legal status of non-Indian wards. Under most conditions, wardship is viewed as a temporary condition, with established standards for cession. Civil guardianship and custody law must allow people who have been deprived of their civil rights means of regaining them in accordance with the Due Process Clause of the United States Constitution. As developed by the BIA, however, Indian wardship has no standard for cession and no ending date. An Indian is defined as a ward regardless of his or her accomplishments or other actions, as the object of a policy that may have misinterpreted Marshall's intent.

Legal scholar Frank Pommersheim writes that "it was in this soil of expansion and exploitation that federal Indian law developed and took root. This was a soil without constitutional loam.... The theory of the trust responsibility with the U.S. government as owner and trustee of Indian land, natural resources, and provider of many services is in direct conflict with any meaningful theory of tribal sovereignty" (Pommersheim, 1995, 38, 445). In other words, as the courts talk a measured sense of sovereignty for reservation residents, the government walks a potent form of colonialism through the trust doctrine.

DOING THE MATH

Around 1991, after having spent a decade badgering federal government officials for explanations of BIA finances, Cobell finally found someone in the Interior Department who was willing to help her: David Matheson, a Coeur d'Alene who was a deputy commissioner of Indian affairs in the first Bush administration. Matheson was about to lose his job, however, when the Clinton administration came into power in January 1993.

Cobell thought she might have trouble finding anyone in the new administration who was willing to listen to her, but Matheson connected her with an influential Washington, DC, banking attorney, Dennis Gingold, who took an interest in the question of Indian trust money. Gingold, who eventually became the lead prosecuting attorney for the case, was quoted in the *Los Angeles Times* as saying of his first meeting with Cobell, "From my experience, American Indians were not involved in banking. I was looking for a bunch of people with turbans" (Kennedy, 2002). Gingold admitted that he had a great deal to learn about how the government had separated Native Americans from their trust assets. Gingold recommended to Cobell that she file a suit against the government, but she initially was reluctant to do so, hoping that Congress would take action to correct the problems.

As part of its rehabilitation efforts, the Interior Department in 1992 hired the Arthur Andersen accounting firm to report on just how much of a mess the BIA had created and how much money would be required to fix it. When the due bill arrived four years later—the firm said it would take $108 million to $281 million just to get the Individual Indian Monies program operational at minimal accounting standards—Congress and the Interior Department decided that because such money was not available, they could do nothing. More holders of Individual Indian Monies accounts were doing the math themselves and concluding that they would get nothing by waiting for the government to fix the problems it had created. The number of Native Americans asking for accountings of their accounts increased during the early 1990s.

Some in the government saw the problem coming before Cobell filed suit. In 1992, the House Committee on Government Operations issued a report, *Misplaced Trust: The Bureau of Indian Affairs' Mismanagement of the Indian Trust Fund.* By that time, Congress's General Accounting Office (GAO) was warning of problems with the BIA's trust funds. *Misplaced Trust* found "significant, habitual problems in BIA's ability to fully and accurately account for trust fund monies." By this time, the report noted somewhat whimsically that "BIA continues to move at a snail's pace…. Indeed, the only thing that seems to stimulate a flurry of activity at the BIA is an impending appearance by the assistant secretary of Indian affairs before a Congressional committee. Afterward, all reform activities appear to suspend until shortly before the next oversight session" (Johansen, 1997, 16–17).

Several times between 1992 and 1996, reports from the GAO said that resolving problems with the Individual Indian Monies and other trust funds would pose a challenge, in large part because record keeping never met the minimal standards of the banking industry. Compelled by congressional action, the BIA in 1994 investigated its own mismanagement, including investment of some Indian monies in failed savings and loans, and pledged reform. Hearings were called and a special office created in the Interior Department to investigate and hopefully resolve the matter. In 1994, Congress passed the Indian Trust Fund Management Reform Act, with the stated aim of cleaning up the mess. The House also established a task force on the problem. Trust reconciliation had become an issue with inside-the-Beltway credentials. For a time, this provided some hope to Cobell, but no movement toward compensation ensued. Life rarely has been so simple at the Interior Department, even before there was a Beltway.

With broad Native American support, the Department of Interior hired Paul Homan, a former director of Riggs Bank and an expert at cleaning up failing private financial institutions, as special trustee for American Indians. Homan, having taken stock of the situation, later quit in disgust as he described a banker's nightmare. Day by day, piece by piece, the Individual Indian Monies inquiries were producing evidence of what must have been the world's sloppiest banking record keeping. Even Cobell was amazed at the sorry state of the BIA's banking system, if it could be called that.

Homan soon beheld the world's worst excuse for financial accounting. The BIA never had established an accounts receivable system, so its bankers never knew how much money they were handling at any given time. More than $50 million had not been paid to individual Indians because the BIA had lost track of them or because they had not left forwarding addresses. Approximately 21,000 accounts listed the names of people who were dead. Large numbers of records were stored in cardboard boxes in leaky warehouses and slowly were being destroyed.

"Years after our lawsuit was filed," said Cobell, "Someone discovered a barn filled with discarded and missing trust records in Anadarko [Oklahoma]. These records were being watched only by the rats in that leaky building. Interior officials testified that when the barn filled up, they just tossed out the oldest records and stacked in newer ones." "As for the leases of Indian lands that were supposed to be the sources of trust account funds," she continued, "Thousands of those leases were never recorded. So how can the trust records be accurate? They can't" (Cobell, April 22, 2005).

In the meantime, a Republican-controlled Congress was funding the trust-fund cleanup at about only $1 million per year, barely enough to keep the paper flowing in Homan's office, much less solve the problems and get Indians their money. The BIA, meanwhile, was spending $21 million building a castle of reports, such as the *Tribal Trust Funds Reconciliation Project,* an *"Agreed-upon Procedures and Findings Report,* and the *IIM* [Individual Indian Monies] *Related System Improvement Project Report.* The reports basically outlined how to implement the cleanup required by law since 1994, pending availability of money, and primarily repeated earlier reports.

Once again, the infrastructure called for in the maze of reports indicated just how haphazard the Interior Department's work as a banker for Indians had become. The reports called for such banking basics as "a proper, accurate, and timely accounting for trust-fund balances," "the preparation of accurate and timely reports to trust account holders," regular audits, a general ledger and general accounting system, a national archives and records center, and so forth (Johansen, 1997, 23). Meanwhile, Homan's office stressed that "Indian Trust Asset reform efforts are critically needed to ensure that the government meets its fiduciary obligations to Indian tribes and individual American Indians." Homan's office began to assemble a comprehensive strategic plan to implement the American Indian Trust Management Reform Act of 1994 (Johansen, 1997, 23).

SENATOR MCCAIN'S SOLUTION

By the first half of 1996, the BIA accounting mess became the subject of hearings before the Senate Committee on Indian Affairs, chaired by Senator

John McCain, Republican of Arizona. McCain himself presented an indictment of the BIA's accounting problems in economic, demographic, and historical contexts that are worth noting. Also worth noting was McCain's proposed solution: that trust accounts be privatized and how that fit in with a more general effort by former Senator Slade Gorton and his allies to get the government out of the so-called Indian business altogether, invoking code words for abrogating treaties.

"I am committed to bringing real and substantive changes to the Bureau of Indian Affairs," McCain said. "For those who may be inclined to resist change, let me paint you a picture. Indian families are living in poverty at three times the national average. Nearly one in three Native Americans in this nation is living in poverty. One-half of Indian households headed by a female are living in poverty. One half of Indian children under the age of six living on reservations are living in poverty. For every $100 earned by a non-Indian family, an Indian family earns $62. The per capita income for an Indian living on a reservation is $4,478" (Johansen, 1997, 18).

McCain continued to paint his statistical picture: "The mortality rate for Native Americans for tuberculosis exceeds the national average by 400 percent. The mortality rate for diabetes exceeds the national average by 139 percent. Native Americans are four times more likely to die of alcoholism than other Americans. The incidence rates for fetal alcohol syndrome among Native Americans is six times the national average." All of this after, according to McCain, "This administration has focused a great amount of energy on reforming the nation's health-care system over the last two years" (Johansen, 1997, 18).

McCain then narrowed the issue to the handling of Native American monies by the government: "Throughout history, American Indians and Alaska Natives have relied on the Bureau of Indian Affairs as the principal agency of the Federal Government to meet this nation's trust obligations to Native Americans. And yet, based on their own studies and investigations, the Bureau of Indian Affairs has failed miserably to carry out this nation's solemn obligations to American Indians. We have no idea how many thousands of Native Americans have been deprived of revenues that belong to them," McCain said. "We should be ashamed of a system that is a living example of our nation's inattention to its trust obligations to Native Americans" (Johansen, 1997, 18–19).

Next, McCain began to assert his political agenda by assigning blame to the obvious (and historically rich) record of bureaucratic bumbling by the BIA:

> In acting as the trustee for Indian tribes and their members, the BIA has failed to meet even minimal fiduciary obligations in the management of Indian trust funds. Over $2.1 billion in Indian trust funds cannot be accurately reconciled. It will cost the federal government over $390 million just to reconcile the trust fund accounts. Government auditors report that there are $1.9 billion worth of construction project costs that cannot be reconciled. It has also been reported that over $3.2 billion in BIA assets cannot be accounted for.

As a financial manager, the BIA has failed miserably. It has been estimated that through mismanagement and poor investments, the BIA has lost between $25 million and $30 million of tribal and individual Indian monies.... The long history of the failings of the Federal government to carry out its responsibilities to American Indians brings new meaning to the phrase "a parade of horribles." ... For all our efforts to reform the BIA and to improve the conditions on most reservations in this nation, we need just to look at the statistics in the recent census to see our failures. (Johansen, 1997, 19–20)

McCain certainly sounded like a "friend of the Indian," and he seemed to see himself in that role. One will recall, however, that so-called reformers played a major role in passing the 1887 Allotment Act. Many Native American leaders believe that McCain's attack on the BIA has an ulterior political motive. He, along with a number of other Republicans in the Senate and the House of Representatives, had voiced support for privatization of the BIA and the entire federal structure that supervises Indians' lives. Some Native leaders found themselves in the paradoxical position of supporting the agency that has defrauded them because they see privatization efforts as an undercover form of termination, an end to the relationship between the federal government and Native nations. How does one privatize a treaty correctly?

With every BIA gaffe, the privatization advocates were counting on the agency's monumental incompetence to build Native Americans' acceptance of the Great White Father's demise. Most know their history too well to be tempted. The phrase one hears most often around Indian Country for plans to privatize Indian Affairs is *The New Termination*.

THE DIMENSIONS OF THE INDIVIDUAL INDIAN MONIES MESS

Meanwhile, the Individual Indian Monies melodrama played on. "Honestly, I have never seen anything like it in my 30-year career as a banker," Homan told the Senate Committee on Indian Affairs in June 1996 (Johansen, 1997, 18). About $695 million in Native funds had been sent to the wrong Indian group, tribe, or nation. Some of the funds never were sent at all. Some funds had been posted to the wrong accounts. One property record valued three garden-variety chain saws at $99 million each. In 1996, $17 million in trust fund money simply vanished due to sloppy bookkeeping. Exhumation of the BIA's financial record keeping came to resemble an archaeological dig. Some of the BIA's financial records were contaminated with asbestos, and other records had been paved over under a parking lot.

The Senate hearings into the accounting mess was an eye-opener for some U.S. senators. "I'm rarely startled when I go into a committee hearing, but I have to say I really have been stunned," said Senator Paul Simon, Democrat of Illinois, after he attended the hearings and heard of the BIA's financial incompetence (Johansen, 1997, 18).

"What we've got is a mess. As far as I can see, it's an unprecedented mess," said Dan Press, an attorney for the Intertribal Monitoring Association on Indian Trust Funds, a coalition of several dozen Indian bands and nations, who told the Congressional Subcommittee on Native American Affairs Committee on Natural Resources that Individual Indian Monies accounts should be credited with interest (Johansen, 1997, 18). The association contended that the BIA had been legally obligated to pay interest since 1938. This group also advocated that individuals whose money was lost through the BIA's investments in failed and bogus financial institutions be "made whole."

Before he quit, Homan reported that no one knew just how many people were owed money. Of the 238,000 individual trusts that Homan's staff located, 118,000 were missing crucial papers, 50,000 had no addresses, and 16,000 accounts had no documents at all. Homan further reported that one could assume money had been skimmed extensively from the trust. "It's akin to leaving the vault door open," he said (Awehali, 2003).

Comparing BIA officials' public testimony with the historical record vis-à-vis Indian trust accounts, one must wonder whether both lived on the same financial planet. The government has long lived in the land of wish fulfillment, spin control, and legal fantasy. Testifying before Congress on August 11, 1994, Ada Deer, assistant secretary and head of the BIA, said, "Our goals for trust funds reform are really quite simple. First, we want to provide tribes with an investment approach that ensures both the safety of the funds and a good rate of return. Secondly, we want to assure that all trust fund account holders receive timely, adequate accounting information. Third, we want to ensure that, to the greatest extent possible, previous inaccuracies in accounting and crediting of accounts are identified and rectified. Fourth, we want to ensure coordination of trust funds management among the [Interior] Department's various bureaus. Finally, we want to ensure that tribes which are prepared to manage their own funds are provided the opportunity to do so" (Johansen, 1997, 15). A dozen years later, the government was using its legal talent to stall attainment of Deer's entire list of goals.

COBELL FILES SUIT

More and more, legal action appeared to be the only alternative for account holders. Cobell said that she took a visitor's tour of Washington, DC, just days before filing the lawsuit. She walked past the Lincoln Memorial. Everywhere she went, she saw "government, government, government." Her adversary's power bore down on her. She felt goose bumps, she said, "I was so frightened." Back at her hotel, Cobell called a friend and expressed her doubts. "I don't know if I can do this," she told her friend. "If not you, who?" her friend asked (Szpaller, 2005).

In 1996, Cobell finally became fed up with government inaction after Attorney General Janet Reno reneged on a promise to look into the matter. The Native American Rights Fund (NARF) announced the class-action suit on behalf of the

300,000 (later 500,000) holders of Individual Indian Monies accounts. Attorneys pointed to people such as Bernice Skunk Cap, an elderly Blackfeet, who lost her cabin to fire in 1994. Planning to build a new home, Skunk Cap applied to the BIA for $2,400 from her Individual Indian Monies account but was told she could have only $1,000 of it. She was forced to move into a nursing home.

John Echohawk, executive director of NARF and Cobell, project director of the Individual Indian Monies Trust Correction and Recovery Project, announced the filing of the class-action lawsuit against Assistant Interior Secretary Ada Deer, Interior Secretary Bruce Babbitt, and Treasury Secretary Robert Rubin. Said Echohawk, "We are in court because we have been unable to persuade the executive and legislative branches of government to honor the United States' solemn trust and legal obligation to 300,000 individual Indian account holders…. The complete failure of the United States government to properly discharge its trust responsibility implicates what we believe is the largest and longest-lasting financial scandal ever involving the federal government. In our view, it represents yet another serious and continuing breach in a long history of dishonorable treatment of Indian tribes and individual Indians by the U.S. government" (Johansen, 1997, 21–22).

Particularly disturbing, said Echohawk, "is the cavalier acknowledgement by the executive branch and Congress that the federal government has failed to account for our trust monies, yet the federal government continually refuses to take the necessary steps to fix the system…. The very government that is required by law to protect and advance [American Indian] interests" (Johansen, 1997, 22)

Echohawk said that neither NARF nor the accounting firm it had retained, Price Waterhouse, would collect a contingency fee from this case. "Fully 100 percent of the recovery in this class-action lawsuit will go to the Individual Indians who lost and continue to lose their money daily at the hands of the federal government" (Johansen, 1997, 22).

Echohawk outlined the goals of the class-action suit: "The suit asks the court to declare that the defendants have breached, and continue to breach, their trust obligations to 300,000 class members. It further asks the court to order the defendants to follow the law, fix the system, provide the account holders with an accounting, and make restitution. Finally, we seek to assure that the Special Trustee [Paul Homan] has the tools he needs to fix the system—and to get the job done right—as Congress mandated when it enacted the Trust Management Reform Act of 1994" (Johansen, 1997, 22).

"This was our last resort," said Cobell. "It's mismanagement, and if this was a bank it would be called stealing, and it's been going on for more than 150 years. The federal government has no idea how much of our money it has, no idea how much of our money it should have, and no idea how much of our money it has lost," she continued (Johansen, 1997, 22). Echohawk elaborated on just how sloppy the BIA's bookkeeping had become: "They have no idea how much has been collected from the companies that use our land and are unable to provide even a basic, regular statement to account holders. Every day we wait they are losing more and more of our money" (Johansen, 1997, 22).

Of Senator McCain's suggestion that Indians might be better off with accounts at private banks, Cobell said as the NARF filed its class-action suit, "That would be a natural way for the government.... They transfer it—say, to Wells Fargo— and then who's responsible for historical wrongs?" (Johansen, 1997, 22). During the late 1980s, without asking anyone, the BIA had spent $1 million trying without success to unload its trust-fund problems on private banks. The House of Representatives had to order a halt to these efforts five times before the BIA finally stopped, according to the House report *Misplaced Trust*. The BIA then gave the originator of the plan a $5,000 award.

The Native American Rights Fund was filing suit in large part because the government, for all practical purposes, had decided that fixing the Individual Indian Monies accounts was too expensive to pursue administratively. The route to this conclusion was a classic in the art of bureaucratic politics, BIA style. First, the BIA ignored the problem or fired nettlesome employees, such as Henry, who raised it. By about 1990, the problem became too large to ignore, so the BIA built a bureaucratic card castle around it. The trust-fund problem acquired a considerable amount of inside-the-Beltway cachet, as has been previously noted. A great deal of hearing testimony and fact-finding was arranged and many reports written and filed.

Cobell realized that large legal actions were massively expensive. Her years of activism and her experience as the Blackfeet's accountant had suggested some sources of support, however. She contacted the Arthur Bremer Foundation of St. Paul, Minnesota, and won a $75,000 grant and a $600,000 loan. In 1997, a year after she filed the class-action suit, Cobell also received, quite unexpectedly, a $300,000 genius grant from the John D. and Catherine T. MacArthur Foundation, most of which went into the case. Shortly after that, J. Patrick Lannan of the Lannan Foundation read about Cobell's MacArthur grant and traveled to Browning to meet with her. Lannan eventually donated $4 million to the cause. By mid-2002, the cost of the legal action had reached $8 million, still barely a drop in the proverbial bucket next to the hundreds of millions of dollars in tax money that the federal government has spent to defend itself.

Cobell and NARF finally filed suit because all of the federal government's previous moving and shaking had been undertaken without any assurance that even one thin dime of actual compensation might reach Individual Indian Monies account holders. Indian account holders thus rediscovered a time-honored principle of life on Capitol Hill: It is easy to pass a law full of all sorts of professed good intentions but much more difficult to get the money to make reality of it. This is the state of trust in today's world, in today's dollars, down the Mall from the Capitol, at the bank that Indian money built.

John Echohawk made this point in more legalistic language as the class-action lawsuit was announced: "The Department of the Interior has no plans or money to do any historical accounting regarding the IIM [Individual Indian Monies] accounts, to determine how much money the IIM account holders may have lost and continue to lose each day.... In short, the federal government continues to turn its back on 300,000 individual Indian account holders." The longer the stall, the more expensive the fix, said Echohawk. "The longer it is permitted to continue, the more expensive it will be to fix the system … the price goes up every day" (Johansen, 1997, 23).

News of the NARF lawsuit percolated at the Interior Department for six months before something of a response surfaced in a departmental report to Congress: Interior proposed a settlement of up to $600 million, a sort of savings-and-loan-style bailout for the BIA The proposed plan was short on details and again reminded many Native Americans who had banked with the BIA of past broken promises and rubber checks. As the amount in arrears grew to tens of billions during subsequent years, Interior's initial low-ball bid looked even more ridiculous.

PEN-AND-INK WITCHCRAFT

With the government's mismanagement of Indian accounts so widely known, a sensible person might have concluded that the time had come to find a way to reimburse the many Native people who had been cheated. If you were one of the 500,000 Native Americans who unwillingly did your banking with the BIA, when might you expect a corrective check in the mail? Do not hold your breath. If the George W. Bush administration has its way, you could turn a very deep shade of blue before the guarantor of your trust makes you, as they say in financial litigation circles, whole. These prospects hardly improved once the case entered the maze of the adversarial legal system.

The spin doctors in the Interior Department probably did not realize that their actions resembled some treaty negotiations for its Alice-in-Wonderland quality (things were never what they seemed). In 1791, the famed Ottawa speaker Egushawa, observing treaty negotiations, called such machinations "pen-and-ink witchcraft." What Egushawa witnessed had nothing on the trust-money mess. After more than ten years of legal shuck and jive by the federal government, the central fact of the case was this: The BIA and Treasury Department never built a record-keeping system capable of tracking the money owed to Native Americans based on income from its superintendency of their resources. Locked in an adversarial relationship with the plaintiffs, the government was even less willing to admit error, much less make good on it.

As time passed (the system, in its modern incantation, began with the advent of the Allotment Act in 1887), the lack of a functioning banking system made record keeping worse; the sloppiness of errant (or nonexistent) record keeping was compounded, for example, because of divisions of estate required by generations of fractional Native inheritances. By the time Cobell and a few other banking-minded Native Americans began asking, seriously, what had become of their Individual Indian Monies, the Interior Department, by and large, did not have a clue.

In an average year, $500 million or more was deposited into the Individual Indian Trust from companies leasing Native American land for grazing, oil drilling, timber cutting, and mining of coal and other natural resources. According to law and financial theory, the money was collected by the Interior Department and sent to the Treasury Department, where it should have been placed into individual trust accounts. Problems began with the approximately 50,000 accounts that lacked names or correct addresses. One such account contained $1 million (Awehali, 2003). Along the way, it also was learned that some exploiters of Native resources simply neglected to pay as required; they soon learned that, much of the time, no one seemed to be watching. They began to act as if the system simply did not exist.

As early as 1999, the plaintiffs' legal team discovered that the Departments of Interior and Treasury had "inadvertently" destroyed 162 boxes of vital trust records during the course of the trial then waited months to notify the court of the so-called accident. "You tell me if that's fair," Cobell told Mike Wallace in a *60 Minutes* interview shortly after the discovery. "When they have to manage other people's money according to standards, why aren't they managing our money to standards? Is it because you manage brown people's money differently?" (Awehali, 2003).

JUDGE LAMBERTH'S RULINGS

The chief judge in the case, Royce C. Lamberth, was a Republican appointee, a Texan with a taste for fancy boots and large cars, who seemed, on the surface, unlikely to take a serious interest in a Native American class-action suit. Lamberth, however, also possessed a keen knowledge of bureaucratic politics and an ability to read and comprehend vast amounts of information. He also was a serious jurist—so serious that the government soon sought to remove him from the case. Like fishing-rights judge George Hugo Boldt (also a Republican appointee), Lamberth also had a sharp sense of justice, regardless of vested interests. He was, in other words (also like Boldt), hardworking and ruthlessly honest.

A native of San Antonio, Lamberth, 63 in 2006, earned his undergraduate and law degrees from the University of Texas. He was drafted out of law school in 1967 and entered the Army Judge Advocate General Corps during the Vietnam War. Until he was appointed to the federal bench in 1987, Lamberth worked in the civil division of the U.S. Attorney's Office in Washington, DC (Talhelm, 2005b).

On December 21, 1999, Judge Lamberth, who was overseeing the case in the Washington, DC, Federal District Court, issued his first (phase one) opinion (the case is divided into two phases). The 126-page opinion stated that the government had baldly violated its trust responsibilities to Native Americans. He called the Individual Indian Monies mess the "most egregious misconduct by the federal government" (Johansen, 2004, 26). Although *Cobell v. Norton* is certainly a big-stakes case, such a superlative overstated its historical scope. Perhaps it is the most egregious example of financial misconduct in a trust relationship by the U.S. government—which, in its two-plus centuries, has done worse to Native Americans than lose several billion dollars.

Judge Lamberth later ordered the government to file reports quarterly describing in detail its efforts to account for the monies. The judge also ordered the Interior and Treasury Departments to compile an audit of the Individual Indian Monies trust-fund system, reaching to its origins in 1887. At present, the Bush administration's unwillingness to follow Lamberth's order constitutes the legal line of scrimmage in what may turn out to be a decades-long battle.

Judge Lamberth was shocked when he discovered, in the course of the lawsuit, that Interior and Treasury had, as a matter of course, destroyed accounting documents and filed false reports with the court. In the course of the litigation, 37 past and present government officials, including Bush's Secretary of the Interior Gale Norton and Clinton's Interior Secretary Bruce Babbitt, have been held in contempt of court. On August 10, 1999, Lamberth ordered the Treasury Department to pay $600,000 in fines for misconduct.

As he delved into the trust-account debacle, Lamberth found that some records were stored in rat-infested New Mexico warehouses. Others were dispersed haphazardly on several remote reservations. When the Interior Department kept computerized records at all, they were so inadequate and insecure that hackers could set up their own accounts (and, presumably, draw money from them).

LAND OF THE MIDNIGHT RIDER

In September 2003, Judge Lamberth ordered the Interior Department to conduct a thorough investigation into money that was supposed to have been paid to Indians for oil, gas, timber, and grazing activities on their land, dating back to 1887. He said that the accounting must be completed by 2007.

Responding to Lamberth's first-phase opinion and this directive, Cobell was enthusiastic at the time. "This is a landmark victory," she said. "It is now clear that trust law and trust standards fully govern the management of the Individual Indian Trust and that Secretary Norton can no longer ignore the trust duties that she owes to 500,000 individual Indian trust beneficiaries" (Awehali, 2003).

The idea of a complete accounting, which sounded so simple, suddenly became very problematic in the land of pen-and-ink-witchcraft. Interior and Treasury, with their allies on Capitol Hill and in the Bush White House, prepared a hastily inserted so-called midnight rider to a federal spending bill that forbade spending that would have implemented Lamberth's directive. Funding, according to the rider, was to be frozen for a year, or until an accounting methodology could be agreed upon by Interior, Treasury, and Congress.

In the meantime, the Interior Department was reported by several news organizations as complaining that the type of historical accounting required by Judge Lamberth's ruling would take 10 years and cost $6 billion to $12 billion. Some feat of accounting that would be; the accounting equivalent, perhaps, of building the Panama Canal or putting many men on the moon—a rubber figure with an odor of obstructionist politics.

To illustrate just how rubbery this estimate was, let us crunch a few round numbers. At $100,000 each per year, very good pay for an accountant, $10 billion would hire 100,000 accountants. Even if they worked ten years each, $10 billion would still pay 10,000 number crunchers. Add a few zeroes here and there, and soon we are talking some very serious money. Bear in mind that the folks who came up with these quick estimates worked at the same agencies that lost track of all that Native American money to begin with.

In the meantime, before a dime has been paid to any of the 500,000 Native people who are part of the class action, the Bush administration seemed to have established some sort of perpetual-motion lawyer-employment fund. It requested $554 million in the 2004 budget to reform the trust fund, an increase of $183.3 million over the $370.2 million budgeted in 2003. *Reform* in this case meant, to a large degree, paying legal talent to cover Uncle Sam's ass against the class-action suit; as with John Ashcroft's Patriot Act, the terminology here is highly Orwellian. In a January 2001 interview with Harlan McKosato on the national radio show *Native America Calling,* Cobell noted that "just by not settling the case, it's costing the government and taxpayers $160,000 an hour, $7 million a day, $2.5 billion a year" (Awehali, 2003).

With a federal budget deficit approaching $400 billion per year (including the wars in Iraq and Afghanistan and reconstruction liabilities running at least $87 billion per year), the Bush administration and the Republican-controlled Congress seemed unwilling to seriously consider paying up a century-plus of Indian-trust money bills that could cost as much as $40 billion—the final bill that could come out of the second phase of the case, once Interior and Treasury assessed the due bills, as ordered by Judge Lamberth. The midnight rider was sponsored in large part by a Republican-controlled executive branch and Congress that has added 721,000 federal jobs to the payroll since George W. Bush assumed office. To those concerned that the United States can not afford a *Cobell v. Norton* settlement, Cobell replied, "It's not your money and never was" (Whitty, 2005).

About fifty Republicans voted against the appropriations bill containing the rider, however, led by Representative Richard Pombo, Republican of California, chairman of the House Resources Committee, with Representative J. D. Hayworth, Republican of Arizona, cochair of the bipartisan House Native American Caucus. Pombo, who favors a legislative solution to the court case, called the rider a "poison pill that was added to the legislation in blatant violation of House rules and protocol" (Reynolds, 2003). The rider passed narrowly, 216–205.

The Senate passed the spending bill (with the midnight rider attached) 87–2 on November 4, 2003, and sent it to Bush, who affixed his signature on November 10. Cobell sharply criticized the Bush administration, including Interior Secretary Norton, for sponsoring the rider. Said Cobell, "What this vote shows is the length that the Interior Secretary and the Bush administration will go to in their efforts to deny Indians the accounting for funds that belong to Indians—not the federal government. Now American Indians are being victimized once again by politicians in Washington" (Reynolds, 2003). Cobell said that she expected the courts to strike down the rider as an illegal interference with the judicial process, a violation of the Constitution's separation of powers.

"It's a clear act of bad faith to seek a stay based on an unconstitutional statute," said Gingold ("Appeals Court," 2003). The Senate's legal counsel and House members from both parties said the provision was probably unconstitutional because the administration can not dictate to the courts how to interpret the law.

In July 2005, Judge Lamberth wrote, "For those harboring hope that the stories of murder, dispossession, forced marches, assimilationist policy programs, and other incidents of cultural genocide against the Indians are merely the echoes of a horrible, bigoted government past that has been sanitized by the good deeds of more recent history, this case serves as an appalling reminder of the evils that result when large numbers of the politically powerless are placed at the mercy of institutions engendered and controlled by a politically powerful few" (Whitty, 2005).

During the first phase of the case, many experts testified that Interior and Treasury lacked the records to render any semblance of a true accounting for the monies that the government was supposed to have been managing. Instead, the plaintiffs have suggested various methods of estimating what is owed. For example, the Geographic Information System (GIS) might use satellite-mapping technology to estimate the amount of oil produced by wells on native lands and thereby derive an idea of royalties owed.

Bureaucratic venality posed another problem. The BIA also fought back in small-minded ways by hassling Indians who spoke out. "Among the Indians who filed affidavits about these BIA tactics was Verna St. Goddard, an elderly Blackfeet," according to one account.

> She ran into problems when she visited the BIA office in Browning last February. For more than 35 years St. Goddard has withdrawn funds for the developmentally disabled Roseline Spotted Eagle, her former foster child. Following her inquiry, however, a BIA official ordered St. Goddard to drive to Great Falls and ascertain the price of the goods she wanted to buy for Spotted Eagle, then drive back to the BIA office to request a check, and then return to Great Falls to purchase the items and back again—480 miles altogether. (Whitty, 2005)

This was a perfect example, St. Goddard said, of what the BIA really stands for: "Bossing Indians Around." When she asked the BIA official why he would not give Spotted Eagle her money, as he has for years, he blamed the Eloise Cobell lawsuit.

A VICTORY FOR THE PLAINTIFFS

In a major victory for the plaintiffs, Judge Lamberth ruled on September 29, 2004, that all sales and transfers of Indian-owned land by the Department of the Interior's Bureau of Indian Affairs must include a detailed, court-approved notification of landowners' rights as trust beneficiaries and class members. For the first time in history, individual Indian landowners would be informed of their rights as trust beneficiaries and class members before the sale of their lands.

The court ruled that each beneficiary who decides to sell trust assets has an absolute right to a full and accurate accounting. Failure by the Interior Department to provide accounting effectively was said by Judge Lambert to rob those beneficiaries of the cash value of their rights. The court ruled that an attempted BIA auction of Indian-owned land in Oklahoma in September 2004 violated a 2002 court order stating that Interior could not communicate with Cobell class members about matters relating to the trust or the litigation without prior approval of the court. The court found that the owners of some of the land that was scheduled to be auctioned were not fully informed of the consequences of such sales with respect to the lawsuit, and in some cases it seemed that the landowners may have been unaware that their land was up for sale.

Surveying this situation, Cobell said, "For more than a century, the U.S. government has sold our land out from under us without consent, without appraisal and without informing us of our rights as trust beneficiaries. That ends today" (Press Release, 2004).

THE DUE BILL RISES

Estimates of the size of the due bill for the trust-moneys mess kept growing as the litigation dragged on. An account in *The New York Times* put the total amount owed from oil, timber, grazing, and other leases since the program began at $137 billion (File, 2004). The dimensions of the scandal also continued to grow. From $2 billion to $3 billion at its initiation during 1996, the total due all plaintiffs was, by 2005, estimated by their attorneys to be $176 billion.

Early in April 2004, Special Master Alan Balaran, a court-appointed investigator of the Individual Indian Monies scandal, resigned from his job probing the federal government's management of the funds, charging that the Bush administration worked to thwart his work. Beginning during summer 2003, he said, Bush appointees began working to block his description of a two-decade-old practice by Interior officials of negotiating leases with oil and gas companies that gave Indian landowners a small fraction of the royalties that private landowners received in similar deals.

Balaran accused the Department of Justice and the Interior Department of trying repeatedly to have him removed from the case "to prevent any further investigation" of the lopsided deals. According to a *Washington Post* report, "A full investigation into these matters might well result in energy companies being forced to repay significant sums to individual Indians," Balaran wrote. "Interior could not let this happen.... Billions of dollars are at stake." According to the same account, Interior Department officials called Balaran's charges "preposterous" and "based entirely on innuendo, supposition and baseless speculation—just the sorts of things to which a competent judicial officer would give no credence" (Leonnig, 2004, A-7).

Balaran described a specific case involving the Interior Department's chief appraiser in New Mexico who, he said, repeatedly negotiated for energy companies to pay Indians less than market value for use of their land. For a San Juan Basin pipeline, the appraiser arranged for a gas company to pay $4.50 per yard to run pipeline across Indian-owned lands that Interior managed, whereas the same energy company paid private landowners $104 per yard for running the same pipe on their adjoining land (Leonnig, 2004, A-7).

INTERIOR WINS ONE

The Cobell case, eight years old by 2004, settled into an adversarial boxing match familiar to anyone who reports legal affairs. Although the government's 100 lawyers got little sympathy from Judge Lamberth, they did win an occasional round in the appeals courts. In a victory for the government, a three-judge panel in federal appeals court on December 10, 2004, unanimously threw out most of Judge Lamberth's orders designed to force the Interior Department to account for Individual Indian Monies. The appeals court panel told Judge Lamberth that he could no longer "micromanage" the Individual Indian Monies system ("Court Rejects," 2004). The ruling permits the Interior Department to propose its own plan to account for the missing money then allows Lamberth to assess its proposal from the bench.

The appeals court thus agreed with the Interior Department that Lamberth's order for an accounting exceeded his judicial authority. "Rather than acting to assure that 'agency action' conforms to law, the court has sought to make the law conform to the court's views as to how the trusts may best be run," Judge Stephen F. Williams wrote for the appeals panel ("Court Rejects," 2004). Interior officials had complained that an audit that Lamberth had ordered, reaching to the origins of the Individual Indian Monies system more than a century ago, could cost up to $12 billion.

At the behest of the Bush White House, Congress intervened in November 2003, approving legislation that prevented an accounting from going forward until Congress had defined the scope and methods to be used.

The court said that the monumental nature of the bookkeeping necessary for such a thing might take 200 years. In essence, the government had botched its accounting so badly that reconstructing the books would cost, by its own estimate, as much as $12 billion. The government had thus ruined Individual Indian Monies accounting badly enough, by the court's circuitous reasoning, to be let off the hook. A three-judge appeals panel agreed, calling Lamberth's decision "ill-founded" and an abuse of discretion that was not favored by either side in the lawsuit (Talhelm, 2005a).

Interior Secretary Gale Norton said that she was pleased by the decision. "Thus far, the department has expended more than $100 million in its historical accounting effort and has found ample evidence that monies collected for individual Indians were distributed to the correct recipients," she said (Talhelm, 2005a).

THE PLAINTIFFS MAKE AN OFFER

On June 20, 2005, several prominent Indian leaders, including Cobell, convened in Washington, DC, to announce 50 principles for legislation that they said could settle the case. Most significantly, they said they would settle the case for $27.5 billion—a figure they said was a very substantial discount from the $176 billion their accountants calculated would be owed in royalties and interest if allotment holders were to be fully compensated. The $27.5 billion offer also acknowledged that some money had been paid over the years (Nieves, 2005, A-19). "It is discounted quite substantially," Cobell said at a news conference, "but I think we all understand that there's a lot of suffering in Indian country. Many people will die before the money is approved" (Nieves, 2005, A-19).

By late 2005, "According to Cobell's forensic accountants, the government owed $176 billion to individual Indian landowners, averaging $352,000 per plaintiff, making this monetarily the largest class-action lawsuit ever launched" (Nieves, 2005, A-19). The Indian leaders said they had been asked by Senate and House members, including Senators John McCain, chairman of the Indian Affairs Committee, and Byron L. Dorgan of North Dakota, senior Democrat on the panel, to come up with a plan they could use as a road map for a congressional resolution to the lawsuit.

Cobell said that a timely settlement of the suit and payment of money would markedly change many Indians' lives. The shame, she said, is that the government is fighting some of the poorest people in the country over money it owes them at the same time that it reneges on its treaty obligations by cutting funding for Indian programs. "They took our land and said they would provide health care and education," she said in an interview with Evelyn Nieves of the *Washington Post* after the news conference. "And every single year they cut the funds" (Nieves, 2005, A-19).

The Indian Health Service, for example, is so underfunded that it will not allow patients to see specialists unless they have a life-threatening condition, Cobell said. "They're pulling young people's teeth out because it's cheaper to do that than fill cavities." She added that her husband did not receive proper care for his diabetes until it became severe. "His leg is amputated now," she said (Nieves, 2005, A-19).

Cobell said of the proposal: "It is a good, commonsense bargain for the government and Indian people. It responds to repeated calls by Congress to settle this case promptly. It gives Congress a bold opportunity to reach out to the nation's first citizens and end a national disgrace that dates to 1887. Our nine-year court fight has documented those wrongs. But the great tragedy of this issue has been that the government has known for decades that the accounts were not being handled properly. Study after study has confirmed that the Indians were short-changed and that the government simply kept the excess in Washington. Now, 118 years later, we finally have a practical way to put back the word 'trust' in the Indian trust account system. Equally important, we have an honorable way to remove the stain from the government's dealings with thousands of Indians who were denied access to the money that they should have had decades ago" (Cobell, July 14, 2005).

Dan DuBray, speaking for the BIA, said that the $27.5 billion the plaintiffs were requesting "is greater than the combined [annual] budgets of the departments of the Interior and Commerce and the Environmental Protection Agency.... It really is a paradox that faces the plaintiffs. They brought the case on the foundation of a 1994 law that requires the government to provide an accounting for Indian beneficiaries. They brought the suit seeking that accounting. Now they're saying that they are not seeking an accounting, they are seeking money" (Nieves, 2005, A-19). True, perhaps, but has not money been the object of the accounting all along? Of what use could an accounting be without a resolution of the resulting claim?

THE GOLD STANDARD FOR MISMANAGEMENT

At this point, Judge Lamberth repeated his belief that the Interior Department's conduct in this case "sets the gold standard for mismanagement by the federal government." DuBray said after the news conference that the department has spent $100 million thus far to provide an accounting and has found "no evidence" of fraud or any major systemic error. (Yes, but it spent $100 million mainly on legal costs, not a dime to the plaintiffs.) Out of 47,500 accounts studied, he said, the department found underpayments in 11 accounts ranging from $57 to $263 (Nieves, 2005, A-19).

In April 2005, citing the government's admission of computer-security problems, lawyers asked Lamberth to impose a temporary restraining order on the Interior Department to prevent computer hackers from damaging thousands of individual Indian trust accounts. The plea by lawyers in a class-action lawsuit came as government lawyers acknowledged that Bureau of Land Management computers holding trust account information had been penetrated by a government contractor last month during a security check.

Accounting for past mismanagement was one thing. Keeping track of the Indian monies system itself was another. Warning that Indian Trust records continued to be in imminent risk of being manipulated and destroyed by computer hackers, Lamberth on October 20, 2005, ordered the Interior Department to disconnect from the Internet all computer systems that housed or provided access to Individual Indian Monies records. Lamberth cited as overwhelming evidence, testimony and documents introduced during hearings before his court indicating that the department's computers are easy prey to attackers as well as poorly designed and managed with regard to security. Lamberth said that the computers should be reconnected only to issue payment checks.

Gingold said that the government's computer security is no better in 2005 than it had been nine earlier when the lawsuit was filed. "Here we are nine years into this litigation and nothing has changed," Gingold told Lamberth during a two-hour hearing ("Lawyers Seek," 2005). Gingold urged Lamberth to disconnect from the Internet any Interior computers containing trust data because of the continuing uncertainty over their security. His request came after the department's inspector general disclosed that it had found serious computer problems in an unnamed Interior agency.

By 2006, the U.S. government showed little inclination to solve the money-funds problem. Instead, Interior's small army of attorneys was going to federal appeals court to get Judge Lamberth removed from the case, arguing that he was biased in favor of the plaintiffs. "It is exceptionally rare for us to make this request we are making today, and we make it urgently," Assistant Attorney General Peter Keisler told the appeals court in Washington, DC, on April 11, arguing that Lamberth should be removed from the case to "restore the appearance of fairness" (Talhelm, 2006). The attorneys complained after an opinion by Lamberth in July 2005 that included phrasing such as:

> Alas, our "modern" Interior Department has time and again demonstrated that it is a dinosaur … the morally and culturally oblivious hand-me-down of a disgracefully racist and imperialist government that should have been buried a century ago, the last pathetic outpost of the indifference and Anglocentrism we thought we had left behind. (Talhelm, 2006)

Keisler told a three-judge panel at the U.S. Court of Appeals for the District of Columbia, "Even in cases involving convicted criminals, judges don't use language this way." If the appeals court removes Lamberth, said Keith Harper, lawyer for the Indian plaintiffs, "It will send a very clear message to the government that all their malfeasance … is exonerated." "We think that would fundamentally undermine the appearance of justice and justice itself" (Talhelm, 2006).

WHITHER THE TRUST-FUND BILLIONS?

Leaders of the Senate Indian Affairs Committee, Senators John McCain and Byron Dorgan, in 2005 introduced legislation to amend the Indian Trust Reform Act. The senators sought to end the decades of fruitless litigation and give the Indians involved a settlement. The bill called for the Treasury and Interior Departments to figure out how much money had flowed through the individual accounts since 1980 and use that as a basis for an estimate of what the overall amount owed should be. During hearings on the bill in late July 2005, Cobell pointed out that the bill would do nothing to uphold her consistent victories in court and in fact would end the court's role in this case. "What's worse," commented an editorial in *The New York Times,* "It would do nothing to reform the supervision of individual Indian trust accounts" ("Fixing an Old Injustice," 2005).

So, whither the trust-fund billions? When all is said and done, will the plaintiffs in *Cobell v. Norton* ever get anything close to what they are owed? Although optimism is always in season, and justice sometimes does actually prevail, there is ample precedent in U.S. legal history vis-à-vis Native Americans to create doubts that right and reasonable outcomes follow the opinions of courts presided over by hardworking, honest judges, even after the government has copiously admitted its errors.

Some historical parallels present themselves: John Marshall, chief justice of the U.S. Supreme Court, found in favor of the Cherokees' sovereignty; President Andrew Jackson ignored him and his court, leading to the Trail of Tears. (Jackson's action was an impeachable offense because contempt of the Supreme Court was a violation of his oath of office. It was never prosecuted because Georgia made a states' rights case that could have started the Civil War thirty years before it actually began.)

More recently, during the mid-1970s, the courts found in favor of a 250,000-acre land claim for the Oneidas. Thirty years later, they have yet to receive any land from this legal proceeding.

Might *Cobell v. Norton* end up being another perpetual-motion employment engine for lawyers and another reminder that sometimes the legal system talks the talk as the executive branch fails to walk the walk of justice? Or might the contending parties, with Judge Lamberth's prodding, find a way to at least estimate what is owed the plaintiffs and take the necessary steps to pay them? The next few years may provide an answer, after the second phase of *Cobell v. Norton* is adjudicated and a final ruling is issued by Judge Lamberth.

Senator Ben Nighthorse Campbell, who is Cheyenne, has insisted that all parties to the Cobell litigation must work together to resolve the case; he believes, otherwise, that it may not be resolved it at all. "We have one year to reach settlement on this issue," he said during a hearing of the Senate Committee on Indian Affairs, as it considered his bill, S 1770, to encourage individual beneficiary settlements in the lawsuit (Reynolds, 2003).

BLACKFEET HISTORY AT GHOST RIDGE

"I've heard from friends that the government thinks I'm tired and that they'll wear me down, so that I'll just go away," Cobell reflected (Awehali, 2003). Near Cobell's home town, a marker describes the winter of 1883–84, when 500 Blackfeet died of starvation and exposure while awaiting supplies promised them by the federal government. The dead were buried in a mass grave that is now called Ghost Ridge. During the more difficult stages of the lawsuit, Cobell said she visited Ghost Ridge, thinking of her ancestors who perished in the cold 120 years ago, while waiting for the government to fulfill its promises (Awehali, 2003).

During the winter of 1883–84, as the cattle of white settlers grazed illegally on Indian lands, the Blackfeet began to die of starvation and a streptococcal epidemic. The following spring, they ate their last government-provided seed potatoes; by June, they were stripping cottonwood trees and chewing their inner bark; and by the time BIA officials in Washington, DC, finally responded with extra rations, a Blackfeet man called Almost-a-Dog was said to have cut 555 notches in a willow stick, one for every Indian who had died—one in every four Blackfeet in the state of Montana (Whitty, 2005).

As the Blackfeet starved, Indian Agent John Young hoarded food. "All the Blackfeet know," says Cobell, "that the Agency man was black-marketing the Indians' rations, and that the reservation was enclosed in barbed wire" (Whitty, 2005). So much for trust and wardship.

By 2006, the federal government was gathering all its money-trust records in one place, in an industrial park a half hour southwest of Kansas City, 70 feet beneath the prairie near Lenexa, Kansas, "filling limestone caverns protected by guards and a bomb-sniffing dog with truckloads of American Indian financial and cultural records…. Two years and $120 million into the accounting [in 2006], the archive has amassed 140,000 boxes with 300 million pages of old leases, bills, ledgers, account statements, school records, maps, letters and black-and-white photographs" (Heilprin, 2006). The government estimated at the time that the mere archiving of the records would take seven years and cost $335 million.

In an area the size of a professional football stadium, "The shelves are coated with an electrostatically charged powder to resist corrosion or chemical action. The air within the painted cavern walls is kept at 60 degrees F. and 40 percent humidity. High-efficiency air filters catch 99 percent of all microscopic particles…. The boxes come from about 100 of the Interior's Bureau of Indian Affairs offices and National Archives record centers around the country. At a nondescript warehouse nearby, 100 workers sort through the boxes and log their contents into computers" (Heilprin, 2006).

The U.S. Court of Appeals for the District of Columbia Circuit in July 2006 took Judge Lamberth off the case at the Interior Department's request, arguing that he had been biased. The removal, a rare event in judicial circles, came even as the court echoed much of what he had said about the nature of the Department of Interior's conduct on the case. The court called Lamberth "an experienced judge who, having presided over this exceptionally contentious case for almost a decade, has become 'exceedingly ill disposed towards [a] defendant' that has flagrantly and repeatedly breached its fiduciary obligations" (Weiss, 2006, A-13).

The court also cited Lamberth's own words to illustrate why he should be removed from the case, now titled *Cobell v. Kempthorne*, including a July 2005 opinion in which he called the Interior Department "a dinosaur—the morally and culturally oblivious hand-me-down of a disgracefully racist and imperialist government that should have been buried a century ago, the pathetic outpost of the indifference and anglocentrism we thought we had left behind" (Weiss, 2006, A-13).

FURTHER READING

"Appeals Court Halts Indian Trust Accounting." *Billings Gazette,* November 14, 2003. <http://www.billingsgazette.com/index.php?id=1&display=rednews/2003/11/14/build/nation/42-indiantrust.inc>.

Awehali, Brian. "Fighting Long Odds: Government Continues to Shred, Evade, Obstruct, Lie, and Conspire in Indian Trust Case." LiP Magazine. December 15, 2003. <www.lipmagazine.org/articles/featawehali_300_p.htm>.

Cobell, Eloise. "Indians Not Being Told Truth." *Daily Oklahoman,* April 22, 2005: n.p.

Cobell, Eloise. "Restoring Trust and Ending a National Disgrace." *Indian Country Today,* July 14, 2005. <www.indiancountry.com/content.cfm?id=1096411230>.

Coulter, Robert T., and Steven M. Tullberg. "Indian land Rights." *The Aggressions of Civilization.* Ed. Sandra L. Cadwallader and Vine Deloria Jr. Philadelphia: Temple University Press, 1984, 185–214.

"Court Rejects Judge's Plan in Indian Case." Associated Press, December 11, 2004 (in LEXIS).

Deloria, Vine, Jr., and Clifford Lytle. *American Indians, American Justice.* Austin: Texas University Press, 1983.

File, John. "One Banker's Fight for a Half-Million Indians." *The New York Times,* April 20, 2004: n.p.

"Fixing an Old Injustice." Editorial. *The New York Times,* August 4, 2005. <http://www.nytimes.com/2005/08/04/opinion/04thu2.html>.

Heilprin, John. "Counting Up What American Indians are Owed." Associated Press, May 7, 2006. (in LEXIS).

Henry, David. *Stealing from Indians.* Billings, MT: Thunder Mountain Press, 1995.

Johansen, Bruce E. "The BIA as Banker: 'Trust' Is Hard When Billions Disappear." *Native Americas* 14, no. 1 (Spring 1997): 14–23.

Johansen, Bruce E. "The Trust Fund Mess: Where Has All the Money Gone?" *Native Americas* 21 (Fall/Winter 2004): 26–33.

Kennedy, J. Michael. "Truth and Consequences on the Reservation." *Los Angeles Times Sunday Magazine,* July 7, 2002. <www.aaanativearts.com/cat186.html>.

"Lawyers Seek Court Order to Keep Indian Trust Accounts Secure." Indian Trust ListServ, April 20, 2005. <http://www.indiantrust.com/index.cfm>.

Leonnig, Carol D. "Interior Dept. Is Denounced; Investigator of Indian Funds Resigns, Alleges Obstruction." *Washington Post,* April 7, 2004: A-7.

Nieves, Evelyn. "Indian Leaders Seek to Settle Lawsuit over Leasing of Land Principles Outlined Include Payment of $27.5 Billion." *Washington Post,* June 21, 2005: A-19.

Pommersheim, Frank. *Braid of Feathers: American Indian Law and Contemporary Tribal Life.* Berkeley: University of California Press, 1995.

Press Release, Plaintiffs. *Cobell v. Norton.* Washington, DC, September 30, 2004.

Reynolds, Jerry. "Bush Administration Likely behind Cobell Appropriations Rider." *Indian Country Today,* November 1, 2003. <http://www.indiancountry.com/?1067709828>.

Szpaller, Keila. "Cobell Speech Inspires, Shames." *Great Falls* (Montana) *Tribune,* July 4, 2005: n.p.

Talhelm, Jennifer. "Appeals Court: Indian Money Accounting Would Be Impossible." *Colorado Daily,* November 16, 2005a. <http://www.coloradodaily.com/articles/2005/11/15/breaking_news/news1.txt>.

Talhelm, Jennifer. "Cowboy Judge in Indian Case Holds Little Back." Associated Press, November 28, 2005b (in Lexis).

Talhelm, Jennifer. "U.S. Wants Judge off Indian Case." Associated Press, April 11, 2006 (in Lexis).

Weiss, Eric M. "At U.S. Urging, Court Throws Lamberth Off Indian Case." *Washington Post,* July 13, 2006: A-13.

Whitty, Julia. "Accounting Coup." *Mother Jones,* September/October 2005. <http://www.motherjones.com/news/feature/2005/09/accounting_coup.html>.

Wilkinson, Charles F. *American Indians, Time, and the Law: Native Societies in a Modern Constitutional Democracy.* New Haven, CT: Yale University Press, 1987.

CHAPTER 3

◦∕

Economic Revival: Up from the Bottom on the Reservation

Reservation poverty is an enduring cliché in Indian Country. As Walter Lippmann wrote when he coined the term, however, all stereotypes grow from a nub of reality to some degree, and thus reservation poverty still rings true, even today. There are signs of economic revival on the reservations, however. In addition, many Native people have been returning to their homelands from cities, bringing with them education, assets, and entrepreneurial energy. New technology also makes conduct of business from a rural base easier and more efficient. Niche markets—such as many that operate from reservations—may be enhanced by Internet technology. Native reservation residents have learned how to use exemptions from state taxes (even as the states mount extensive efforts to collect this money). Land bases and other assets also have been acquired through enforcement of laws such as the Non-Intercourse Acts of 1790 (and later years), which forbade state governments and individuals from purchasing or otherwise taking Native land without federal approval, laws that were routinely flaunted in the eighteenth century. On-reservation banking (such as efforts by the Blackfeet Eloise Cobell, described in chapter 2) has been an essential element in this economic revival.

Some of this new economic activity is due to the infusion of gambling money. Although gaming has spawned its own set of socioeconomic problems on reservations, it has brought some seed money for other enterprises. Is gambling the answer, the new buffalo as some Native Americans have called it? Some places, such as the Pequots' Foxwoods in Connecticut and some other locales, have been enriched by gaming. In other places, such as the New York Oneidas' lands in upstate New York, gambling has provided an enriched upper class the means to hire police to force antigambling traditionalists from their homes. Among the Mohawks at Akwesasne, people have died over the issue. Akwesasne's position on the United States-Canada border also has made smuggling of cigarettes, liquor, other drugs, weapons, and human beings a major industry.

Even today, however, a survey of contemporary reservation economic conditions is a corrective for anyone who thinks that modern-day reservation gambling has made all Native Americans rich. Aside from some of the poorest counties in the United States, Native peoples also occupy some of Canada's most desolate real estate, as characterized here by the village of Pikangikum, which has one of the highest suicide rates of any community in the world. Alcoholism is still a plague in the cities as well as on rural reservations. Readers will become acquainted in this chapter with the hamlet of Whiteclay, Nebraska, where the major business is selling beer and other alcoholic beverages to Indians of the neighboring Pine Ridge Indian Reservation, where such sales are illegal.

A GROWTH IN BUSINESS ENTERPRISES

Beginning in the late 1980s, Indian Country witnessed an explosion in Native American enterprises (not all of them legal) involving the retail of cut-rate tobacco and gasoline as well as gambling establishments, from simple bingo halls to Las Vegas–type casinos, that now operate on a hundred or more reservations. Sovereignty is increasingly being interpreted as economic independence as Native Americans seek more control over resource development on their lands. Business profits, in many cases, are being used to buy back parcels of land that had been sold to non-Indians decades or centuries ago. On the Northern Cheyenne reservation in southeastern Montana, for example, land is being repurchased from non-Indians and turned over to tribal members who intend to use it for cattle ranching.

Oneidas in New York and Wisconsin have been steadily acquiring formerly alienated lands with profits from casinos and using the proceeds to start other businesses as well as to preserve language and culture. By 1997, the unemployment rate on the Oneida reservation in Wisconsin (near Green Bay) had fallen to 4.2 percent, below the national average for all workers. The Wisconsin Oneidas are now one of the largest employers in the Green Bay area. They also spend almost $1 million per year on adult education. In 1995, the Wisconsin Oneidas purchased, for $40 million, a 49 percent stake in Airadigm Communications, a mobile telephone company that serves Wisconsin and Iowa. The Oneidas also spent $22 million in a joint venture with Plexus, a circuit-board assembly company. The Oneidas of Wisconsin also own a one-third stake in Bay Bank of Green Bay and maintain a $5 million revolving loan fund to provide start-up capital for small businesses.

The Mississippi Band of Choctaws in the late 1970s borrowed $500,000 from a federal program that made guaranteed loans and sank most of it into a factory to make wire harnesses for automotive electronics. The business now also makes car stereos for Ford and Chrysler. The Mississippi Choctaws also opened a greeting-card plant in a joint venture with American Greetings as well as other enterprises, including an 18-hole golf course. By the late 1990s, less than 3 percent of household income on the Mississippi Choctaw reservation came from welfare programs, compared to almost 70 percent twenty years earlier. Unemployment on the reservation has fallen to less than 3 percent, and the tribe is the largest employer in its geographical area. Roughly half the tribe's work force is non-Indian (Darlin, 1997, 88).

The White Mountain Apaches of Arizona have increased their income dramatically by operating elk-hunting expeditions for which seven-day permits cost about $14,000. Some of these permits have been auctioned for as much as $50,000. Fishing permits go for $200 per day. The White Mountain Apaches make about $1 million per year from such permits, money that has helped fund development of a ski resort, a modest casino, and ecotourism package tours that feature white-water rafting and mountain climbing (Darlin, 1997, 88).

Some Indian reservations experienced remarkable employment growth in the late twentieth and early twenty-first centuries. In what is probably part of a national pattern, the Affiliated Tribes of Northwest Indians Economic Development Corporation has compiled figures illustrating an explosive growth of individual Indian entrepreneurship. Statistics compiled by this group assert that the number of businesses owned by American Indians in Oregon nearly doubled (from 333 to 618 firms) between 1987 and 1992. In the state of Washington, businesses owned by American Indians also nearly doubled during the same period, from 682 to 1,335. These figures are probably representative of the United States generally.

Between 1980 and 2002, employment on the Leech Lake Reservation in Minnesota rose from 75 to 348. One of the most successful businesses at Leech Lake is a firewood company, which cuts, seasons, and markets wood for home heating. On the White Earth Reservation in Minnesota, a company was started to freeze-dry fishing bait. On the Grand Portage Reservation of Minnesota, the 100-room Grand Portage Lodge and Conference Center was built in 1973. Ojibway Forest Products at White Earth cuts lumber for export.

Six weeks after Hoopa Modular Building Enterprise opened its doors in mid-August 2005 to begin constructing modular built-to-order homes, it had three months' worth of orders. The company, owned collectively by the Hoopas, aims to create jobs and affordable housing. The vast majority of the 60 workers employed at the new facility are Hoopas, who earn significantly more than minimum wage (Rushton, 2005). Inside the airplane hangar-size factory, the modular homes' walls, floors, and roofs are constructed separately and then assembled into the more recognizable house shapes, which are then moved along the assembly line by cranes (Rushton, 2005). The modular homes range in size from 800 square feet to 3,000 square feet. Orders have come from Eureka to San Diego, with most of the homes going to buyers in the Los Angeles area. As of 2005, the homes could not be sold outside of California due to regulations, but the company was working with the Washington and Oregon governments to allow the homes to be shipped there (Rushton, 2005). The modular homes cost about $100 per square foot, less than half the average cost of traditional dwellings. Costs vary depending on which cabinets, flooring, and other fixtures are selected.

CULTURE AND ECONOMIC COMPETENCE

Native American economic resurgence requires access to capital with which to build reservation infrastructure. John C. Mohawk, professor of Native American Studies at the State University of New York–Buffalo, wrote:

[F]or too long, apologists for the failure of United States Indian policy have asserted that the primary cause of Indian poverty is the culture of the Indians. The proposal that Indian culture causes poverty completely ignores the fact that the essential ingredients for economic growth—access to means and opportunity—have been forcefully absent from Indian life. (Mohawk, 1992, 46)

Professor Mohawk continued:

If you want to do successful economic development in Indian country, you eventually have to conclude that you must do it on the Indians' own terms. You come to understand that economic development in Indian country is not just organizing the materials and labor to produce wealth. It is also coming up with a way that people are comfortable in moving forward, in doing what they need in order to meet their needs. (Mohawk, 1989, 56)

By the last years of the twentieth century, these means and opportunities were becoming more available to urban and reservation Indians who also were doing their best to maintain their traditional cultures. The 1990s witnessed an explosion in business ventures by Indian tribes: fish canneries operated by the Quinault, Lummi, and Swinomish of the Pacific Northwest and office and industrial parks operated by the Oneidas of Wisconsin and the Gilas of Arizona. The Warms Springs Reservation of Oregon now includes a large sawmill and a tourist resort.

David Lester, executive director of the Council of Energy Resource Tribes (CERT), who is Creek, wrote:

While Indian peoples still lag other Americans in socioeconomic indicators, for the first time in over 200 years we are witnessing tribes as pillars in their regional economies. We see a consensus across Indian America that developing stable, diversified economies is key to other important tribal goals, such as cultural continuity, retention of the federal trust, tribal self-governance, and the protection of Indian treaty rights.... The Indian vision is to effectively govern our own land ... to master the tools of modern technology to protect our cultural heritage, and to develop strong local economies that give expression to our tribal values in economic terms. (Lester, 1997, G-1)

HISTORICAL ROOTS OF NATIVE AMERICAN POVERTY

Today's reservation economic conditions have a long history, as do government statistics describing them. Shortly after 1920, a wave of sympathy emerged in response to the cruelties imposed on Native American peoples during the nadir of the reservation era. This wave of political opinion produced Lewis Meriam's report (1928), which documented horrid economic conditions on Indian reservations under the Bureau of Indian Affairs' (BIA's) wardship.

By 1923, a group of influential Indians and non-Indians, the Committee of One Hundred, was lobbying for more respectful and humane treatment of surviving American Indians. John Collier was an early member, along with William Jennings

Bryan, Clark Wissler, Gen. John J. Pershing, Bernard Baruch, William Allen White, and the Seneca Arthur C. Parker. Parker was elected presiding officer at a convention in Washington, DC, in December 1923. Under his aegis in 1924, the group published its findings under the title *The Indian Problem*. This document formed the basis for the better-known Meriam Report four years later.

The Indian Problem provided graphic evidence of just how badly the government's wards were being treated. Infant mortality on Indian reservations, for example, was found to be nearly three times that of European-descended Americans generally. Large numbers of Indians were dying from tuberculosis, measles, and other diseases that had been largely eradicated in non-Indian populations. In this sea of disease, health services on reservations were ill-equipped and lacking sufficiently trained staff. Diets laden with cheap commodity carbohydrates were producing malnutrition in people who were otherwise overweight. The government provided an average of 11 cents per day to feed students at its boarding schools and skimped on equipment and salaries for teachers. Schools were often unsanitary. Per capita income for Native reservation residents was less than $200 per year at a time when national average earnings were $1,350.

Belief that government should address its mistakes with regard to Indian affairs by bolstering Native economies became a popular political theme after the release of the Meriam Report. Even before John Collier (who had been accused of communist tendencies during the so-called red scare of the early 1920s) became Indian commissioner under Franklin Delano Roosevelt, Herbert Hoover drew the erudite Ray Lyman from the presidency of Stanford University to become his secretary of the interior. Hoover also chose Charles J. Rhoades, a devout Quaker, as commissioner of Indian Affairs. Rhoades quickly set about to try to implement the findings of the Meriam Report. Thus began a bit of momentum for radical reform to restore some economic integrity to reservation life.

In certain ways, life for some Native people living on reservations was getting more difficult as the twentieth century ended. By 1990, the Pine Ridge Oglala Lakota (Sioux) Reservation in southwestern South Dakota, whose people are descended from Crazy Horse and Red Cloud and which was the site of the 1890 massacre at Wounded Knee and the 1973 confrontation there, had become the poorest area in the United States.

In the 2000 U.S. census, the rankings were little changed. Buffalo County, home of the Lower Brule Indian Reservation, had the lowest per capita income in the United States. The second lowest ranking was Shannon County, home of the Pine Ridge Indian Reservation. In Buffalo County, 61.8 percent of the children lived in poverty, the highest rate in the United States, followed by Zieback County (61.2%) and Shannon County (61%). These rates were much higher than those in any urban area.

The 2000 census indicated that South Dakota as a whole had the largest percentage increase in the United States for household median income between 1990 and 2000. At the same time, Buffalo County, home of the 3,500-member Crow Creek Sioux, exchanged places with Shannon County as the two poorest in the United States. In Buffalo County, the largest and most successful business

during the 1990s was the Lode Star Casino. Shannon County has benefited somewhat from federal empowerment-zone status that brought the county millions in
federal dollars for economic development and a visit from President Bill Clinton.

In 1989, nearly seven of every ten people in Shannon County were unemployed, and virtually the only work, except for a few private businesses, came
from government agencies and the underground economy. Pine Ridge village, the
largest town on the reservation, had no railroad or bus connections and no bank,
theater, clothing store, or barbershop. Meanwhile, the pervasiveness of poverty
shattered families and caused people to turn to alcohol and other drugs. Infant
mortality at Pine Ridge was 29 per 1,000 children, three times the national average. The death rate from homicide was also three times the national average.
People at Pine Ridge die from alcoholism at 10 times the national rate (not taking into account damage caused by fetal alcohol syndrome). The death rate from
adult diabetes was four times the national average. The tribal housing authority
had a waiting list of 2,000 families for subsidized lodging, at least a quarter of the
people on the reservation.

The indications of poverty in South Dakota were nearly duplicated in neighboring states. In Nebraska, unemployment on the Omaha reservation stood at
71 percent in the late 1980s; among the Santee Sioux, unemployment was 55
percent, compared to 65 percent among the Winnebago (Suzuki, 1991, 27–28).
Nationwide, the civilian unemployment rate among Native Americans on reservations was about 30 percent in 1990. Unemployment on the Navajo reservation,
with its workforce of 87,000 people (the largest in the United States), was 29.5
percent.

Nationwide, Native Americans' income level was falling in 1990 as measured
against all other ethnic groups in the United States. According to the U.S. Census
Bureau, the median household income for Native Americans (adjusted for infla-
tion) fell from $20,541 in 1980 to $20,025 in 1990, whereas the same figure for
citizens of European heritage rose from $29,632 to $31,435. The percentage of
Native Americans defined as living below the poverty line increased from 27.5
percent in 1980 to 30.9 percent in 1990, whereas the percentage for European
Americans rose from 9.4 percent to 9.8 percent. In 1990, the Census Bureau
found that 29.5 percent of blacks, 14.1 percent of Asians, and 25.3 percent of
Hispanics lived in poverty. In 1989, the Children's Defense Fund found that 66
percent of Native American children in Minneapolis were living in families with
incomes below the poverty line.

Native American income levels have risen since 2000 in the United States and
poverty rates have stabilized, but as a group they remain among the poorest in
the nation, according to the U.S. Census Bureau. From 2004 to 2005, the average
U.S. household earned $46,326, an increase of 1.1 percent, the first year since
1999 that the median household income rose. Incomes for American Indian and
Alaska Native households from 2003 to 2005, averaged $33,627, lower than any
other broadly defined ethnic group (white, Asian, and Hispanic). Only African

American households, with a median income of $31,140, ranked below Native households (Census Bureau, 2005).

There are still 37 million people, or 12.6 percent of the population, and 7.7 million families in poverty nationwide. Among American Indians and Alaska Natives, the picture was much worse. According to a 3-year average of data, 25.3 percent of Native Americans are living in poverty. This was actually a slight increase from the 24.3 percent that the Census reported in its 1990 study on income and poverty. The figure translated to 537,000 American Indians and Alaska Natives who were below the poverty line. As defined by the Office of Management and Budget, the poverty threshold for a family of four in 2005 was $19,971; for a family of three, $15,577; for a family of two, $12,755; and for unrelated individuals, $9,973 (Census Bureau, 2005).

MIXED SOCIOECONOMIC EVIDENCE

Although many statistics indicate that Native Americans often were experiencing intensifying poverty at the end of the twentieth century, some indicators revealed improvement in some areas of health and welfare. For example, the Indian Health Service reported that the homicide rate for Native Americans (per 100,000 people) declined from 23.8 in 1955 to 14.1 in 1988 as the homicide rate for all ethnic groups in the United States increased from 4.8 to 9.0. Between 1966 and 1988, 57 percent of murders of blacks and 47 percent of murders of whites involved guns (according to the Federal Bureau of Investigation (FBI), only 29 percent of Indian murders involved firearms). Thirty-two percent of murdered Indians were killed with knives. Deaths from alcoholism among Native Americans declined from 56.6 per 100,000 in 1969 to 33.9 in 1988, whereas the alcoholism death rate for all races in the United States declined only slightly, from 7.7 to 6.3 per 100,000. Put another way, in 1969, the alcoholism death rate for Native Americans and Alaska Natives was 7.4 times that of the general population. In two decades, that figure fell to 5.4 times, according to the Indian Health Service.

According to Jeffrey Wollock, writing in *Native Americas,* from 1996 to 2001, crime rates on reservations rose, whereas they fell elsewhere. Indians 12 to 20 years old are 58 percent more likely to be victims of crime than are whites and blacks. Indians younger than age 15 are murdered at twice the rate of whites (Wollock, 2003, 30).

The contemporary murder rate on Indian reservations is five times the average in the United States as a whole: 29 per 100,000 people, compared to 5.6. The average in U.S. urban areas is 7 per 100,000 ("Crime Rate," 2003, 11). An Indian Country Crime Report, compiled from 1,072 cases prosecuted in U.S. district courts, did not include felonies committed by non-Indians on reservations. Some small reservations have very high murder rates, according to this report. The Salt River Pima Maricopa Community in Arizona, for example, had six murders among 6,405 people, a murder rate 17 times the national average. The Gila River Reservation, with 11,257 enrolled members, suffered 11 murders, a similar rate

("Crime Rate," 2003, 11). According to Mac Rominger, an FBI agent on the Hopi and Navajo reservations, often-blamed problems such as alcoholism and poverty were being compounded by isolation. "Ninety-five percent of the violent crime out there is directed towards family and friends," he said ("Crime Rate," 2003, 11).

Youth suicide among Native Americans is twice the rate of non-Indians. The American Medical Association reports that one in five Indian girls attempts suicide before leaving high school. The alcoholism death rate is four times the national average (Wollock, 2003, 30). Additionally, more than 40 percent of Native Americans in the United States live in substandard housing, compared with an average of 6 percent for the rest of the population. The crisis for Native American young people is closely tied to loss of culture, with youth "stuck between two worlds" (Wollock, 2003, 30). Many more Native youth, compared to earlier times, can not speak their own languages and have little grasp of their traditional culture and history.

Similar statistics can assume a terrifying profile when they are described in personal context of on a small village. Take, for example, the Ojibway-Cree village of Pikangikum, about 200 miles northeast of Winnipeg, Manitoba.

PIKANGIKUM'S CONTINUING DESOLATION ESCAPES CANADA'S MINISTRY OF INDIAN AFFAIRS

The Ojibway-Cree village of Pikangikum, about 200 miles northeast of Winnipeg, Manitoba, has the highest documented suicide rate in the world. It is a place where the main recreational pastime for young people is glue-sniffing. The reserve's only school was closed for more than a year because of a fuel leak. Pikangikum's water-treatment plant was closed nearly as long, also because of an accidental fuel leak. Eighty percent to 90 percent of the adults in Pikangikum are unemployed. The village is so overcrowded, with 400 homes for 2,100 people, that some people sleep in shifts to make beds available for others. All food is flown in, so prices are about five times the average for the rest of Canada.

What did Canada's Ministry of Indian Affairs do about all of this? When people in the village asked for help, it suspended the fiscal authority of the village band council, provoking anger at Pikangikum. On May 17, 2001, Indian Affairs Minister Robert Nault took control of the Pikangikum First Nation's $9 million (Canadian) annual budget and then gave control to a private consulting firm, A. D. Morrison and Associates, Ltd., of London, Ontario, an arrangement known within the Canadian Indian bureaucracy as third-party management. When the residents of Pikangikum refused to cooperate with Nault and the third-party managers, Nault, whose riding (district) in Canada's Parliament includes Pikangikum, suspended federal transfer payments to its council, meaning that most of the 10 percent of the town's adults who had jobs with the council stopped receiving paychecks.

The local council called Indian Affairs' actions paternalistic. The band council had no observable financial problems when the government removed its authority. It was not running a deficit when its financial powers were removed;

it had passed previous financial audits. Chief Louis Quill, a spokesman for the Pikangikum council, said the community was shocked to learn that the new colonialist agent was a First Nations–operated company. "I don't think that's the way to treat other Natives," said Quill. "We shouldn't be going after our own people on behalf of Indian Affairs." Quill said the third-party managers "are not welcome in our community" ("Federal Paternalism Angers Pikangikum," n.d.).

A WAVE OF SUICIDES

While Ottawa played bureaucratic Great White Father in Pikangikum, more than forty young people killed themselves there during the 10 years ending in 2002. The same rate, per capita, would have yielded 70,500 suicides in a city of 3 million people. In 2000, the community's rate of suicide was 380 per 100,000 population. The national average suicide rate in Canada is 13 per 100,000. "If [third-party management] is being forced on the community [Pikangikum] from the outside ... that just increases the sense of not having control, and that increases the distress," said David Masecar, president of the Canadian Association of Suicide Prevention (Elliott, June 7, 2001, A-15).

Most of the suicides were women who hanged themselves (Elliott, June 7, 2001, A-15). In 2000 alone, nine Ojibway girls aged 5 to 13 killed themselves in Pikangikum. Those suicides sent the year's suicide rate up to 470 deaths per 100,000, 36 times the Canadian national average. Three more young women killed themselves between mid-May and mid-June 2001. "When young women who are the bearers of life start to kill themselves, it's a real reflection on the health of the community," said Arnold Devlin of Dilico Child and Family Services in Thunder Bay, Ontario (Elliott, November 30, 2000).

Since 1995, the Pikangikum Youth Patrol, a team of young volunteers, has scoured Pikangikum almost every night looking for huddles of gas-sniffers "whose spine-chilling howls permeate the community at night, but the young addicts often scatter into the darkness before patrollers can reach them. At peak suicide times like ... summer and fall, there's an attempt or two every night" (Elliott, November 30, 2000).

Louise Elliott wrote for Canadian Press, "The [suicide] problem, while worst in Pikangikum, is region-wide. On Monday, another 13-year-old girl took her life in Summer Beaver, a reserve 300 kilometers east of Pikangikum, bringing the total suicides on northern Ontario reserves this year [2000] to 25. 'This is the worst year on record [for suicide],'" said Arnold Devlin, of Dilico Child and Family Services in Thunder Bay" (Elliott, November 30, 2000).

"It's very, very difficult," said band councilor Sam Quill, his eyes welling with tears. Quill, who recalled Pikangikum's first rash of youth hangings in 1993 and 1994, included the suicides of his daughter and granddaughter (Elliott, November 30, 2000). Nault had his own take on the rising suicide rate across Ontario's north country. In a letter, he said that Pikangikum band leaders had "perpetuated" the community's suicide crisis by talking to the media. "I'm very concerned that the decision to pursue a media approach may in fact perpetuate the suicide crisis," Nault wrote, adding that a 1996 report by the Royal Commission on Aboriginal peoples "suggests the more publicity given to suicides, the more suicides that follow in their wake" (Elliott, June 22, 2001).

Joseph Magnet, a University of Ottawa law professor who undertook a constitutional challenge to Nault's decision to take over the band's finances, said the letter unfairly blamed the community's interviews with media in recent weeks for the suicide epidemic. "It's a weird thing to say—'we shouldn't bring our lawyers in, we shouldn't call the press, we should let our kids die in private.'" Magnet said of Nault's letter. "It's ridiculous" (Elliott, June 22, 2001).

A DISTRAUGHT DOCTOR

Michael Monture, a Grand River Mohawk who is also a medical doctor, became lost in the bush while serving a rotation on the reserve, despite his reputation as a skilled hunter who was at home in the backcountry. Five doctors rotate in Pikangikum; the reserve has no other medical services. The entire community joined in a search for Monture because he was so well-loved. People who had shared a meal with Montour the evening before he departed for the bush said Monture lost his bearings after he was devastated by the horrible conditions in Pikangikum.

The previous week, according to a report in the *Brantford* (Ontario) *Expositor,* during his second visit to Pikangikum, Monture had tallied up some of the dire social ills that plague the 2,100-member community and was angry. Bonnie-Jean Muir, had shared a dinner with Monture the evening before he went into the bush, beginning a two-day ordeal. About 12:30 A.M. he went out for a long walk, intending to spend the night in the bush. With little food and dwindling gasoline supplies, town residents used their own all-terrain vehicles and boats to comb the area in their search for Monture. They set out each morning of the search from a base camp north of Pikangikum. Spotted by an Ontario Provincial Police helicopter, Monture emerged from the bush seven miles from Pikangikum after two-and-a-half cold, wet days. According to one news account, Monture said that "The suffering and desperation ... on the remote reserve of Pikangikum ... prompted him to set out on a spiritual quest for help" (Elliott, June 18, 2001, A-14).

Like each visiting physician in Pikangikum, Monture was given a large box of food for his rotation. Monture gave most of his food away. "The most common concern was the lack of food. What am I supposed to do? Write a prescription for food for these people?" Monture told Canadian Press (Gamble, n.d.). Monture had henceforth decided to dedicate much of his medical practice to the people of Pikangikum. He moved to Sioux Lookout, near Pikangikum, so that he could fly in to offer medical treatment to the community once or twice a month when not on rotation.

"I was concerned and frustrated at the lack of resources," Monture said after he was rescued. "What galvanized me was how people were lacking in basic food and necessities," he said. "It's not a question of *what* you're going to eat, it's *whether* you're going to eat." Monture described seeing young children huddled near a burning pile of refuse at Pikangikum. "They have a fire going in the garbage dump to keep warm while looking for things to eat," he says. "It's very upsetting to think that this is Canada" (Elliott, June 18, 2001, A-14).

Chief Quill said that Monture's actions had raised the community's profile and its spirits, according to Canadian Press reports, which noted, "Residents, apparently overwhelmed by the doctor's actions, circled around him as he prepared to fly off the reserve Saturday night, reaching out to touch him as though he were a hero" (Elliott, June 18, 2001, A-14). "It was a political stance he was taking," said Muir. "He could not believe what he saw" (Elliott, June 22, 2001, A-16). Stan Beardy, the grand chief of Nishnawbe-Aski Nation, the political organization that represents northern Ontario First Nations reserves, says he believed that fury over the government's appointment of an Indian agent to take control of Pikangikum's finances also played a role in Monture's sojourn into the bush.

FAILED INFRASTRUCTURE

About 200 students lost access to education when Pikangikum's only school closed for about a year after 6,300 gallons of diesel oil was accidentally pumped into the crawl space under the school building. In addition, on October 2, 2000, the Pikangikum water-treatment plant flooded, leaking more than 250 gallons of fuel oil into the town's reservoir. According to a report in a local newspaper, the *Anishinabek News,* "Health Canada closed down the water system and closed the hotel. The workers working on the school had to leave as well…. Chief Peter Quill has stated that unless the water situation is dealt with immediately, the impact of the community will be devastating—both in terms of water-related medical problems and youth suicide" (Goulais, 2000). Many Pikangikum residents were forced to buy water at the local store for $5.99 (Canadian) per four-liter jug. Residents who could not buy drinking water used bottled water that was occasionally, owing to weather conditions, flown in by Indian Affairs. Otherwise, they boiled lake water.

Canadian Indian Affairs provided $1.3 million in repairs to the water plant, which were completed on January 22, 2001. "Canada's Indian Affairs Department asserted that no residents of Pikangikum were without clean water. In addition, the department also flew in a portable Zenon water plant at a cost of $4,500 per month. The community continues to use this portable plant. (A local news account said, "The water situation is no stranger to the communities of the Anishinabek Nation. In August, Gull Bay First Nation tested positive for e-coli contamination in their water supply. According to Chief Oliver Poile of Gull Bay, somebody may have died as a result of that contamination" (Goulais, 2000).

Pikangikum also has been grappling with $10 million in failed infrastructure projects. In March 1999, workers were putting finishing touches on a business center in Pikangikum, including a 1,080-square-meter business center that houses a hotel, full-service restaurant, offices, rental space and classroom facilities, which created 15 permanent jobs in Pikangikum. Two years later, Indian Affairs' embargo on funding closed the hotel.

The list of woes afflicting Pikangikum included construction delays and legal disputes with contractors over an all-weather road and a power line intended to connect the community to the provincial power grid—two necessary steps toward building the kind of infrastructure community members say is necessary.

Meanwhile, at Pikangikum, according to Louise Elliott of the Canadian Press, "On the roads ... young children play on makeshift sleds—sharp-edged fragments of wainscotting they've pulled from stalled construction projects. Band leaders say the community doesn't have enough electricity right now to fix its water treatment plant, or to keep up with the need for new houses. A grid line to pipe in electricity from Balmertown, 100 kilometers south, is only half-finished—it stalled when the contractor walked off the job last summer.... Outside the graffiti-scrawled homes with no indoor plumbing, crosses marking the graves of old and young are lined up seven or eight meters from the front doors, in a unique Pikangikum custom. No one seems to know where this tradition began—some say it happened when people left their traditional church for another, and could no longer use the church graveyard" (Elliott, 2000).

AKWESASNE: THE DOWNSIDE OF GAMBLING AND SMUGGLING

Today on the Akwesasne Mohawk reservation (St. Regis) in upstate New York, the main highway is lined with businesses that did not exist two decades ago, and not just the usual cheap gas and cigarettes, but the everyday goods that sustain people who live there. Many Mohawk-owned businesses have secured government-backed loans and grants resulting in the building of a small strip mall and enterprises ranging from lacrosse-stick manufacturing to large-scale construction companies. This curious mixture of legitimate and illicit economies brought unparalleled material wealth to the Mohawks, but it was not without conflict.

Doug George Kanentiio, who has lived at Akwesasne most of his life, reports that by far the most lucrative money-generating activity was drug smuggling. The risks of carrying narcotics had risen since 2001, but the rewards were substantial. Teenagers were actively solicited by the smuggling cartels because they were told it was unlikely they would be imprisoned if they were caught. A few hours on a boat netted them more money than their parents earned in a month, or so went the rationale.

The local newspaper, Indian Time, also is flush with advertising of Akwesasne businesses, including a First Americans Food Store, the Village Currency Exchange, EScentULee (manicures, pedicures, facials, etc.), Little Bear Design (embroidery and design), Burning Sky Office Products, Four Seasons Lawn Care and Snow Removal, Grace and Allan's Discount Tobacco Products, St. Regis Mohawk Senior Center, CKON Radio, Broken Arrow Truck Stop and Gift Shop, Physical Limits Fitness Club, Clyde N Performance Plus (boats and motors), Akwesasne Mohawk Casino, Trade Zone Gasoline Station, Oakes Heating and Cooling, and Bear's Den Restaurant and Motel.

Although gambling has brought benefits to some Native American communities, it has brought violence to the Akwesasne Mohawks. The violence erupted in part over the issue of gambling. As many as seven casinos had opened illegally along the reservation's main highway as the area became a crossroads for illicit smuggling of drugs, including cocaine and tax-free liquor and cigarettes.

Tension escalated after early protests of gambling in the late 1980s (including the trashing of one casino and the burning of another), to attempts by gambling supporters to brutally repress this resistance. Residents blockaded the reservation to keep the casinos' customers out, prompting the violent destruction of the same blockades by gambling supporters in late April 1990.

At Akwesasne, the rhetoric of Native American sovereignty has been called into service to justify growth of smuggling and gambling as well as the rise of a paramilitary Warrior Society, whose ideological basis was laid by Kahnawake Mohawk Louis Hall. Factions at Akwesasne collided violently in conflicts over commercial gaming during the middle and late 1980s.

By the time of the April 1990 blockade and its subsequent destruction, gambling at Akwesasne was generating $100 million per year in revenues and $7 million per year in untaxed profits to the owners of six establishments, which employed about 500 people. At that time, the casinos were the largest employers on the reservation; 1 in 10 working Mohawks had a job at a casino.

By that time, violence had spiraled into brutal beatings of antigambling activists, drive-by shootings, and nightlong firefights that reminded some observers of gun battles in Belfast, Northern Ireland, and Beirut, Lebanon. The battles culminated in two Mohawk deaths during the early morning of May 1, 1990. Intervention by several police agencies from the United States and Canada followed the two deaths; outside police presence continued for years afterward.

Many Native nations in North America face environmental problems, and commercial gambling also has become an issue on many reservations in the United States. At Akwesasne, however, these crises hit with a special force because the reservation is dissected by the Canada–United States border. As violence related to the debate over gambling hit its peak at Akwesasne in spring 1990 with the shooting deaths of Mathew Pyke and "Junior" Edwards, press reports described a "Mohawk civil war." Such a limited perspective ignores the important role of the international border in the intensifying agony of Akwesasne.

The United States–Canada border has complicated the governance of Akwesasne immeasurably. The reservation is divided between two national governments (the United States and Canada; three if Quebec becomes independent). The borders of New York and the provinces of Quebec and Ontario also converge within the borders of Akwesasne. Internally, the United States recognizes the St. Regis Tribal Council, whereas Canada recognizes the Mohawk Council of Akwesasne. Many Mohawks reserve their political participation for the traditional Council of Chiefs, which draws its constituency from both sides of the border but is recognized by neither the United States nor Canada.

The conflict at Akwesasne was usually characterized in the press as a battle between Mohawk factions over gambling. Although the events that shook the Mohawk reservations of Akwesasne, Kahnawake, and Kanesatake did pit Mohawks against Mohawks (often estranging members of families), and although gambling was a major issue, the root cause was not personal animosity, smuggling, guns, or gambling alone. The events were rooted in the loss of a productive land base and a way of life that once was based upon it.

AKWESASNE'S ROOTS OF STRIFE

The strife that paralyzed Mohawk Country in 1990 was not a series of events isolated in time but the violent culmination of many events and issues that grew out of the ruination of the traditional way of life. This attempt at tracing the recent history of Mohawk Country is really a case study of how the modern industrial state can crush a Native way of life. Without loss of the land and the way of life that Mohawks had based on it, the nationalistic Warrior Society, a paramilitary group whose image mesmerized headline writers in the northeastern United States and most of Canada during that violent summer of 1990, might never have arisen. Had the construction of the Saint Lawrence Seaway shortly after World War II and the subsequent industrialization of the area not destroyed traditional ways of making a living in Mohawk Country, gambling and smuggling might never have emerged as avenues of economic survival there.

The Saint Lawrence Seaway brought ranks of manufacturing plants to Mohawk Country that profited from ready access to the open ocean and cheap power. This industrial base generated the pollution that ruined the farming, fishing, and hunting economy at Akwesasne and its sister Mohawk reserves. In a historical sense, the deaths of Mohawks Mathew Pyke and "Junior" Edwards, as well as the murder of Marcel Lemay (the Quebec police officer killed at Oka in 1990), may be attributed to the rise of industry and its attendant pollution along the Saint Lawrence.

The destruction of the natural world, along with erosion of the Mohawk land base, made living by the old ways nearly impossible and prompted many Mohawks to look for other ways to survive in the cash economy. During the first half of the twentieth century, many moved away; some became the legendary "Mohawks in high steel," the men who constructed large parts of the urban skylines from Montreal to New York City. Some later returned home to ply the smuggling trades and, later, build a gaudy gambling strip along Highway 37 across Akwesasne.

THE GROWTH OF SMUGGLING

A steep rise in Canadian taxes on tobacco opened opportunities in smuggling of cigarettes, which were sold at smoke shops on the Mohawk reserve of Kahnawake, near Montreal. Ancillary smuggling in alcohol, illicit drugs, and weapons followed. The smuggling trade provided the precedent and the seed money for gambling that was never regulated according to U.S. law. Very little of the gambling revenue went to meet tribal needs.

In addition to smuggling, the paramilitary Warrior Society was growing at all three Mohawk reserves. The Warrior Society fed on the frustrations of Mohawks whose old ways had been destroyed and whose lives were deteriorating day by day as factories poisoned the lands that had not been taken from them. Although many Mohawks disparaged the violent tactics of the Warrior Society that often made them feel like hostages in their own homes, everyone in Mohawk Country understood the roots of the problems that had led to the rise of tension and conflict.

Smuggling has remained an enduring economic force at Akwesasne despite efforts by police on both sides of the border. In June 1997, 21 Mohawks were arrested by federal officials in what was called the largest bust of a smuggling ring in U.S. history. The indictment sought to recover $680 million in property allegedly purchased with profits from cigarette, liquor, and gun smuggling that crossed Akwesasne territory, including boats, cars, and real estate. Among those arrested was L. David Jacobs, former chief of the St. Regis Mohawk Council, who was accused of taking several hundred dollars worth of payoffs.

Everyone who is familiar with Akwesasne Mohawk Territory knows it has been the scene of considerable smuggling between the United States and Canada, but no one knew the extent of the traffic until its volume drew the attention of prosecutors and police in both countries. By late 1999, with several convicted smugglers awaiting sentencing, the size of the smuggling industry outlined in court records was astounding even to veteran observers. The evidence presented by prosecutors outlined the largest smuggling operation since the United States-Canada border with land access on both sides was established.

As the only Native American reservation that straddles the United States-Canada border, Akwesasne has long provided a smuggling route for anything illegal that may be in demand on either side. This cargo varies from cigarettes and hard liquor (which are taxed much more heavily in Canada than in the United States) to several varieties of illegal narcotics, automatic weapons, and even human beings. Immigration authorities at one point broke a smuggling ring that was ferrying people (most of them illegal immigrants from Asia) across the border at a cost of $45,000 to $50,000 each.

The right of Mohawks to cross the border unimpeded is recognized by the Jay Treaty (1794), which Canadian authorities occasionally have contested. Various enterprising Akwesasne residents have become adept at selling their connections as border middlemen, the central link in the smuggling chain. A few years ago, a story floated around the reservation that a local kingpin was negotiating to buy a small island in the Saint Lawrence River for about $225,000 for use as a smuggling base. After the two parties agreed on the price, the new owner walked to a closet in his home, which was stacked floor to ceiling with cash in large denominations. He peeled an inch or two off the top of the stack to pay for the island.

The Canadian federal government has asserted that taxing authorities in that country lost $750 million in potential revenue because of smuggling through Akwesasne between 1991 and 1997, when the biggest smuggling ring was busted. Nearly as much money was laundered through an armored-car business in Massena, New York. Prosecutors requested that U.S. district court Judge Thomas McAvoy sentence John "Chick" Fountain of Massena to seven years in prison and forfeiture of an unspecified amount of personal property for his role in laundering

$557 million through his armored-car and currency-exchange businesses. Before he started this business, Fountain previously had lived much more modestly as a New York state trooper.

Fountain, convicted on November 3, 1998, was one of 27 people whom prosecutors alleged had important roles in a smuggling ring that at its height operated large warehouses and squads of motorboats that were used to ferry goods and people across the Saint Lawrence River. When the river was frozen, smuggling often took place in automobiles. The smuggling ring drew some well-known names at Akwesasne into its ambit, including longtime gambling developer Tony Laughing and former St. Regis tribal Chief Leo David Jacobs, who was convicted of taking $32,000 in kickbacks paid to link alleged kingpin Larry Miller with a number of Akwesasne businessmen. One of these businessmen was Loran Thompson, owner of a marina, a restaurant, and what New York radio reporter Neil Drew of Malone, New York, called "a very busy cigarette warehouse along the St. Lawrence River ... where millions of cartons were purchased for smuggling into Canada" (Drew, 2001).

The alleged kingpin of the smuggling cartel was Larry Miller of Massena, who traveled the world in a Lear Jet and owned five houses in Las Vegas as well as an estate not far from the source of his income: the porous international border through Akwesasne. According to court records, Miller made as much as $35 million per year at the height of the operation. Prosecutors suggested that Judge McAvoy fine Miller $160 million in cash and personal assets in addition to a sentence of 17 to 22 years in prison.

ALCOHOLISM: THE CONTINUING TOLL

Second only to the ravages of smallpox and other diseases, alcoholism has been the major cause of early death and other forms of misery for Native Americans since the so-called discovery of the Americas by Columbus. Scarrooyady, an Iroquois sachem, told Pennsylvania treaty commissioners in 1750, "Your traders now bring us scarce anything but rum and flour. The rum ruins us.... Those wicked whiskey sellers, when they have got the Indians in liquor, make them sell the very clothes from their backs!" (Johansen, 1982, 68). In 1832, the sale of alcoholic beverages to Indians was made illegal, an act that was not repealed until the early 1950s, when it became evident that prohibition produced a bootlegging industry little different from that which had flourished in the United States during the 1920s and early 1930s.

Alcoholism continues to be a major problem today and is the leading single cause of death in many Native American communities. Today, the sharpest increases in alcoholism are being suffered in faraway places such as Alaska and the Canadian North, where Native peoples only recently have been deprived of their traditional ways of life. In Manitoba, for example, several hundred Native people whose lands were flooded have been moved to settlements where they are no longer allowed (or able) to wrest a living from the land. Alcoholism and other forms of social disorientation have followed suit. As many as 90 percent of adults have abused alcohol and other drugs, and juveniles frequently engage in fights.

In 1960, before widespread energy development on Alaska's North Slope, the suicide rate among Native people there was 13 per 100,000, comparable to averages in the United States as a whole. By 1970, the suicide rate had risen to 25 per 100,000; by 1986, it was 67.6 per 100,000. Homicide rates by the mid-1980s were three times the average in the United States as a whole, between 22.9 and 26.6 per 100,000 people, depending on which study was used. Death rates from homicide and suicide were related to rising alcoholism. In the mid-1980s, 79 percent of Native suicide victims had some alcohol in their blood at the time of death. Slightly more than half (54%) were legally intoxicated.

In 1969, the Indian Health Service appointed a Task Force on Alcoholism that, a year later, concluded that alcoholism was one of the most significant health problems facing American Indians and Alaska Natives. Seven years later, the American Indian Policy Review Commission, established by the U.S. Congress, found that alcoholism and its medical consequences were the most serious and widespread health problem among American Indians. According to the Indian Health Service, alcoholism has an insidious multiplier effect. Not only does it contribute to elevated rates of traffic deaths but it also contributes to the majority of Indian homicides, other assaults, suicides, and other mental-health problems.

Even today, among Plains Indians, 80 percent to 90 percent of Native American men drink alcohol, as do 50 percent to 60 percent of Indian women. By age 17, a majority of Indian boys and a large minority of Indian girls are steady drinkers. Drinking among Indian young people has been related directly to the highest suicide rate in the United States for any age group. Alcohol abuse also relates to low educational achievement, poor health, high rates of unemployment, and crime among Indian youth.

Nationwide, Indians have, for several years, averaged 12 times the number of arrests, per capita, compared to the general population. Three-quarters of these arrests are alcohol-related, almost twice the national average. In 1973, the General Accounting Office surveyed six Indian Health Service hospitals and found that 60 percent of the caseload could be directly or indirectly attributed to alcohol use. Cirrhosis of the liver was a frequent cause of hospitalization and, eventually, death. According to the Indian Health Service, cirrhosis of the liver occurs in American Indians at five times the rate of the general population. The Indian Health Service also reports that many child-battering cases are alcohol-related.

A major cause of Indian alcoholism is deprivation and poverty, rejection by European Americans as inferiors, deterioration of traditional cultures, and a generally high level of anxiety that attends day-to-day reservation life. The Klamaths, who were dispersed by federal government termination policies during the early 1950s, had a high rate of arrests for alcohol-related crime, even when compared to the averages for all Indians, which are 12 times those for non-Indians. By contrast, the Pueblo Indians of New Mexico, who have maintained most of their traditional way of life through 150 years of U.S. domination (and two centuries under Spain and Mexico before that), have relatively low rates of alcohol-related arrests.

Given the history of Indian alcoholism, treatment for it is a relatively recent development. As late as the mid-1960s, intoxicated Indians arrested in Gallup, New Mexico, simply were put in jail until it filled. On winter nights, those who were not arrested ran a risk of freezing to death. In a routine winter, many Indians froze to death on the streets of Gallup.

For a number of reasons, most of them cultural, traditional non-Indian treatments, from hospitalization to non-Indian chapters of Alcoholics Anonymous, had very little success dealing with Indian alcoholism. In the late 1960s, along with a general thrust of Indian self-determination, Native treatment programs began to open. The idea of Indians treating Indians was hailed as revolutionary in some quarters, but it is not really new. Since at least the days of the Iroquois spiritual leader Handsome Lake in the early nineteenth century, Indian religious figures have opposed the use of alcohol and achieved moderate success in sobering their followers.

THE POLITICS OF MALT LIQUOR

During the 1990s, protests from Native groups arose in several states regarding the sale of Crazy Horse Malt Liquor. The beverage was being sold by Hornell Brewing Company of New York in 40-ounce bottles bearing a likeness of Crazy Horse, the nineteenth-century Lakota leader. The brew was being manufactured by G. Heileman Brewing Company.

In Congressional hearings, U.S. Surgeon General Antonia Novello and representatives of Native American groups contended that Crazy Horse Malt Liquor was specifically aimed at underage Native American drinkers. The surgeon general also attacked other brands of alcohol, as well as cigarettes, that appeared to be aimed at minorities, women, and teenagers. The campaign already had resulted in the removal from shelves of PowerMaster, also a malt liquor, after complaints that it was targeted at young blacks.

Crazy Horse Malt Liquor was not the first marketing attempt aimed specifically at Indians, of course; traders have been getting them addicted to liquor since the earliest days of contact. It also was not the first alcoholic product to enter into contemporary Native politics. In the late 1980s, Native groups across the northern tier of states (roughly from Wisconsin to Washington) protested the marketing of Treaty Beer by sportsmen's-rights groups raising funds to annul Native agreements with the federal government. At the time, the fund-raising brew was called "the Klan in a can" by Indians in Washington (Johansen, 1988, 13).

WHITECLAY: THE BUSINESS IS BEER

On June 26, 1999—123 years and one day after their ancestors had removed George Armstrong Custer's scalp—Lakotas gathered in Whiteclay, Nebraska, to demand details describing how Wilson "Wally" Black Elk and Ronald Hard Heart had died. Their partially decomposed bodies had been found on June 8. Many people at the Pine Ridge Indian Reservation believe that the way in which Black Elk and Hard Heart died was similar to how two other Lakota, Wesley Bad Heart Bull and Raymond Yellow Thunder, were killed in 1972—beatings to death by white toughs having what they regarded as a sporting time with inebriated Oglala Lakotas.

A month and more after the killings of Black Elk and Hard Heart, the men's reservation relatives knew little or nothing, officially, of how they died. Law enforcement officials in Nebraska and FBI agents talked vaguely of "foul play" and "following leads" while anger spread at Pine Ridge. Pine Ridge tribal police chief Stan Star Comes Out told the *Omaha World-Herald* that the remains of the two men had been wounded and bloody. He also said the two men had been bludgeoned to death. The bodies were found on the Pine Ridge (South Dakota) side of the state line, but many Lakota believe the men were murdered in Nebraska, closer to Whiteclay, after which their bodies were dragged across the border.

Lakota community responses to the deaths of Yellow Thunder and Bad Heart Bull defined the American Indian Movement in 1972 and provided a provocation (one of many) for the occupation of Wounded Knee the next year. Yellow Thunder was kidnapped and beaten to death during mid-February 1972 in Gordon, Nebraska (about 25 miles southeast of Whiteclay and 13 miles south of Pine Ridge), by several white toughs. Four young men were charged with manslaughter (not murder), and two of them were convicted. By March, Gordon was the scene of rallies of more than 1,000 Lakota and allies demanding justice for Yellow Thunder. Two brothers who were convicted of manslaughter served 10 months (of a two-year sentence) and two years (of a six-year sentence), respectively.

Shortly after the murder of Yellow Thunder in 1972, Lakota Wesley Bad Heart Bull was stabbed to death by a young white man near Custer, South Dakota (in the Black Hills southwest of Rapid City). The assailant was charged with second-degree manslaughter, provoking demonstrations, some of which turned violent, at the courthouse in Custer, organized by the American Indian Movement (AIM).

In 1999, some of the major organizers were the same ones who had been in Gordon and Custer—AIMsters with many more lines on their faces. They listened to speeches by Russell Means, Clyde Bellecourt, and Dennis Banks, among others, protesting basic injustices, such as young white men's penchant for taking out their aggressions (sometimes with fatal results) on drunken Indians near the dusty streets of Whiteclay, population 24, where the main business is selling $3 million of beer per year to the people of Pine Ridge (Johansen, 1998, 5).

In reaction to the murders of Hard Heart and Black Elk, a Rally for Justice—250 people walking and accompanied by about 150 automobiles—traversed the two-lane blacktop to "take Whiteclay back" on June 26. As the larger rally was breaking up in Whiteclay, about 25 to 30 people trashed a grocery store, V. J.'s Market, in Whiteclay. It was said that V. J.'s owner, Vic Clarke, had treated Lakota in a demeaning manner. The store's freezer cases were destroyed and its cash registers doused with lighter fluid. Groceries were strewn through the store.

Claims of Lakota control to the ground on which Whiteclay sits are based on surveys taken for the Fort Laramie Treaty of 1868, which place Whiteclay within reservation borders. Documents related to the Dawes (Allotment) Act, notably legislation passed by Congress in 1889 to break up what was then called the Great Sioux Nation, also support this assertion. An executive order issued in 1882 by President Chester A. Arthur created a 50-square-mile buffer zone (which includes the site of Whiteclay) south of the Pine Ridge Indian Reservation expressly to curtail the liquor trade. This order was rescinded on January 25, 1904, by President Theodore Roosevelt with the rationale that non-Indians needed the land.

For years, Nebraska officials had been warned by activist Frank LaMere and others that the situation in Whiteclay could explode. One day during summer 1997, LaMere, a Winnebago who was executive director of the Nebraska Inter-Tribal Development Corp., visited Whiteclay. He counted 32 intoxicated Indians on the town's streets at 5:15 A.M. and 47 drunks on the streets during the afternoon, some of whom were fighting with each other. Several other Indians were passed out at the intersection of Nebraska Highway 87 with the road that leads to the reservation. A few of them were urinating on the street (Johansen, 1998, 5).

Shortly after he visited Whiteclay, LaMere asked the Nebraska Liquor Control Commission to shut Whiteclay down. "I don't know what constitutes infractions of liquor laws in Whiteclay, but my good sense tells me there is something terribly wrong," LaMere told Toni Heinzl of the *Omaha World-Herald.* "What I saw … in Whiteclay would not be acceptable in Omaha or Lincoln," LaMere continued (Johansen, 1998, 5).

The Pine Ridge Reservation in 1996 had an alcoholism-related death rate of 61.9 per 100,000 people, twice the average for Native American reservations and nine times the national average of 7.1. On the two-mile highway between Pine Ridge village and Whiteclay, tribal police issue at least 1,000 driving-while-intoxicated citations per year. Despite the police presence, residents who live along the road are constantly pestered by drunks. Several family dogs have been shot to death along the road as well.

A PROTEST MARCH IN WHITECLAY

On Saturday, July 3, 1999, about a hundred sheriff's deputies and state patrol officers, many of them in riot gear, barricaded Whiteclay's business district. Ironically, the Nebraska State Patrol had met one of the protesters' demands: for Friday and Saturday, at least, the beer stores of Whiteclay would be closed, on one of their busiest weekends of the year. During Friday afternoon, caravans of cars from Pine Ridge circled Whiteclay and its barricades in an air of ghostly quiet, using several back roads.

Aside from a few rocks thrown and nine brief arrests (one of them Russell Means), the July 3 march came and went without notable physical contact between the Lakota Sioux and the hundred SWAT officers barricading Whiteclay. Many participants in the march stressed the spiritual nature of their actions. Marchers stopped four times to pray (and to give elderly marchers some rest) during the hour-and-a-half it took the group of several hundred people to move from Pine Ridge to Whiteclay on a hot and unusually humid day.

As they approached Whiteclay, marchers debated whether to cross a line of yellow plastic tape that police had strung across the road into the village. Most urged restraint, but Russell Means urged the group on. One man on a pinto pony tried to run the line but was stopped by police. Means and the eight others who were arrested also stepped over the line, briefly, and were cited for failure to obey a lawful order, to establish a basis for a later court case (the activists contended that their arrests were illegal). They were released an hour later. Other marchers threw mud at the helmeted troopers. A few spit on them and cursed. One protester plastered a bumper sticker reading "YOU ARE ON INDIAN LAND" across one officer's helmet.

As the dust settled in Whiteclay following the second rally, the beer stores opened briefly Monday morning but closed once again after Clyde Bellecourt told Stuart Kozel, owner of the Jumping Eagle Inn, that opening his store would provoke another confrontation with AIM. Another beer outlet with a distinctly Indian-sounding name, the Arrowhead Inn, also remained closed for an extra day.

On Saturday, July 10, a smaller rally was held, followed by another march and motorcade from Pine Ridge to Whiteclay. Roughly 100 people on foot and in cars sang and drummed as they paraded up and down Whiteclay streets, unimpeded by police this time. AIM members posted eviction notices on the four beer stores then withdrew to tepees and tents erected on the site where the bodies of Black Elk and Hard Heart had been found on June 8. The people in the camp pledged to maintain it (along with weekly demonstrations in Whiteclay) until the border town went dry.

In the meantime, LaMere, one of nine people who had been arrested at the initial rally, appealed again to the Nebraska Liquor Control Commission to shut down Whiteclay's beer businesses permanently. Once again, the board did not act; within days the activists were gone, and most of the Indians on the streets of Whiteclay were, once again, falling down drunk.

BILL CLINTON VISITS PINE RIDGE

President Bill Clinton visited Pine Ridge later the same summer. The White House called the tour (which included communities in Appalachia, the Mississippi Delta, South Phoenix, the Watts area of Los Angeles, as well as Pine Ridge) the New Markets Initiative. The main purpose of the four-day tour was to lobby for business development of impoverished areas. Some White House planners had suggested that the federal government match certain forms of private investment in such areas.

When President Clinton arrived at Pine Ridge on July 7, 1999, he found a page out of the Meriam Report, a state of reservation life in many cases little changed from the days of Franklin Roosevelt or Dwight Eisenhower. The Pine Ridge and its neighboring Rosebud Sioux reservations are among the poorest 10 counties in the United States. Clinton arrived at Ellsworth Air Force Base, near Rapid City, South

Dakota, early in the morning and, after a lengthy drive, arrived at Pine Ridge village by midmorning. The president ceremonially signed documents creating an empowerment zone at Pine Ridge (the first such zone on an Indian reservation), toured a few housing areas, gave a speech at Pine Ridge High School, and was on his way back to Ellsworth after lunch.

Clinton thus completed a three-hour visit to Pine Ridge that made him the first sitting U.S. president to visit an Indian reservation since Franklin Delano Roosevelt as well as the first to visit Pine Ridge since Calvin Coolidge (in 1927). During his 20-minute speech at Pine Ridge High School, Clinton greeted the 4,500 people in Lakota and promised such things as a doubling of the number of federal-backed mortgages at Pine Ridge, a move meant to add 1,000 homes to the reservation within a few years. As Clinton spoke, the waiting list for housing there stood at 4,000 units.

GAMBLING: THE NEW BUFFALO?

The arrival of gaming has brought dividends to some Native peoples and controversy culminating in firefights and death to others. At the same time, during the late twentieth century, commercial gambling has become a major source of income on many Indian reservations across the United States. On reservations where gambling is collectively controlled, revenue from gaming establishments sometimes has helped repurchase formerly alienated land and build infrastructure. Gambling benefits vary widely from reservation to reservation. The Mashantucket Pequots' income at Foxwoods, more than $1 million per person per year, compares to gaming income of only $167 per year per member of Native nations in South Dakota (Giago, 1997, 24; Murphy, 2000, A-1).

The concept of placing bets on sporting contests was known to several Native American peoples in precontact times; the Iroquois, Ojibways, and Menomines, for example, placed bets on games of snow snake. The scale of such gambling was usually small, and noncommercial. Although many Native American cultures today practice forms of gambling as a type of ceremonial sport, there was no traditional experience with gambling as a large-scale commercial enterprise.

Marion Blank Horn, principal deputy solicitor of the Interior Department, described the fertile ground gambling enterprises found in Indian Country:

> The reasons for growth in gambling on Indian land are readily apparent. The Indian tribal governments see an opportunity for income that can make a substantial improvement in the tribe's [economic] conditions. The lack of any state or Federal regulation results in a competitive advantage over gambling regulated by the states. These advantages include no state-imposed limits on the size of pots or prizes, no restrictions by the states on days or hours of operations, no costs for licenses or compliance with state requirements, and no state taxes on gambling operations. (Johansen, 1993, xxix)

The history of reservation-based commercial gambling began during 1979, when the Seminoles became the first Native nation to enter the bingo industry. By early 1985, 75 to 80 of the 300 recognized Indian tribes in the United States were conducting some sort of game of chance. By fall 1988, the Congressional Research Service estimated that more than 100 Indian nations and tribes participated in some form of gambling, which grossed about $255 million per year. By 1991, 150 of 278 Native reservations recognized by non-Indian governmental bodies had some form of gambling. According to the Interior Department, gross revenue from such operations passed $1 billion that year. By 2006, the number of Native American groups in the United States hosting some sort of gaming topped 300.

In 1996, American Indian casinos in the United States grossed about $6 billion, compared to $100 million in 1988. Indian gambling revenues increased 3,500 percent from 1985 to 1995, from $1.25 million to $4.5 billion. The increase in revenues has prompted attempts by some in Congress to collect taxes from these revenues. One outspoken advocate of such measures has been Bill Archer, Republican of Texas and chair of the House Ways and Means Committee.

Individual prizes in some reservation bingo games were reported to be as high as $100,000, whereas bingo stakes in surrounding areas under state jurisdiction sometimes were limited to $100. The reasons for growth in gambling on Indian land were readily apparent. Native governments sensed an opportunity for income that could make a substantial improvement in their economic conditions. A lack of state or federal regulation provided them a competitive advantage over off-reservation gambling regulated by the states. These advantages included a lack of state-imposed limits on the size of pots or prizes, no restrictions by the states on days or hours of operations, no costs for licenses or compliance with state regulations, and (unless they were negotiated) no state taxes on gambling operations.

By the 1990s, gambling was providing a small galaxy of material benefits for some formerly impoverished Native peoples. One of the most successful reservation gambling operations in the United States was the Little Six Casino in Minnesota, which opened as a 1,300-seat bingo parlor in 1982, drawing customers from Minneapolis-St. Paul with free shuttle buses. The casino was a half-hour's drive from the Twin Cities, and blackjack players crowded 41 tables while 450 other players stared into video slot machines inside the tepee-shaped Little Six Casino, operated by the 103 members of the Shakopee Mdewakanton Sioux. By 1991, each member of the tribe, as a shareholder in the casino, was receiving a monthly dividend check averaging $2,000. In addition to monthly dividends, members became eligible for homes (if they lacked them), guaranteed jobs (if they were unemployed), and full college scholarships. The tribal government took out health insurance policies for everyone on the reservation and established day care for children of working parents.

Within a year of its founding, the Little Six had paid off its mortgage and paved its parking lot as well as the driveways of several Shakopee-Mdewakanton reservation homes. Gambling opened under management by a non-Indian company that received 45 percent of the profits. The rest went into common funds. By 1984, Little Six's profits passed $12 million per year, and it had become the largest employer in Prior Lake, Minnesota. Profits were used by the Mdewakanton Sioux to build a health clinic, day-care center, and cultural center. Everyone on the reservation who wanted a job was able to work.

By 1998, the Shakopee's Little Six Casino had been enlarged and expanded as the Mystic Lake Complex:

> [The casino] rises like Oz from the rolling countryside; beams form a circle of spotlights intersecting high above in the darkness to form a teepee of light. Down below, there are about 2,600 slot machines, at least 140 gaming tables, five restaurants, and a luxury hotel. The tribe is Scott County's largest employer by far. Twenty-four hours a day, throngs of gamblers stuff quarters, dollars, and even hundred-dollar bills into the machines with glazed-eyed intensity. (Farney, 1998, A-1)

By 1997, 6 million visitors surged through its gambling facilities, earning the Mdewakanton Dakota $600,000 for each of its 270 members, who lived on 248 acres granted reservation status in 1969. Almost three decades later, the tribal casino complex, the only gambling of its type in the Minneapolis-St. Paul area, employed 3,900 people, most of them non-Indians, and bringing $100 million per year to the regional economy (Farney, 1998, A-6).

According to the National Indian Gaming Association, Indian gaming by 2002 contributed approximately $120 million in state and local tax receipts annually. Gaming patrons spent an estimated $237 million in local communities around Indian casinos (Marquez, 2002). Of the 562 federally recognized Native American governmental entities in the United States at that time, 201 participated in class II or class III gaming by 2001. Class II includes such games as bingo, pull-tabs, lotto, punch boards, and certain card games permissible under individual state laws. Class III includes everything else, such as casino-style table games like roulette and craps and card games such as poker and blackjack. Indian casinos operated in 29 states under a total of 249 separate gaming compacts (Wanamaker, April 5, 2002).

A FEW CASINOS MAKE MOST OF THE MONEY

A General Accounting Office (GAO) study conducted during the late 1990s disclosed that only a few reservations had casino windfalls. Ten casinos generated almost half the $7 billion in annual revenues generated by Indian tribes (with a net income of $1.6 billion per year), according to the GAO. Nearly all of them were located close to major urban areas that supply a large number of non-Indian gamblers. Only 5 percent of the nearly 500 tribes in the United States had made large profits from gambling. The typical casino was a small operation serving a limited clientele in a rural area. The Oglala Lakota, for example, grossed about $1 million a year from its casino, which was housed in three double-wide trailers on concrete blocks. Their revenues for a year equaled those generated at the Pequot casino at Foxwoods in half of an average day. The biggest moneymakers were the small number of casinos situated close to large non-Indian markets. Nearly 80 percent of casino profits went to 5 percent of Native nations and tribes.

The largest casino to open by mid-1991 was the $3 million Sycuan Gaming Center on the Sycuan Indian Reservation near El Cajon, a suburb of San Diego, California. The casino's rakish neon sign flashed against a rocky patch of land onto which the government forced the tribe to move more than a century ago. The sign was visible miles away over scrub-covered hills.

The Sycuan Gaming Center's gaming revenue grew to $10.6 billion in 2000, representing 16 percent of the $64.9 billion generated by gaming in the United States as a whole (Wanamaker, May 16, 2002). By 2002, Indian gaming revenue had grown to $14.5 billion.

THE ONEIDAS OF NEW YORK: A BUSINESS CALLED A NATION

In few areas is the conflict regarding gambling as sharp as among the Haudenosaunee, or Iroquois Confederacy, where New York governor George Pataki promoted plans to open as many as six new Native-controlled casinos in an attempt to jump-start a state economy that had been badly damaged by the attacks of September 11, 2001. The experiences of the New York Oneidas with gambling has been a particularly raw example of conflicts that have beset many Native American nations that have attempted to address problems of persistent poverty and economic marginalization by opening casinos. Supporters of the casinos see them as the so-called new buffalo, whereas opponents look at them as a form of internal colonization, an imposition of European-descended economic institutions and values upon Native American peoples.

Around 1970, the New York Oneidas' landholdings were down to 32 acres east of Syracuse, with almost no economic infrastructure. Three decades later, the New York Oneidas owned a large casino, the Turning Stone, which had incubated a number of other business ventures. Many of the approximately 1,000 Oneidas who resided in the area were receiving substantial material benefits. The Turning Stone Casino, 25 miles east of Syracuse, produced more than 4,000 jobs and has become, according to Oneida Nation representative Ray Halbritter, the fifth most popular tourist attraction in New York.

Eighty-five percent of the Turning Stone's employees are non-Indian. An expansion of the Oneidas' casino and hotel accommodations during the late 1990s was expected to increase the Oneida payroll to 2,600, making it the largest employer in the region. Although Halbritter pointed to the economic benefits of the Oneidas' growing payroll, local public officials complained that the Oneidas' business ventures paid no sales or excise taxes to cities, counties, or the state. Additionally, land purchased by the Oneidas was taken off the property-tax rolls. In September 1997, the Oneidas attempted to assuage these criticisms by paying Oneida County $71,080 and Verona County (in which the casino is located) $55,230 in lieu of property taxes. The payments have been pledged on an annual basis (Kates, 1997, 25).

By 2003, Turning Stone was earning an estimated net profit of $70 million per year on $230 million gross income. Approximately 4.2 million visitors passed through the casino's doors each year (many of these were repeat visits). The casino's influence on the tax base of nearby small towns was enormous. James Chapell, mayor of the town of Oneida, for example, said that the Oneidas had taken so much land off the tax rolls that the town's tax revenues fell from $700,000 to $139,000 in one year (Randolph, 2003). The town of Oneida has resisted requesting financial help from the Oneida Nation, but nearby Verona, which faced similar declines in tax revenue, negotiated funding for a water project as well as $800,000 for local services (Randolph, 2003).

The Oneidas used some of their gambling profits to start other businesses, such as the Oneida Textile Printing Facility in Canastota, their first effort at diversification outside of gambling. Oneida Textile, located in a renovated 6,000-square-foot structure, printed and marketed T-shirts, sweatshirts, and other items of clothing. A 285-room luxury hotel was opened in September 1997, adding 450 jobs; it was expanded eight years later. Casino profits also have been used to build a council house; health-services center; a cultural center and museum; a recreational center with a swimming pool, gymnasium, and lacrosse box; scholarship programs; medical, dental, and optical facilities; job training; legal assistance; Oneida language and music classes; elder meals; and day care. A convention center-arena and golf course are planned.

The recent experience of the Oneidas of New York raised several significant questions for Indian Country as a whole. Is the Oneida model of an economic powerhouse key to defining the future of Native American sovereignty in the opening years of the twenty-first century, as many of its supporters believe? Materially, some of the New York Oneidas have gained a great deal in a quarter-century, including repurchase of 14,000 acres of land. Have these gains been offset by an atmosphere of stifling totalitarianism and a devastating loss of traditional bearings, as many Oneida dissidents attest?

DISSENT IN ONEIDA COUNTRY

A substantial dissident movement has grown among Oneidas who assert that Halbritter, so-called nation representative of the New York Oneidas, was never voted into such an office. This group is centered in the Shenandoah family, which includes the notable singer Joanne Shenandoah and her husband, activist Doug George-Kanentiio. They believe that the New York Oneidas under Halbritter have established a business, called it a nation, and acquired the requisite approvals from the New York and the U.S. federal governments to use this status to open the Turning Stone Casino. On various Internet sites and chat rooms, supporters of Halbritter accused the Shenandoah family of supporting antitreaty groups, whereas opponents of the Oneidas' corporate structure routinely called Halbritter "the king" and "the despot."

The dissidents' benefits as Oneidas were eliminated after they made these points, in 1995, in a march for democracy (Johansen, 2002, 25–43). The New York Oneidas under Halbritter's aegis also appointed a men's council (a body unheard of in traditional matrilineal Iroquois law or tradition), which issued a zoning code to beautify the Oneida Nation. This code enabled his 54-member police force (patrolling a 32-acre reservation) to "legally" evict from their homes those Oneidas who opposed his role as leader of the New York Oneidas. Halbritter's control also was supported by the acquisition of a number of other businesses, a phalanx of public-relations spin doctors, several lawyers, and ownership of *Indian Country Today*, a national Native American newspaper. The newspaper carried no news of the evictions.

Dissent against gambling also surfaced in other areas. John Yellow Bird Steele, chairman of the Oglala Sioux Tribal Council in 1992, advocated construction of three casinos to alleviate unemployment and provide private industry on the reservation. The Wounded Knee chapter of AIM opposed the proposal on grounds that that gambling would drive poor people on the reservation farther into alcoholism and debt, regarded by AIM as a modern form of genocide.

PROSPERITY FOR THE WISCONSIN ONEIDAS

For the Oneida of Wisconsin, gambling has been the key to a quarter-century of economic development that reduced reservation unemployment from 75 percent in 1970 to 5 percent in 1995. The Wisconsin Oneidas, with $100 million in gambling revenues annually, have used some of the profits to purchase land taken from them many years ago.

The Wisconsin Oneidas also have become the largest single employer in Brown County, which includes the city of Green Bay. The Oneidas employed 3,600 people, 55 percent of them members, in 1997. By the late 1990s, the Wisconsin Oneidas were bringing more than $1 billion per year in economic activity to the Green Bay area (Johnson, 1995, 17). The Oneidas have diversified into other investments, such as a printing business, telecommunications, and retail stores; revenues from a 301-room hotel owned by the Oneidas helped fund a Green Bay convention center during the mid-1990s.

In 1969, the Oneida government in Wisconsin employed 9 people; by 1995, the payroll was 3,391: 1,611 members, 357 Native Americans who were not Oneidas, and 1,421 non-Indians. The Oneida Nation's annual budget in 1969 was about $50,000, nearly all of which came from federal funds. In 1995, the budget was $158 million, of which 80 percent was generated on the reservation (Johnson, 1995, 17–18).

Tim Johnson wrote that the Oneidas have used Indian gaming to develop reservation infrastructure, including education, in a way that has "merged Indian culture with corporate practices and left the Oneidas in a position to protect, preserve, strengthen, and protect their identity far into the future" (Johnson, 1995, 17). Prosperity has come to the Oneidas of Wisconsin at the same time as a revival of the traditional Longhouse religion.

Non-Indians flock to the Oneidas' casino from a radius of 200 miles, arriving by the busloads to play 5,000 slot machines that can pay off as much as $1 million. Prizes at the bingo tables can be as high as $250,000. "When I walk into that casino, I'm overwhelmed," said Carol Cornelius, a Wisconsin Oneida. "I think, 'My people did all this.'" Cornelius recalled that "Twenty-five years ago when I graduated from high school there were no jobs. As young folks we went to Milwaukee and found out we couldn't handle city life. There just wasn't a future. Now I see all of these young people working and I think, 'all of these people now have job skills'" (Johnson, 1995, 20).

THE FOXWOODS MONEY MACHINE

By 1995, the largest Native American casino was the Mashantucket Pequots' Foxwoods, operated by the Pequot between the urban areas of Boston and New York City. This casino has been notable for the socially conscious use of its profits. By 1995, the Foxwoods casino had become the largest single gambling establishment in the United States, where patrons could sample 3,900 slot machines, dine in 15 restaurants, or can take in entertainment by the likes of Bill Cosby, Ray Charles, and Joanne Shenandoah. The 190,000-square-foot casino complex, which also included several bars, spas, and a shopping center, employed almost 10,000 people on a reservation with 350 permanent residents located on 2,000 acres of trust land within a short drive of the Boston and New York metropolitan areas (Johnson, 1995, 22–23).

Mashantucket means "the much-wooded land." The word *Foxwoods* is a combination of the notion of forest with the Pequots' reputation as "the fox people." Foxwoods started as a very small bingo parlor after approximately 40 banks refused to loan money to the Pequots. The bingo parlor began operating in 1986 and became wildly successful. Having obtained financing from outside the United States, the Pequots opened their full-scale casino in 1992. At the time, Foxwoods was the only gaming establishment on the East Coast that offered poker, which was banned at the time in Atlantic City, New Jersey.

The first day Foxwoods opened, February 14, 1992, its 1,700-car parking lot was full by 10:30 A.M. Approximately 75,000 people passed through the casino's doors during that first day, and 2,000 of them were still present at the casino's 4 A.M. closing time. During the ensuing decade, Foxwoods expanded and become one of the most notable examples anywhere of Native American economic development.

By the year 2000, the Foxwoods complex was drawing about 50,000 people on an average day. By that time, the Foxwoods Resort Casino complex included five casinos housing more than 300,000 square feet of gaming space, 5,842 slot machines, 370 gaming tables, a 3,000-seat high-stakes bingo parlor with $1 million jackpots, a 200-seat Sportsbook, and a Keno lounge. Table games included baccarat, mini-baccarat, Big Six Wheels, blackjack, Caribbean stud poker, craps, Pai Gow, Pai Gow Tiles, Red Dog, roulette, and a number of other games. The Foxwoods casino complex also included four hotels ranging in size from 280 to 800 rooms. In addition to gaming space and its four hotels, Foxwoods also offered 23 shopping areas, 24 food-and-beverage outlets, a movie-theater complex, as well as the Mashantucket Pequot museum and a Fox Grand Theater that featured Las Vegas–style entertainment.

HELPING THE STATE BALANCE ITS BUDGET

Foxwoods quickly became a very large financial success for its sponsors, as well as for the state government of Connecticut, to which the casino's management pledged a quarter of its profits. During the fiscal year beginning July 1, 1999, and ending June 30, 2000, Foxwoods' gross revenues on its slot and video machines alone totaled more than $9 billion. Foxwoods quickly become an pillar of Connecticut's economy and a multimillion-dollar contributor to the state's charities. The Pequots' casino even put up cash one year to help the state balance its budget.

By 2000, the Foxwoods casino complex was paying the state of Connecticut more than $189 million a year in taxes. The Foxwoods and a second, more recently constructed casino, the Mohegan Sun, paid the state of Connecticut more than $318 million during the 1999–2000 fiscal year. The Mashantucket Pequots became Connecticut's largest single taxpayer and, with 13,000 jobs, one of its larger employers. The casino complex employed a staff of lawyers and maintained its own permanent lobbying office in Washington, DC.

At the same time, the Pequots also became a significant contributor to the Smithsonian Institution's new National Museum of the American Indian at $10 million. That amount was soon matched by the New York Oneidas, drawing from its own casino profits. The Mashantucket Pequots also gave $2 million to the Special Olympics and $500,000 to the Hartford Ballet, as well as $5 million to the Mystic, Connecticut, Aquarium. In June 2001, the Mohegans, owners of the neighboring Mohegan Sun Casino, made an equal pledge.

To illustrate the volume of money changing hands in these casinos, consider that Mohegan Sun Casino investors included Trading Cove Associates, headed by Sol Kerzner, creator of the Sun City casino and resort in South Africa. By 2000, this firm had received more than $800 million in fees, a sum the company argued was fair compensation for services rendered.

SOME CASINOS STRUGGLE

Some casinos have not fared well. In late August 1997, the Lummis, in northwestern Washington, closed their casino because it was losing money. At about the same time, the two-year-old Seven Cedars Casino on the Jamestown S'Clallam reservation on the northern Olympic Peninsula laid off more than half of its 500 employees.

In Nebraska and Iowa, two Indian casinos north of Omaha found their profits diminished by the opening of three non-Indian casinos in Council Bluffs, Iowa, closer to the urban area. The Omaha and Winnebago tribes opened casinos in 1992. The Omahas' casino has seen a 30 percent decline in profits since a peak in 1995; the Winnebagos' WinnaVegas has watched profits decline from $10 million per year to $5 to $6 million during the same period. The tribes have been using the profits to build business ventures (such as motels), to provide prenatal care, to fund day care, and to pay some tribal members' college expenses. Per capita payments of $599 per year to both Winnebagos and Omahas, begun when gambling revenues were at their peak, were discontinued as profits fell. Employment at the Omaha Nation casino has declined from 500 to about 350 (Dorr, 1997, 14-A).

Other American Indian nations have decided not to get involved in casino gambling at all. On November 4, 1997, the Navajo reservation's residents rejected a proposal to allow as many as five casinos on their lands in Arizona and New Mexico. ˙Of 33,392 votes cast, 18,087 (54%) were against casino gambling. Navajos rejected gambling despite promises that it would provide $25 million in payrolls and other aid during its first year on a reservation with a 45 percent unemployment rate. The Navajos' oral tradition includes several stories that warn of the perils of overindulgence in gambling.

CULTURAL APPROPRIATENESS AND ECONOMIC DEVELOPMENT

One of the most important—and often most vexing—questions in Indian Country today concerns the creation of reservation economic bases that produce necessary cash income while being culturally appropriate and sustainable. Casinos, the reservation cash cow du jour, sometimes produce mountains of money as they transform parts of reservations into annexes of the non-Indian economy, with all of their imported artifices and vices.

One question that concerns many responsible students of Native American economic infrastructure is what is going to be left behind that is sustainable and culturally appropriate after gambling loses its luster, after non-Indian interests find ways to cash in on the bonanza?

Modern Tribal Development: Paths to Self-Sufficiency and Cultural Integrity in Indian Country (2000) by Dean Howard Smith is one of the first books to stare this question straight in the eye. It is an extension of the author's involvement in programs such as the National Executive Education Program for Native American Leadership (NEEPNAL), which aims to increase "the cultural integrity and sovereignty of the Native American nations … leading to cultural integrity, self-determination, and self-sufficiency" (Smith, 2000, x).

In this context, Smith, an associate professor of economics at Northern Arizona University as well as a Grand River Mohawk, raises some very important questions:

1. How do tribes maintain their cultural individuality and secure their cultural integrity?
2. How do tribes develop their sovereign rights as stipulated in the Constitution and the laws of the United States and the treaties?
3. Most importantly, how do tribes become fully self-determined and self-sufficient, thereby securing their rights and cultures?

Smith's book focuses on the importance of economic development as a means to answer these questions (Smith, 2000, 3).

The term *development* can be beguiling but costly in terms of cultural integrity and self-sufficiency. Early in the history of Native American-European relations, Smith points out that missionaries and merchants introduced guns, after which many Native hunters lost their traditional tracking and bow-hunting skills. "When the shotgun shells ran out," Smith observes, "They became beggars" (Smith, 2000, 8). One recalls the debates engaged by Canassatego, Haudenosaunee (Iroquois) Grand Council Tadadaho (speaker) during the 1740s, regarding whether European artifices should be adopted at all, for just this reason.

Even today, some Native American nations have made conscious decisions to forego the types of economic development that would make money and build infrastructure on a mainstream capitalistic model. The Hopis, for example, have passed up substantial potential income from tourism so that they can maintain their religious traditions. The Hualapai have closed large parts of their lands to outsiders so that they can live unmolested in a traditional manner. The Havasupai have refused uranium mining; they believe that mining uranium desecrates Mother Earth. After many miners' deaths, the Navajos have done the same.

Often, debates regarding the appropriateness of development have split Native nations, sometimes with deadly results. The so-called Akwesasne Mohawk civil war that degenerated to gunfights (and two deaths) in 1990 at its base was a debate over which path economic development should take. One faction interprets sovereignty as the freedom to establish businesses, including gaming, and to smuggle goods across the international border. Another faction opposes the transformation of Akwesasne into a one-stop cash transfusion from non-Indians looking for discount smokes, cheap gas, or a lucky strike on the video slots. The same debate has split the Senecas with a seriousness that has cost several lives.

Smith points out, briefly but cogently, the fact that "Native Americans had extensive and vibrant economic systems of production and trade during the centuries of pre-contact" (Smith, 2000, 23). Extensive trade networks laced the hemisphere long before the arrival of Columbus; some of today's interstate highways follow these original routes. The Senecas, for example, maintained extensive, lush cornfields at which Gen. John Sullivan's soldiers marveled before they were laid waste. The contributions of Native American cultures and peoples to our staple diet (not to mention our political institutions) are well known to serious students of Western Hemispheric history.

Smith is likewise clear and cogent on the point of who and what have caused the widespread economic poverty that has long been associated with the so-called plight of the Indian: "The dire poverty and the concomitant social problems facing Native Americans today are the direct result of federal policy, past and present" (Smith, 2000, 33).

Smith's book is woefully short of specific suggestions circumscribing just how specific peoples, on specific reservations, can implement its theoretical program. The book contains some very good theoretical ideas, but it (and $1.50) will get you a cup of joe in Lame Deer or Macy or Pine Ridge, where the need for sustainable, culturally appropriate economic development is more acute than ever.

Modern Tribal Development does contain some worthwhile general suggestions. For example, it suggests that Native polities find better ways to keep people's money at home, diminishing linkages to border towns that tend to suck Native income off-reservation. Smith also suggests that reservation governments inventory the working skills and employment ambitions of their residents with an eye toward designing enterprises that will take advantage of these skills.

Smith also points out the growing role of tourism on many reservations, meanwhile stressing the need to develop tourism industries that do not disrupt traditional life. Dances, rodeos, and powwows are among the draws. In the meantime, some Native nations face difficulties keeping tourists away from religious ceremonies that are meant to be private. Without cultural education, many non-Indians often can not tell the difference between public and private activities.

This book also stresses the noneconomic (or social) value of infrastructure, quoting Oglala Sioux President John Yellow Bird Steele: "He said it is not hard to understand that when you wake up in the morning realizing that 'not only is today going to be like this, but tomorrow is going to be like yesterday, too. So you go out and get a bottle'" (Smith, 2000, 71). Lack of economic development stifles cultural activity; conversely, development of infrastructure also creates other jobs with cultural value, such as schools that require the employment of teachers.

Smith also airs debate concerning the utility of one obvious route to reservation development: the importation of manufacturing that has little cultural relevance and provides minimum-wage work. In such cases, employers are often looking for cheap labor. The record of such enterprises on reservations has been rather dismal. Instead of being assimilated into an industrial capitalistic system, Smith believes that Native American traditions can be used to design "a new type of system that incorporates competitive behavior, social compatibility and adaptation, and environmental concerns" (Smith, 2001, 77). Smith has a handle on the conceptual framework required to develop reservation economies that will enhance social values and culture rather than simply make money for off-reservation interests. Here, we have a truly exciting beginning. Next, Smith and others will have to face the difficult part of economic development: How do we bring these thoughts to street-level reality?

The final section of *Modern Tribal Development,* titled "Examples and Issues," promises to "explain how the theoretical framework can be put into action" (Smith, 2001, 91). This section also is largely generic and academic. Starting on page 105, however, the author does present case studies of the Rosebud Sioux and Fort Belknap communities (105–122). Many more case studies could be warranted, with specific types of economic activities on specific reservations. What is being done with timber in Taholah? How about uranium in Window Rock? How are the Osages doing with their oil? How are the Wisconsin Oneidas doing as the largest single employer in Green Bay, Wisconsin? Another book rather quickly and easily suggests itself. As the Smith suggests, "Little first steps lead toward larger ones" (148). This book presents some very good ideas that should be adapted to specific community needs.

THE MAINE INDIAN CLAIMS SETTLEMENT ACT

The Penobscots and Passamaquoddies proved in federal court in 1975 that 12.5 million acres of Wabanaki land acquired by Maine and Massachusetts violated the terms of the 1790 Intercourse Act (Brodeur, 1985). The Intercourse Act laws, enacted between 1790 and 1834, made illegal any land purchases from Native governments not attended by a U.S. commissioner and ratified by Congress. Several land claims in the northeastern United States are based on violation of these laws.

In exchange for giving up their claims to nearly two-thirds of Maine, the Wabanakis, principally the Penobscots and Passamaquoddies, during the 1970s received a settlement of $81 million, federal recognition, the right to purchase at least 300,000 acres of land, as well as limited immunity from state laws. Although the Maine Indian Claims Settlement Act was a legal success, 25 years after its enactment many Wabanakis believed that the settlement also presented serious obstacles to their aboriginal sovereignty, economic growth, and environmental health.

The act established a $27 million trust to be shared equally between the Passamaquoddies and Penobscots, tax-free and with interest paid quarterly. It also set aside $54.4 million to buy 300,000 acres to add to Passamaquoddy, Penobscot, and Maliseet territory. These new land acquisitions would be held in trust for the Wabanakis by the United States and subject to oversight by the U.S. secretary of the interior. The act also provided enormous benefits to the state of Maine. Although the federal government paid the $81 million settlement's cost, Maine paid nothing, and the state cleared title to all of its lands.

The settlement also equated the regulatory rights of Indian nations with state municipalities, a compromise of sovereignty. Courts have upheld this stipulation, which has practical implications, including denial of the Wabanakis' request to build casinos.

ALASKA NATIVE CORPORATIONS

The Alaska Native Claims Settlement Act, passed by Congress in 1971, exchanged Alaskan natives' claims to land across most of Alaska for 44 million acres and for shares in 13 regional and 200 village corporations, which were then developed economically with native labor and almost $1 billion in start-up capital provided by the U.S. government.

Alaska native corporations and their 18,000 Aleut and Inuit shareholders acquired a sizable amount of economic clout in the quarter-century after the corporations' formation. In one instance, the town of Pelican, population 160, was saved by native Alaskan capital from closure of its major (and sole) industry, a cold-storage facility, after its abandonment by Japanese owners. The Sealaska Corporation's headquarters dominates the skyline of Juneau, Alaska's capital, where several Alaska natives were elected to the state legislature during the 1980s and 1990s.

A minority of Native shareholders in some of the corporations have voiced concerns that their behavior has become too capitalistic and predatory on the environment. Special attention has been focused on the logging practices of Sealaska and Haida native corporations in the state's panhandle. These practices have been characterized as some of the most environmentally unfriendly in North America. · Natives who continue to fish and hunt (as well as cash dividend checks) assert that insensitive logging is destroying animal herds (especially deer) and poisoning groundwater, diminishing salmon runs. Native corporations on the North Slope of Alaska, which have been major beneficiaries of royalties from the Prudhoe Bay oil fields, have lobbied to have portions of the Arctic National Wildlife Refuge opened for oil drilling, causing bitter debate not only between Native groups but also between the corporations and environmental activists as well.

During the late 1990s, leaders of some of Alaska's 226 recognized Indian tribes and bands had identified another problem with the act creating native corporations that was passed in 1971: It left them without many of the legal protections exercised by Native Americans in other states, such as the right to levy taxes, enforce most laws, and regulate hunting and fishing on their territories. Legally, the Alaska native corporations do not fall within the definition of Indian Country, with its treaty-guaranteed rights of sovereignty. Venetie, a small native village in Alaska (population 200) filed suit to have Alaska natives incorporated within Indian Country, leading to a ruling by a federal district court that the definition did not apply to Alaska natives. On appeal to the Ninth Circuit Court of Appeals in San Francisco, that ruling was reversed in November 1996, creating a major public controversy across Alaska. The court of appeals held that the act creating the Alaska Native Corporations did not adequately address legal issues defining Alaska natives' status. On June 23, 1997, the United States Supreme Court agreed to hear the state government's appeal of the court of appeals' ruling.

The U.S. Supreme Court heard arguments in the Venetie case late in 1997 and ruled in March 1998 in agreement with the state's position. This decision has an impact on one-tenth of Alaska's land area, which makes up roughly 200 Native American communities. At stake is the jurisdiction to levy taxes, a loss the state has sought to forestall by spending more than $1 million on its appeal to the Supreme Court.

The Supreme Court, in a unanimous ruling, said that Venetie does not constitute a reservation or a dependent Indian community as defined under statutes delineating Indian Country.

NATIVE AMERICAN OFFSHORE BANKING

The type of banking secrecy usually associated with Switzerland, the Cayman Islands, and other offshore locations is now available on the windswept plains of southwestern Oklahoma, an hour from Oklahoma City, at First Lenape Nation Bank and the Apaches' First Americans Trust Company. Both are lodged in nondescript office buildings in the town of Anadarko, within a short drive of oil derricks and acres of grazing cattle on a reservation shared by the Delawares and a band of Apaches.

The two banks operate without much of the usual apparatus of commercial banks, such as advertising signs and automated teller machines. Most of the Lenape Bank's advertising is over the Internet (http://www.firstlenapenationbank. com), and most of its deposits arrive in the mail or by wire. Because of the reservation's semisovereign status, the two banks advertise the benefits of offshore banking in the middle of the American heartland: numbered accounts, privacy, and safety from most legal demands for money, notably judgments of U.S. courts. The two banks also do not report deposits of more than $10,000, as federal law requires.

The Delawares' original name is Leni Lenape; *Delaware,* the slightly anglicized name of a French nobleman, became associated with them following European immigration along the Delaware River as the city of Philadelphia was established. At Penn's Landing, less than a mile west of Independence Hall, William Penn was met by the Delaware sachem Tamenund, as both men counseled peace. With the demise of William Penn, greedier members of his family expelled Native Americans from the state named after the Penn family. Some of the Delawares migrated to Ontario, and others endured a forced march that took them from Pennsylvania to Missouri and Texas, both of which were then under Spanish control. After the United States absorbed Texas, the Delawares were removed to western Oklahoma, by which time only 90 members of the Leni Lenape people remained alive. Today Anadarko, sometimes called Indian City, USA, is home to about 7,500 people and has an unemployment rate of 45 percent.

A number of federal and state agencies, including the Department of the Treasury, the Internal Revenue Service, and the FBI have tried to probe the two banks' businesses, which were more than a year old by mid-1998. None of the agencies moved to close the banks, however, largely because federal regulations and legal precedents for offshore banking on Indian reservations are virtually nonexistent. The federal agencies seem to be searching for a pretext to legally challenge these first experiments with independent Native American banking.

The banks have been established as an experiment in Native American sovereignty. They also exist to bring money to the reservation and to build infrastructure. Investigating federal agencies maintain that they are concerned about the banks' potential for attracting shady money seeking secrecy, a concern that leads the United States to seek banking regulation agreements with nations that host offshore banks. These banks offer none of the deposit insurance guaranteed by institutions chartered within the United States. As of mid-1998, eight other banks operated on Indian reservations with federal chapters.

Shortly after the Lenape and First Americans banks opened, the Oklahoma state banking commissioner as well as the federal Office of the Comptroller of the Currency warned banks that it regulates to "exercise extreme caution" in doing business with First Lenape, First Americans, and any other banks that might be set up by Native Americans on the same model. First Lenape responded by saying that it accepts only noncriminal funds for deposit.

THE COUNCIL OF ENERGY RESOURCE TRIBES

The Council of Energy Resource Tribes (CERT) was founded in 1975 by 25 Native American tribes and nations that own substantial reserves of energy and other natural resources. Denver-based CERT, by 2005 a consortium of 57 American and Canadian Indian polities, works to help Native Americans recognize, protect, and exploit energy-related wealth on their lands. A. David Lester has been CERT's executive director nearly since the nonprofit group's inception. CERT pursues a cooperative relationship between private industry, particularly in the energy sector, and American Indian governments. CERT also has become a notable lobbying force for Native American energy interests within the federal government, including Congress and the Interior Department.

Native lands in the CERT consortium produce 380 billion cubic feet of natural gas annually and contain 2 trillion cubic feet of proved gas reserves. Properties overseen by CERT also hold 30 percent of U.S. coal reserves, 5 percent of its oil, and significant amounts of uranium. CERT is governed by the elected tribal leaderships of 53 federally recognized Indian tribes in the United States and four Canadian bands that are affiliated with it. Its members have been working toward self-management of their energy resources, from negotiating agreements to protecting the environment to verifying revenue payments.

CERT played a role in the North American Energy Summit, held April 14–16, 2004, in Albuquerque, New Mexico, which included state, provincial, Native American, and national leaders from three countries and involved diverse interests in seeking to develop a secure, affordable, and environmentally responsible energy system. The conference included presentations by governors Bill Richardson of New Mexico, Bill Owens of Colorado, Janet Napolitano of Arizona, Frank Murkowski of Alaska, Dave Freudenthal of Wyoming, John Hoeven of North Dakota, Mike Rounds of South Dakota, as well as Canadian provincial premiers Ralph Klein of Alberta, Gary Doer of Manitoba, and Joseph L. Handley of the Northwest Territories.

The summit considered capitalizing on renewable energy resources, improving energy efficiency, determining the future of nuclear energy and fossil fuels, providing a reliable and efficient electricity grid, financing infrastructure and making it more secure, and achieving needed international collaboration. The summit also included an Energy Futures Expo, which featured cutting-edge technologies, systems, and alternative-fuel vehicles.

CERT has supported legislation that would allow Native American governmental entities to submit tribal energy resources agreements covering energy and right-of-way leases to the Interior Department that, when approved, may enable agreements to proceed without prior secretarial approval. This stripped-down version of the current process could accelerate energy development on Native American lands.

Although this proposal has widespread support from Republicans, some Democrats fear it could dilute environmental restrictions on oil and gas drilling on Indian land and weaken the Interior Department's trust responsibilities. In addition, according to the Democrats, the hydroelectric language in the energy bill would create a licensing process that favors power providers to the detriment of Native governments, their treaty rights, and the general public, according to a position paper Senate Democrats released at a Native American forum on Capitol Hill. Instead, the Democrats favor proposals to promote transmission development on Indian lands and creating tax incentives for renewable energy that are favorable to Native governments.

Tex Hall, as president of the National Congress of American Indians, has gone on record in support of CERT's assertion that incentives will be required for Native cooperation in exploitation of energy resources residing on Native lands. Hall would like to see the Congressional Budget Office analyze how much money the energy bill would allocate for development of Native American energy resources. He also wants the U.S. Department of Energy to provide a number of $1 million to $2 million grants for wind-energy demonstration projects on land with significant potential, such as the Blackfeet in Montana or Hall's own Mandan, Hidatsa, and Arikara Nation in North Dakota. Federal utilities, military bases, and government agencies also should include preferences for energy supplied by Indian tribes and nations in their procurement contracts, Hall believes.

Through its representatives in Washington, DC, CERT also has been lobbying the U.S. federal government for simplification of many arcane federal, state, and Native governmental tax laws and regulations that discourage development of energy resources on Native lands. The organization also has been pressing Congress to pass a measure that would allow private producers of energy to receive credits on their federal tax returns for tax payments to a given state for Native energy development. In addition to making exploration and production on tribal lands more attractive, such a change would encourage more thorough exploitation of existing wells, Lester has said.

CERT has supported inventories of energy resources with Global Energy Decisions, which has produced a wall map portraying the energy development issues in the West that illustrates the production, transmission, consumption, and land-use patterns. The map contains references to coal mines, oil and natural-gas wells, pipelines, railroads, power plants, and transmission lines as well as public lands (Indian reservations, national parks, national forests, and Bureau of Land Management districts).

In addition to its energy-related activities, CERT also plays a major role in raising money for Native American education. By 2005, CERT had raised nearly $6 million through its American Spirit Award Dinner. CERT and the Morongo Band of Mission Indians on June 21, 2005, hosted the 25th annual American Spirit Award Dinner, a leading fund-raiser for Indian education at the Morongos' $250 million Morongo Casino, Resort, and Spa.

The dinner was part of the three-day Indian Energy Solutions 2005 conference focusing on current Indian energy policies, economic development, energy market trends, alternative and renewable energies, and Native utility formation. More than 500 energy industry officials, state and federal elected leaders, Native representatives, and press attended.

The CERT Tribal Internship Program provides students with opportunities to work alongside senior CERT staff, Native leaders, and energy companies on technical and scientific issues, policies, and projects. Past projects have focused on reservation water-quality studies, cooperative planning on environmental issues with state and local governments, hazardous waste operations training, and biodiversity.

CERT also operates a Tribal Institute for Sustainable Energy and publishes *Red Earth Magazine Online.*

THE FIRST NATIONS DEVELOPMENT INSTITUTE

The First Nations Development Institute seeks to combine Native American cultural strengths with technical support to create economic opportunity within Indian communities. Rebecca Adamson founded the First Nations Development Institute in 1980. Her major goal has been to help Native American communities become economically self-sufficient and thereby reduce their dependence on federal funding. Grants are awarded for projects that benefit Indian communities and provide long-term economic benefits.

Adamson, daughter of a Cherokee mother and a Swedish American father, developed an interest in Native American economic self-sufficiency early in her life as she visited her mother's parents on the Eastern Cherokee reservation in the Great Smoky Mountains of westernmost North Carolina. She cut her teeth as an activist in efforts to gain for Native Americans more control over reservation schools. By 1980, she had borrowed from Third World economic development the idea of microgrants, usually about $500 each, that helped people start businesses in their homes. She won a $25,000 grant from the Ford Foundation to develop the idea, and the First Nations Development Institute was born. The institute's first project was development of a touring exhibition of art by children on the Pine Ridge Indian Reservation, which earned $20,000 in fees that were used to purchase winter clothes for the children.

First Nations Development Corporation grants about $1.25 million each year to reservation communities. Between 1994 and 1997, the organization granted about $3 million to Native Americans belonging to about 240 Native groups in 213 states (Prue, 1997, B-1).

First Nations Development Corporation has helped develop ecotourism projects on several reservations. A health clinic was funded at Porcupine on the Pine Ridge Indian Reservation in one of the 99 grants made by the group in 1997. Other projects include video-rental stores on reservations and a small electric utility on the Hopi territory that generates and distributes solar power.

NATIONAL CENTER FOR AMERICAN INDIAN
ENTERPRISE DEVELOPMENT

The National Center for American Indian Enterprise Development, headquartered in Mesa, Arizona, provides support for Native American small-business development across the United States. Each year since 1987, the organization also has hosted a national Reservation Economic Summit and American Indian Trade Show, which attracts about 500 registrants and about 150 trade booths.

The National Center for American Indian Enterprise Development was started in 1969 by seven Native Americans in Los Angeles as the Urban Indian Development Association. It was incorporated in 1970 and acquired its present name in 1988, when its national conference was attended by Senators Daniel Inouye and John McCain. By the mid-1990s, the organization had opened offices in Los Angeles and Seattle, in addition to its home office in Arizona. The center provides entrepreneurs with contacts in government and private businesses, assists with legal matters, helps with loan applications, and designs marketing strategies. Much of this is done through workshops and other training sessions.

FURTHER READING

Barreiro, José, ed. *Indian Corn of the Americas: Gift to the World.* Special issue of *Northeast Indian Quarterly* 6, no. 1–2 (Spring–Summer 1989): 1–96.

Bristol, Tim. "Gaining Influence." *Native Americas* 13, no. 3 (Fall 1996): 14–21.

Bristol, Tim. "'Indian Country'—Alaska." *Native Americas* 14, no. 2 (Summer 1997): 38–45.

Brodeur, Paul. *Restitution: The Land Claims of the Mashpee, Passamaquoddy, and Penobscot Indians of New England.* Boston: Northeastern University Press, 1985.

Census Bureau, United States. "Income, Poverty, and Health Insurance Coverage in the United States: 2005." <http://www.census.gov>.

Chavaree, Mark. "Tribal Sovereignty." *Wabanaki Legal News* (Winter 1998). <http://www.ptla.org/wabanaki/sovereign.htm>.

Cornell, Stephen, and Joseph P. Kalt. "Pathways from Poverty: Economic Development and Institution-Building on American Indian Reservations." *American Indian Culture and Research Journal* 14, no. 1 (1990): 89–125.

Cornell, Stephen, and Joseph P. Kalt. "Where's the Glue? Institutional Bases of American Indian Economic Development." Malcolm Wiener Center for Social Policy Working Paper Series, H-91-2. John F. Kennedy School of Government, Harvard University, March 1991.

"Crime Rate on Indian Reservations Much Higher than U.S." *Indian Time,* October 9, 2003: 11.

"Crisis at Akwesasne." Transcript, Hearings of the New York Assembly. Albany: State of New York, July–August, 1990.

Darlin, Damon. "Rebellions on the Reservations." *Forbes,* May 19, 1997: 88.

Dorr, Robert. "Tribal Gambling Income Dented by Bluffs Casinos." *Omaha World-Herald,* September 14, 1997: 14-A.

Drew, Neil. Personal communication. July 1, 2001.

Elliott, Louise. "Band Talking to Media May Perpetuate Suicide Crisis, Says Nault." *Canadian Press,* June 22, 2001.

Elliott, Louise. "Hunger and Suicide Stalk Reserve after Feds Cut Funds." *Montreal Gazette,* June 7, 2001: A-15.

Elliott, Louise. "Ontario Native Suicide Rate One of the Highest in World, Expert Says." *Vancouver Sun,* November 30, 2000, n.p.

Elliott, Louise. "Reserve's Doctor Safe After 2-day Walk in Wilderness." Canadian Press in *Montreal Gazette,* June 18, 2001, A-14.

Farney, Dennis. "They Hold the Cards, but, after All, They Do Own the Casino." *Wall Street Journal,* February 5, 1998: A-1, A-6.

Federal Bureau of Investigation. *Crime in the United States.* Washington, DC: U.S. Government Printing Office, 1989.

"Federal Paternalism Angers Pikangikum." *Canadian Aboriginal.* n.d.

Gamble, Susan. "M.D. Shocked at Conditions on Reserve." Brantford (Ontario) *Expositor,* n.p., n.d.

Ganter, Granville. "Sovereign Municipalities? Twenty Years after the Maine Indian Claims Settlement Act of 1980." *Enduring Legacies: Native American Treaties and Contemporary Controversies.* Ed. Bruce E. Johansen. Westport, CT: Praeger, 2004. 25–43.

Giago, Tim. "Gambling Helps Few Indian Tribes." *Omaha World-Herald,* June 6, 1997: 24.

Goulais, Bob. "Water Crisis Latest Plague to Visit Pikangikum." *Anishinabek News,* November, 2000, n.p.

Hornung, Rick. *One Nation under the Gun: Inside the Mohawk Civil War.* New York: Pantheon, 1991.

Johansen, Bruce E. *Forgotten Founders: Benjamin Franklin, the Iroquois, and the Rationale for the American Revolution.* Ipswich, MA: Gambit, 1982.

Johansen, Bruce E. "The Klan in a Can." *The Progressive,* July 1988: 13.

Johansen, Bruce E. *Life and Death in Mohawk Country.* Golden, CO: North American Press/ Fulcrum, 1993.

Johansen, Bruce E. "The New York Oneidas: A Case Study in the Mismatch of Cultural Tradition and Economic Development." *American Indian Culture and Research Journal* 26, no. 3 (2002): 25–46.

Johansen, Bruce E. "Whiteclay, Nebraska: The Town That Booze Built." *Native Americas* 15, no. 1 (Spring 1998): 5.

Johnson, Tim, "The Dealer's Edge: Gaming in the Path of Native America." *Native Americas* 12, no. 2 (Spring/Summer 1995): 16–25.

Kates, William. "Oneidas' Enterprises Bolster Struggling Central New York." *Omaha World-Herald,* November 5, 1997: 22, 25.

Killborn, Peter T. "Poverty Only Sure Bet at Pine Ridge." *Omaha World-Herald,* June 12, 1997: A-1, A-2.

Lester, David. "American Indians Enter a New Era of Renewal, Self-governance." *Denver Post,* April 27, 1997: G-1.

Maine Indian Tribal-State Commission (MITSC). *At Loggerheads—The State of Maine and the Wabanaki: Final Report of the Task Force on Tribal-State Relations.* Hallowell, ME: Maine Indian Tribal-State Commission, 1997. Revised, June 2000.

Maine Indian Tribal-State Commission (MITSC). "Maine Indian Land Claims Case." February 14, 1995. <www.passamaquoddy.com/land_claims/preamble.htm>.

Marquez, Deron. "Indian Gaming is Different." *Indian Country Today,* February 9, 2002. <http://www.indiancountry.com/content.cfm?id=1013188413>.

Meriam, Lewis. *The Problem of Indian Administration*. Baltimore: Johns Hopkins University Press, 1928.

Mohawk, John. "Economic Motivations: An Iroquoian Perspective." *Indian Corn of the Americas: Gift to the World*. Special issue of *Northeast Indian Quarterly* 6, no. 1–2 (Spring–Summer 1989): 56–63.

Mohawk, John C. "Indian Economic Development: The U.S. Experience in Evolving Indian Sovereignty." *Indigenous Economics: Toward a Natural World Order*. Special issue of *Akwe:kon Journal* 9, no. 2 (Summer 1992): 42–49.

Murphy, M. Maureen. "Gambling on Indian Reservations." Congressional Research Service, Library of Congress, April 26, 1985.

Murphy, Sean P. "Congressmen Seeking Probe of Indian Casinos." *Boston Globe,* December 16, 2000: A-1.

Ortiz, Roxanne D., ed. *Economic Development in American Indian Reservations*. Albuquerque: University of New Mexico Indian Studies, 1979.

Pasquaretta, Paul. "On the 'Indianness' of Bingo: Gambling and the Native American Community." *Critical Inquiry* 20 (1994): 694–719.

Pertusati, Linda. *In Defense of Mohawk Land: Ethnopolitical Conflict in Native North America*. Albany: State University of New York Press, 1997.

Prue, Lisa. "Tribal Self-sufficiency Is First Nations' Aim." *Omaha World-Herald,* November 3, 1997: B-1, B-2.

Randolph, Eleanor. "New York's Native American Casino Contributes, but Not to Tax Rolls." *The New York Times,* October 18, 2003: n.p.

Rushton, Nathan. "Tribe's Home Business Booming." *Eureka* (California) *Reporter,* September 30, 2005. <http://www.eurekareporter.com/ArticleDisplay.aspx?ArticleID=4703>.

Schwab, Priscilla Anne. "The Industrial Reservation." *Nation's Business,* August 1981: 57.

Seminole Tribe of Florida v. Butterworth, 658 F. 2d 310 (5th Cir., 1980).

Smith, Dean Howard. *Modern Tribal Development: Paths to Self-Sufficiency and Cultural Integrity in Indian Country*. Walnut Creek, CA: AltaMira Press, 2000.

Suzuki, Peter T. "Housing on the Nebraska Indian Reservations: Federal Policies and Practices." *Habitat International* 15, no. 4 (1991): 27–32.

U.S. Congress, Joint Economic Committee. *American Indians: Facts and Future: Toward Economic Development for Native American Communities*. New York: Arno Press, 1970.

U.S. Department of Health and Human Services. *Trends in Indian Health*. Washington, DC: U.S. Government Printing Office, 1991.

Walke, Roger. "Gambling on Indian Reservations." Congressional Research Service, Library of Congress, October 17, 1988.

Wanamaker, Tom. "Debunking the Myth of Unregulated Indian Gaming." *Indian Country Today,* May 16, 2002. <http://www.indiancountry.com/content.cfm?id=1021399362>.

Wanamaker, Tom. "Indian Gaming Column." *Indian Country Today,* April 5, 2002: n.p. (in Lexis).

Wollock, Jeffrey. "On the Wings of History: American Indians in the 20th Century." *Native Americas* 20, no. 1 (Spring 2003): 14–31.

CHAPTER 4

∽

High-Stakes Genealogy: When Is a Pequot Not a Pequot?

Jeff Benedict, author of *Without Reservation: The Making of America's Most Powerful Indian Tribe and Foxwoods, the World's Largest Casino* (2000), purports to expose the builders of the world's largest casino (Foxwoods, near Ledyard, Connecticut) as faux Pequots. As a salesman of ethnic chauvinism, Benedict has got something going here. Pandering to various racial prejudices did his bank balance no harm. *Without Reservation,* for a time, was rated in the top 100 of Amazon.com's sales rankings (among roughly 2 million listed titles). Arguing that the Pequots who started Foxwoods may actually be white—or is it black?—broaches a sticky historical swamp in which hardly anyone, strictly speaking, is purely anything.

The broader issue here relates to problems parsing racial or ethnic identity by singular standards in a multiethnic world as well as the big money behind such definitions. Mixed genealogy is hardly unusual, and it bedevils creators of racial categories. For example, Crispus Attucks, son of an African American father and a Massachusetts Indian mother, was the first casualty of the Boston Massacre of March 5, 1770, the first death in the cause of the American Revolution. Attucks's father was a black slave in a Framington, Massachusetts, household until about 1750, when he escaped and became a sailor. Attucks's mother lived in an Indian mission at Natick. Poet Langston Hughes, singer Tina Turner, actor James Earl Jones, and civil rights activists Frederick Douglass and Jesse Jackson all have some degree of black American Indian ancestry, and not usually the kind that comes easily sketched in little boxes on charts.

Benedict's book became something of a best seller among members of antisovereignty groups such as the Citizens Alliance, which pumped it on the Internet. This book contains no index, a substantial oversight for a historical work. This book's lack of sources that can be traced by anyone other than the author renders *Without Reservation* nearly useless as documentary history, despite the 650 interviews that the author says he conducted. Still, Benedict must have laughed all the way to the bank as he railed against a riches-to-rags-to-riches story that might have impressed Horatio Alger. Commented one observer, surveying the financial success of Foxwoods so close to Mystic, site of a 1637 massacre that nearly obliterated the Pequot nation, "After a 350 year truce, the Mashantucket may actually have won the Pequot War" (Pequot History, 1997).

Benedict, 35 years of age when *Without Reservation* hit the best-seller charts, once aspired to be a federal prosecutor (Barry, May 14, 2000, B-1). He wrote *Without Reservation* while he was a student at the New England School of Law in Boston. Benedict earlier had authored another expose, *Pros and Cons: The Criminals Who Play in the NFL* (1998).

Benedict probably will never become as wealthy as some of the Mashantucket Pequots who tapped a huge gambling market by opening Foxwoods, in Connecticut, however. Georg Sutterlin, a reporter for *Neue Zurcher Zeitung* of Zurich, Switzerland, described the grand sight approaching Foxwoods, the largest complex of structures committed to gambling in the history of the human race:

> Foxwoods rises like a mirage out of the Connecticut forests. People from New York or Boston, traveling through scattered villages, past fields and woods, do not expect a monumental, ultramodern building complex in this rural area. Traffic lights direct the flow of vehicles into the asphalt desert of the parking lots. (Sutterlin, 2001, 32)

Another book about the Pequots, by Kim Isaac Eisler, an editor at *Washingtonian* magazine, was published in February 2001 (Eisler, 2001). *Revenge of the Pequots: How a Small Native American Tribe Created the World's Most Profitable Casino* expresses wariness about the Pequots' ethnic identities but also describes evidence to support their claims. Eisler notes that the Indians were cheated out of their land because, in part, of their problems with alcohol; now their enrichment has come out of the white man's compulsion for gambling. "A delicious irony," Eisler wrote (Dalla, n.d.). Remarked another observer, "Of course, if the Pequots still were selling firewood and maple syrup, nobody would be concerned about the matter. The debate isn't really about Indian rights or tribal sovereignty. It's about money. The Indians are making money—and lots of it. Some people have a hard time dealing with that fact" (Dalla, n.d.).

HISTORY OF THE PEQUOTS

The purported extinction of the Pequots has been one bit of Connecticut folklore that has made its way into some important precincts of American letters. Alexis de Tocqueville, passing though the area as a tourist, missed several remnants of the Pequot Nation when he declared them extinct in 1833. He also declared extinct all of the Native peoples who had once inhabited New England (including the Narragansetts and Mohicans as well as the Pequots). In *Moby Dick,* published in 1851, Herman Melville explains that the *Pequod,* Captain Ahab's doomed ship, was named after a New England Indian tribe that the narrator believes to be extinct. Melville also missed the scattered remnants that had survived the Puritans' war of extermination (Eisler, 2001, 36).

James Cunha Jr., chief of the Paucatuck Eastern Pequots, recalled rushing home from high school after a teacher had declared the Pequots extinct. His grandfather, dressed in his regalia, walked to the classroom door and glowered, "Tell me that I don't exist" (Barry, December 12, 2000).

Before they were slaughtered in the Pequot War (1636–37), the Pequots were some of the most affluent Native Americans to do business with the early English immigrants. *Pequot* is derived from the Algonquin word *pekawatawog* or *pequt-toog,* meaning "destroyers" (Pequot History, 1997). The Pequots and the Mohegans originated as a single group that migrated to eastern Connecticut from the upper Hudson River Valley in New York, probably the vicinity of Lake Champlain, sometime around 1500. At the time of their first contact with Europeans, the Pequot occupied southeastern Connecticut from the Nehantic River eastward to the present-day border with Rhode Island.

If the Mohegan are included, the Pequot probably numbered around 6,000 in 1620. After a major smallpox epidemic during winter 1633–34 and the departure of the Mohegans, about 3,000 Pequots remained by the mid-1630s. Fewer than half are believed to have survived the Pequot War of 1636 and 1637.

Highly organized, aggressive, and warlike, the Pequot dominated Connecticut before 1637, "a pattern continued later by the closely related Mohegan. Like their neighbors, the Pequot were an agricultural people who raised corn, beans, squash, and tobacco. Hunting, with an emphasis on fish and seafood because of their coastal location, provided the remainder of their diet. Clothing and housing were also similar—buckskin and semi-permanent villages of medium-sized longhouses and wigwams" (Pequot History, 1997).

The Pequot were no larger in numbers than the peoples surrounding them, but they were more highly organized, with strong central authority exercised by a council led by a grand sachem. Their organized nature provided the Pequot a considerable military advantage over their neighbors before the intervention of English immigrants.

The Pequot War began during summer 1636 when a Boston trader, John Oldham, was killed as the western Niantic captured his boat near Block Island. Richard Mather, in a sermon delivered in Boston, denounced the Pequot as the "accursed seeds of Canaan," in effect imagining the confrontation in Connecticut as a holy war by the Puritans against the forces of evil. With these fiery words urging them to action, Massachusetts, without bothering to consult the colonists in Connecticut, sent a punitive expedition of 90 men under the command of John Endecott (or Endicott) to Block Island in August with orders to kill every man and take the women and children prisoner. The English soldiers managed to kill 14 Niantic and an undetermined number of dogs before they escaped into the woods and then burned the village and crops. Endecott then loaded his men back into the boats and sailed over to Fort Saybrook to add some additional soldiers for the second part of his mission—a visit to the Pequot village at the mouth of the Thames River to demand 1,000 fathoms of wampum for the death of Oldham and several Pequot children as hostages (Pequot History, 1997).

MASSACRE AT MYSTIC

The Pequot were furious. During the winter, they plotted revenge and sent war belts to the Narragansett and Mohegan, asking their help in a war against the English. Because of their past actions, however, the Pequot had few friends, and the English found it fairly easy to isolate them. Early in 1637, Sassacus, a Pequot leader, ordered a series of raids against the Connecticut settlements to retaliate for Endecott's raid of the previous summer. Two hundred warriors attacked Wethersfield on April 12 and killed nine colonists (six men and three women). Other victims were 20 cows and a horse. Taking two teenage girls hostage, the war party loaded their loot into canoes and went home on the Connecticut River. Passing the fort at Saybrook, they taunted the garrison by waving the bloody clothes of their victims. The colonists lost 30 people in these raids, and in May the general court at Hartford formally declared war (Pequot History, 1997).

A joint expedition of 90 English and 70 Mohegan warriors under Uncas assembled near Hartford to attack the main Pequot fort at Mystic. Commanded by Capt. John Mason, an experienced soldier, this tiny army departed on what seemed a suicide mission. Passing down the Connecticut River, it stopped at Fort Saybrook to add a few soldiers and then proceeded up the coast only to discover the Pequot waiting for them at Mystic.

When Mason reached the Narragansett villages, 200 warriors joined his ranks, and he received their permission to travel overland through Narragansett territory for a surprise attack on Mystic from the rear. With his force now numbering more than 400 men, Mason left the Narragansett villages and moved westward across the hills of western Rhode Island. The English and their allies arrived at Mystic undetected because the Pequot warriors who usually would have been defending Mystic were absent. Lulled into a sense of false security by the sight of what earlier had seemed to them a retreat by Mason's men, the Pequot had formed a war party to raid settlements near Hartford.

Members of the Massachusetts Bay Colony attacked and massacred the Pequots in their fortified village near the Mystic River on May 26, 1637. The Pequot community at Mystic had gathered for its annual Green Corn Dance ceremony. After they had assembled in a thatched fort at Mystic, mercenaries of the English and Dutch surrounded the fort and set it aflame, trapping the Pequots inside. Pequots who sought to escape the flames met the business end of Puritan muskets at point-blank range, and witnesses left descriptions of Pequot flesh sizzling as the strings on their bows melted in a holocaust of roaring fire.

A few Pequot bowmen stood their ground amid the flames, until their bows singed and they fell backward into the fire, their flesh sizzling like bacon on a hot griddle. The massacre even frightened some Puritans. William Bradford recalled, "It was a fearfull [sic] sight to see them thus frying" (Covey, 1966, 200). The English, Dutch, and their Indian allies held their noses against the stench of burning flesh. The roaring inferno burned itself out less than an hour after the torching had begun. During that hour, between 600 and 700 Pequots died.

> Trapping 700 Pequot inside the fort (mostly women, children, and old people), Mason and his men set it afire. Those Pequot not burned to death were killed when they tried to escape. Following Mason's orders, the Narragansett and Mohegan finished any Pequot the English missed but were aghast when the English indiscriminately slaughtered Pequot women and children. Their grim work completed, Mason made a hasty retreat (actually, a headlong rush) to his boats waiting at a rendezvous on the Thames. Sassacus' village was only five miles away, and his warriors were in hot pursuit. Hartford declared June 15th as a day of prayer and thanksgiving for the "victory" at Mystic. (Pequot History, 1997)

Although a few Puritans remonstrated regarding the violence, many (Bradford included) soon placed the massacre in the category of God's necessary business, along with all sorts of other things, from smallpox epidemics to late frosts and early freezes.

The outcome of the Pequot War during summer 1636 radically altered the demographic balance in New England. Before it, the English colonists were a tiny minority. Afterward, the immigrants held a slight majority. The terms of a peace treaty signed after the Pequot war systematically dismembered the Pequot as a people (Pequot History, 1997). After the Pequot war, most captured warriors were executed, and the English sold the remainder as slaves to the West Indies. Some of the women and children were distributed as servants to colonial households in New England. Some of the survivors also were divided as slaves among the Indians who had supported the Puritans: 80 to Uncas and the Mohegans, 80 to Miantonomo and the Narragansetts, and 20 to Ninigret and the Niantics. No Pequots were thereafter allowed to inhabit their traditional lands. The name *Pequot* was to be expunged; survivors were instructed to take the names of the Native nations to which they had been given.

Some surviving Pequots were adopted by the Mohegans. The Mohegans treated their Pequots so badly that by 1655 the English were forced to remove them. Two reservations were established for the Pequot in 1666 and 1683. By 1762 there were only 140 Pequot; their population decline continued to a low point of 66 in the 1910 census.

THE WAR OF GENEALOGIES

The largest casino in the United States sprang from exceedingly humble beginnings. *Mashantucket* means "the much-wooded land." The word *Foxwoods* is a combination of the notion of forest with the Pequots' reputation as "the fox people." By 1972, the 214-acre Western Pequot reservation housed only one resident, Elizabeth George, "The Iron Lady," who died of a heart attack in 1973. George "could not have foreseen the radio call-in shows devoted to her bloodlines, or the press releases, or the ethnographic commentary of Donald Trump, who said that the Pequots who trace their lineage through George's family 'don't look like Indians'" (Barry, May 14, 2000, B-1). By 2000, Foxwoods had become the largest single gambling complex in the world, a place where "Indian genealogy is a current event" (Barry, May 14, 2000, B-1). Much of Benedict's story centers on George's grandson, Richard (Skip) Hayward, who, with attorney Tom Tureen, led a group that sued to regain 800 acres of Western Pequot land sold by the state in 1855 on grounds that the sale was illegal under the Nonintercourse Acts.

According to one observer, "What remained of the [Pequot] tribe was concentrated on a few hundred acres near the Rhode Island border. In 1856, the state of Connecticut—in an act that would typify much of the acrimony between the U.S. government and Native Americans—sold off nearly 80 percent of the Pequot's land (an act later judged to be illegal by the federal courts). That left the tribe with only 213 acres. Descendants faced the bleak prospect of no jobs on the reservation. Many were forced to take jobs in cities. The tribe's population dwindled with each passing year" (Dalla, n.d.).

By October 1983, the Western (Mashantucket) Pequots had won 800 acres, $900,000 to pay for it, as well as federal recognition as an Indian tribe. From that point, the Mashantucket Pequots acquired more land, with an eye toward establishing businesses. At the time, the Pequot tribal roll (Benedict spells this term *role* at least twice, without editorial intervention) contained 42 reservation residents and 153 other Pequots.

Ellen Barry, a reporter for the *Boston Globe,* observed, "So began the latest Indian war—the war of genealogies. Once the territory of academic researchers, the federal recognition process has come under pressure from millionaire investors who want to speed it up and angry state officials who want to stop it cold. Liberal-minded Yankees are commissioning opposition" (Barry, December 12, 2000).

Foxwoods started as a small bingo parlor because some 40 banks had refused to loan money to the Pequots. The bingo parlor began operating in 1986 and became wildly successful. After the U.S. federal Indian Gambling Regulatory Act was passed the following year, the Pequots signed an agreement with the state that 25 percent of revenues would be paid in taxes. (By the fiscal year beginning July 1, 1999, and ending June 30, 2000, Foxwoods' gross revenues on its slot and video machines alone totaled more than $9 billion.)

The first day Foxwoods opened, February 14, 1992, its 1,700-car parking lot was full by 10:30 A.M. Approximately 75,000 people gambled there during the first day, and 2,000 of them were still present at the casino's 4 A.M. closing time. During ensuing years, Foxwoods expanded and became one of the most notable examples anywhere of Native American economic development. When it opened, Foxwoods was the only gaming establishment on the East Coast offering poker, which was banned at the time in Atlantic City, New Jersey.

THE SIZE OF FOXWOODS

By 2000, the Foxwoods complex was drawing about 50,000 people on an average day. The Foxwoods Resort Casino complex included five casinos housing more than 300,000 square feet of gaming space, 5,842 slot machines, 370 gaming tables, a 3,000-seat high-stakes bingo parlor with $1 million jackpots, a 200-seat Sports-book, a Keno lounge, and pull tabs. Table games include baccarat, mini-baccarat, Big Six Wheels, blackjack, Caribbean stud poker, Craps, Pai Gow, Pai Gow Tiles, Red Dog, roulette, and a number of other games. The Foxwoods casino complex also includes four hotels ranging in size from 280 to 800 rooms and suites. In addition to gaming space and its four hotels, Foxwoods also offers 23 shopping areas, 24 food-and-beverage outlets, a movie theater complex, as well as the Mashantucket Pequot museum and a Fox Grand Theater with Las Vegas–style entertainment.

Foxwoods quickly has become an integral pillar of Connecticut's economy and a multimillion-dollar contributor to Connecticut charities. The Pequots' casino even put up cash one year to help the state balance its budget. By 2000, the Foxwoods casino complex was paying the state of Connecticut more than $189 million per year. The Foxwoods and the Mohegan Sun casinos, combined, paid the state of Connecticut 20 percent of their slot-machine profits, more than $318 million during the 1999–2000 fiscal year. The Mashantucket Pequots also became Connecticut's largest single taxpayer and, with 13,000 jobs, one of its larger employers. The casino employed a staff of lawyers and its own permanent lobbying office in Washington, DC.

The Pequots became the largest single contributor to the Smithsonian Institution's National Museum of the American Indian—at $10 million, the largest contribution to any Smithsonian project. They gave $2 million to the Special Olympics, $500,000 to the Hartford Ballet, and $5 million to the Mystic Aquarium (Eisler, 2001, 212–13). In June 2001, the Mohegans, owners of the neighboring Mohegan Sun Casino, made an equal pledge.

To illustrate the volume of money changing hands in these casinos, consider this fact: Mohegan Sun Casino investors included Trading Cove Associates, headed by Sol Kerzner, creator of the Sun City casino and resort in South Africa. By 2000, this firm had realized more than $800 million, a sum the company argued was "fair compensation" for services rendered (Murphy, 2000, A-1).

Foxwoods also has funded a $200 million Mashantucket Pequot Museum and Research Center, which houses "dioramas of Pequot villagers, mastodons, and a trailer very much like the ones occupied by tribal members living on the reservation in the 1970s" (Barry, May 14, 2000, B-1). Construction of the 90,000-square-foot museum and research center began in 1993.

Entering the museum, visitors pass through a simulated glacial crevasse, complete with cold air and creaking ice, which leads to an exhibit showing how glaciers shaped modern-day landforms in Pequot country. Computer animation and sound animates a diorama, 50 feet in diameter, of an 11,000-year-old caribou kill. A 22,000-square-foot immersion environment depicts a sixteenth-century Pequot village that features life-size, naturalistic, handcrafted figures taking part in everyday activities.

The museum also includes a re-created Pequot village, circa 1550, and a palisaded area, circa 1620, that comprises 12 wigwams, a sweat lodge, dugout canoes, stone tools, woven cattail mats, weapons, food-storage pits, a waterfall, and streams. The exhibit includes 29 full-scale hickory, white oak, black gum, and chestnut trees, as well as some 25 animal species, amid hundreds of other items typical of life during the sixteenth and seventeenth centuries. A state-of-the-art sound system employing 110 speakers and hundreds of sounds, from seagulls to crickets, has been added to the re-created village. Sensory inputs enable visitors to hear hundreds of village sounds and smell the woodlands and the aroma of a campfire as they walk among the oaks, chestnuts, and wigwams. A realistic model and three-dimensional interactive computer displays re-create a seventeenth-century Pequot fort, discovered in 1992 just 600 feet from the Museum and Research Center. The interactive display enables visitors to navigate through the fort as designers believed it existed about 300 years ago.

In an outdoor, eighteenth-century farmstead, re-created on approximately two acres of land, visitors walk through an orchard and gardens, learning about eighteenth-century tools and farming techniques. Other presentations illustrate life on the reservation up to present times, including a gallery of portraits of contemporary Pequots. Thirteen original films and video programs explore various aspects of everyday Pequot life, including the making of clothes, preparation of food, as well as construction of canoes and wigwams. The manufacture of wampum also is illustrated. One of the films, *The Witness*, recounts the Mystic massacre of 1637, seven miles from the site of the museum, where 600 to 700 Pequot were burned alive in a thatched fort by the English. The Research Center also houses a library devoted to American and Canadian Native histories and cultures. A 185-foot stone-and-glass tower provides visitors with sweeping views of the region.

More than 200 Native American artisans, craftspeople, consultants, and contractors from approximately fifty Native American tribes and nations contributed to the permanent exhibits through creation of original artwork, crafting of reproduction artifacts, and gathering of authentic materials. They also acted in the films and shared oral histories. Profits from Foxwoods also have financed archaeological digs in the area. Findings from these digs suggest that the Pequots "not only endured but also maintained many native practices—what they ate, how they cooked, how many family members lived together and more—through at least the eighteenth century" (Dobrzynski, 1997). Inside the 1670s fort is the remains of a village of eight to ten houses, "yielding a trove of fragments from iron kettles, pothooks, pottery pots with Pequot marks, pipes stamped with English makers' marks, wampum, musket balls, gun flints, arrow points, spear points and decorative objects" (Dobrzynski, 1997).

Laurence M. Hauptman, a history professor at the State University College at New Paltz, New York, and a coauthor of *The Pequots in Southern New England: The Fall and Rise of An American Indian Nation* (1990), said that "Village sites are hard to find because most are now other towns, like New London.... We Europeans didn't discover the geopolitical or economic importance of certain sites" (Dobrzynski, 1997).

The archaeologists have found trace remnants of a fortified Pequot village, probably built in 1670 and abandoned in 1675, and several eighteenth-century dwellings. These findings are beginning to sketch the story of how the Pequots persevered after the English forbade mention of their name following the Mystic massacre in 1637. Traces also have been found indicating that the Pequots' remote ancestors occupied the area possibly 10,000 years ago. Other Foxwoods profits have been invested in fisheries and a shipyard and used to make an annual payment to all members. The Pequots also used some of Foxwoods' profits to build roads, schools, and a power plant.

THE NONINTERCOURSE ACTS

Native American legal self-preservation is not solely a twentieth-century idea. Within years of the genesis of the United States as a national entity, the federal government passed several laws aimed at preventing the taking of Indian land by local investors or state-level interests. The laws, called the Nonintercourse Acts, forbade land-dealing without federal approval. The aim was to prevent fraud, of which there was plenty. The aforementioned local interests routinely ignored these acts, committing a raft of illegalities that would come back to haunt many landowners the better part of two centuries hence. In such a manner, the Pequots came to be reconstituted as a nation.

Legal actions under the aegis of the Nonintercourse Acts during the 1970s netted the Passamaquoddys and Penobscots of Maine a land base and economic infrastructure. *Without Reservation*'s early pages contain a fascinating brief legal history detailing the roles played by Tom Tureen, then a young attorney, and John Stevens, tribal governor of the Passamaquoddy. This was the first time that a federal court ever has ordered a federal department (Interior, in this case) to sue a state, an instructive story for anyone interested in the practical rudiments of Native sovereignty.

Before the land-claims settlement, the Passamaquoddy had inhabited a small and shrinking reservation; at one point, U.S. Route 1 was built through the reservation, and non-Indian families moved in without asking permission or paying for the land. In 1957, documents were discovered indicating that a treaty signed in 1794 between the Passamaquoddy and officials of Massachusetts had never been approved by Congress. Therefore the treaty, by which the Indians had ceded much of Maine, was not legally valid. At one point, the Penobscots and Passamaquoddys claimed rights to 12 million acres, two-thirds of the state of Maine, much of it large tracts owned by some of the world's largest wood-products companies, including Scott Paper, Georgia-Pacific Corporation, St. Regis Paper Company, and the International Paper Company. The story of the Nonintercourse Acts is extremely important to contemporary treaty interpretation and will have an influence on land claims to come, including Iroquois claims in New York.

In 1980, the Passamaquoddy and Penobscot each were awarded $40.3 million to settle their claims. Instead of distributing money to each tribal member in per capita payments, the Passamaquoddy and Penobscot decided to invest the money in land and business ventures to reestablish collective identity.

The two tribes suddenly found themselves holding the largest pool of investment capital in Maine. One-third of the Passamaquoddys' settlement money was spent on 300,000 acres of land. Another third was placed in conservative financial investments; the interest and dividends of these investments were earmarked for payments to members each year. The remaining third was invested in business ventures under a tribal-management firm, Tribal Assets Management. The Passamaquoddys invested a large portion of their capital in one of Maine's largest blueberry farms. The farm was so profitable that the tribe recovered its investment in two years. In 1983, the Passamaquoddys bought the only cement plant in New England. They sold the plant five years later at a profit of $60 million.

The same set of laws that was applied to the Maine tribes was found to have been ignored during the long history of land transfers that reduced the Mashantucket Pequots' landholdings to 214 acres, enabling the legal rebirth that gave rise to the Foxwoods casino complex. Thus began the story of the Pequots' rebirth, with acquisition of land, federal recognition as a Native polity, construction of Foxwoods, and the ensuing squabble, exploited by Jeff Benedict's *Without Reservation,* regarding how much blood makes a Pequot "authentic."

BLOOD QUANTUM AND ETHNIC IDENTITY: WITHOUT RESERVATION'S CONTRADICTIONS

Without Reservation badly needed critical editing before its publication. The book, as published, suffers from several embarrassing contradictions that reflect Benedict's ignorance of Pequot history. On page 31, for example, before the reader is introduced to Elizabeth George, Benedict declares that the Western Pequots "had died away generations ago," evidencing, as absolute fact, his opinion that none of the Indian movers and shakers in this story meet his definition of Mashantucket Pequot heritage. On page 37, Benedict writes that the Western Pequot reservation was founded before the town of Ledyard, after which he declares (on the same page) that the reservation was placed in a remote area "to keep the Indians out of sight." "Out of sight of whom?" a reader might ask. If the reservation was founded before the town, how is this possible?

To call *Without Reservation* Anglocentric would be something of an understatement. One notable example is the way in which Benedict describes Skip Hayward's ethnic heritage. When Benedict introduces Hayward (on page 34), he is, without qualification, "a white person." By page 57, however, he is sitting with his grandmother Elizabeth George acquiring "Native American culture." On the next page, Benedict resolves the ambiguity he has created by saying that though Hayward has some Pequot blood, "the bloodline to the Pequots was tissue-thin." All along, the author uses Anglo-American, not Native American, definitions of kinship.

Throughout *Without Reservation,* Benedict seems enamored of a simple concept of race, by which each and every person can be described with a one-word label. Based on blood quantum (a governmental definition), the most any of the present-day Mashantucket Pequots can claim is one-eighth blood (Dobrzynski, 1997). This singular fact, like no other, seems to rile Benedict and his European American readership. To them, one-eighth blood is seven-eights something other than Pequot, making the Mashantucket Pequot nation, as presently constituted, more a marriage of economic opportunity than a Native American nation.

Regarding Skip Hayward's Pequot heritage, Kim Isaac Eisler wrote, "On his mother's side, Skip was about one-sixteenth Indian, at most. On his father's side, he was as American as pumpkin pie," whatever that means (Eisler, 2001, 56). In defense of mixed bloodlines, one may observe that John Ross, hero of the Cherokees' resistance to the removal that became the Trail of Tears was exactly one-eighth Cherokee. At some point, blood quantum and ethnic identity do sometimes part ways.

How vexing it must be to Benedict when Kenneth Reels, the chairman of the Mashantucket Pequot after Hayward, described his complicated ethnic heritage. Reels explained on a local cable show that his great-grandfather, Paul George, was a Pequot leader around the year 1800. "I can go back on a lot of sides and show all my blood," Reels said on the local access channel's *Renshaw Report,* hosted by New London plumber Murray Renshaw, "I'm a Western [Pequot] an Eastern [Pequot], a Mashantucket, a Niantic, a Narragansett. I'm black, I'm Caucasian, and I'm Portuguese. I'm proud of who I am" (Associated Press, 2000). Reels continued, "We are a proud people, and we will not stand by and cater to anyone who may be racist or jealous of our hard work and success" ("Farm Land Sits," n.d.). Reels's ancestors include full-blooded Pequots, he said, a fact affirmed by a family Civil War pension document. *Without Reservation* ignores this (Scarponi, May 12, 2000). Professor Hauptman said he would not give Benedict "even a C-minus for research." Hauptman said that Benedict is "ill-informed about Native Americans, about American and Connecticut history, and even about law, his chosen profession" (Barry, May 14, 2000, B-1).

Reading *Without Reservation,* one hears the engine hum of some very imaginary late-model welfare Cadillacs in the background. Benedict sheds a quick tear for the historical circumstances that reduced the Pequots' numbers so drastically (including a very brief description of the 1637 Mystic massacre), but he seems ready to ratify the upshot of genocide by declaring that the Pequot, by lack of numbers, now have no right to a Native American identity.

Benedict introduces the present Western Pequot chairman Kenneth Reels, who defeated Hayward for the chairmanship in November 1998, with the same welfare Cadillac treatment. On page 230, Benedict says that Reels's birth certificate (at Wakefield, Rhode Island, on April 18, 1960) identifies him as "a Negro." Benedict then lavishes attention (as he did with Hayward) on selective recall regarding Reels's dysfunctional parents: a mother who was "destitute and constantly pregnant" (231) and a father who served nine years in prison for manslaughter in the death of Bonnie Jean Hay, who had filed a complaint that Hayward abused her 16-month-old baby. To his credit, Benedict admits that the younger Reels graduated from high school (having pointed out that both his parents dropped out), kept himself out of trouble with the law, and excelled at basketball. Still, Benedict finds him as "black" as he found Hayward "white," arguing from town records that often had no Native American category. Pequots had been defined out of existence.

The Single-Ethnicity Question

The single-ethnicity question that vexes Benedict is the same one facing the U.S. census, which has been struggling for years with systems to describe (and count) people with multicultural heritages. The 2000 census form, for the first time, allowed respondents to mark one or more of 14 boxes representing six races and subcategories or "some other race." In all, as many as 63 combinations were possible. This is a considerable demographic advance from the days before the Civil War, when the U.S. census contained two categories: white and Negro, for the sole purpose of determining congressional representation under the three-fifths compromise that counted blacks as 60 percent of a human being. Only recently has the census been worded with an eye to demographic value. Town records also reflected these trends.

During his diligent efforts to discern who is and is not Pequot, Benedict displays an instinct for finding exactly what he wants to see in conflicting historical records, ignoring all contrary evidence. For example, Benedict ignores an 1857 state-court ruling that determined that the family from which a number of the Western Pequot are descended is, indeed, of Pequot lineage. Pequot officials have produced a 1857 Connecticut Superior Court petition and have asserted that it establishes a line of genealogical descent from the late 1700s to present Pequot Tribal Chairman Kenneth M. Reels and other members. Benedict believes that the document identifies Reels's ancestor as a Pequot and a Mohegan on different pages. "That document doesn't prove that Kenny Reels is descended from Pequots," Benedict has said. "What it proves is that there are a litany of documents that say conflicting things." Benedict has palmed off the document by saying, "The courts aren't always right" (Scarponi, May 12, 2000).

Benedict is not always right, either, of course. He also uses historical sources without reference to their inherent biases. Commented Hauptman:

> Benedict's conclusions on who is or was a Pequot is largely based on southeast-
> ern Connecticut town records. Reflecting the racial bias of the times, the only
> categories for classifying peoples were often either "white" or "black," an easy
> way to write Indians out of history. Benedict ignores the more reliable Connecti-
> cut State Overseers' records—state officials who directly administered these and
> other Connecticut Indians from before the Revolution to 1973—records that
> clearly show the continuity of the Mashantucket Pequot as a distinct Indian
> community with a leadership over time. (Hauptman, 2000)

Without Reservation's richly detailed anecdotal nature induces a bogus sense of the familiar that creates a fuzzy zone between fact, as most historians and journalists understand it, and partially fictionalized accounts that sound as if the author was a fly-on-the-wall witness of many events that he most probably never saw. Witness Benedict's descriptions of Hayward beating his first wife Aline during the early and mid-1970s, around page 50. Benedict does this again on pages 88 to 92, as he lavishes detail on the way in which Aline separated from and finally divorced Hayward in 1976, after seven years of marriage. One could swear from the precision of Benedict's descriptions and the large number of direct quotes that the author was sitting right there, taking notes for a book to be published a quarter-century later. As a matter of fact, Benedict started writing *Without Reservation* in 1998.

Benedict firmly believes that Hayward and others have adapted a Pequot motif to ride an affirmative-action gravy train and builds his case to fit. Benedict repeats the same theme on page 123 ("After organizing his [Hayward's] relatives into an Indian tribe") and again on page 138 ("Bestowing sovereign status on Skip and his family"). On page 151, Benedict does his best to assemble a case that not even Elizabeth George was a Pequot. Benedict believes that George lived on the reservation not out of any attachment to her ethnic identity or culture, but solely because her residence was rent-free.

To the point of repetitive boorishness, Benedict drives home his central theme that Hayward and the rest of the Western Pequots are fakirs. There are no real Pequots, he tells us on page 62, and, on page 100, "The real Pequot tribe has been non-existent for years." Benedict pegs Hayward and the rest of the Western Pequots as increasingly sophisticated scam artists. "If they did pull off a scam, it's probably the most brilliant scam in American history," said Michael Bernz, who grew up in the area and hosts a morning call-in show on WBMW in Ledyard (Barry, May 14, 2000, B-1). Although many non-Indians in the area have complained about the casino, most businesses in the vicinity of Foxwoods have profited handsomely since it opened, including local suppliers, retailers, hotels, and restaurants.

THE COMMON NATURE OF MIXED GENEALOGIES

Benedict's version of ethnic cleansing aside, mixed genealogies are very common in the United States. For example, the mother of Frederick Douglass, the famed black abolitionist, a slave, was probably partially Native American. Douglass was born Frederick Augustus Washington Bailey on a farm on Lewiston Road, Tuckahoe, near Easton, Talbot County, Maryland, in February 1818, son of an unknown European American father and Harriet Bailey, a slave who may have been partially Native American. No traces remain of which Native tribe or nation with which he may share ancestry. As a boy, Douglass's owner, Aaron Anthony, referred to him as his "little Indian boy."

In some cases, Native Americans and escaped slaves made common cause in sizable numbers. On such example are the Black Seminoles, who are sometimes called Seminole Maroons by ethnologists, who live today mainly in Oklahoma, Texas, the Bahamas, and Coahuila, Mexico. Their ancestors were runaways from the plantations of South Carolina and Georgia between the late seventeenth and mid-eighteenth centuries who sought refuge in Spanish-controlled Florida. The name *Seminole,* derived from the Spanish word *cimaroon,* meaning "fugitives" or "wild ones," was incorporated into the Native language. The word *maroon,* in English, stems from the same Spanish word.

Fugitive slaves from Charleston arrived in Spanish St. Augustine, Florida, as early as 1687, where many began new lives as free men and women in a multicultural community. Some of the men worked as cartwrights, jewelers, butchers, and innkeepers, and women were employed as cooks and laundresses. Some also owned small businesses. In 1838, the Spanish authorities established a settlement for escaped slaves, Gracia Real de Santa Teresa de Mose, where some 100 men, women, and children came into contact with various bands of Native Americans living nearby.

The Seminoles, originally one of the five Civilized Tribes (the others being the Cherokee, Choctaw, Chickasaw, and Creek), were chased into Florida by armed forces under the command of Gen. (and later U.S. president) Andrew Jackson. Jackson's pretext for invading Florida (over Spanish diplomatic objections) was pursuit of freed slaves as well the Seminoles. For several decades, through the first half of Frederick Douglass's life, escaped slaves made common cause with the Seminoles, sometimes mingling and at other times establishing a separate identity and preserving their own culture and traditions. In the meantime, the Seminoles fought the U.S. Army to a stalemate. To avoid capture, the Black Seminoles developed skills at guerilla warfare. They also became very adaptable, finding ways to survive in new environments that other people regarded as uninhabitable or marginal, such as the Florida Everglades.

In 1818, Gen. Andrew Jackson's troops chased the Seminoles into Florida, which was still under Spanish jurisdiction (the area was ceded to the United States in 1821). The Seminoles, many of whom were descended from Creeks, had elected to ally themselves with the Spanish rather than the United States, an act of virtual treason in General Jackson's eyes. In addition, the Seminoles were giving shelter to escaped slaves. The pretext of Jackson's raid thus was recovery of stolen human property. After Florida was purchased from Spain by the United States, slave-hunting vigilantes invaded the area en masse, killing Seminoles as well as blacks. Later, during the 1830s, when President Jackson proposed to remove the Seminoles to Indian Territory, they refused. Moving deep into the swamps of southern Florida (an area that, ironically, was being used as a removal destination for other Native peoples), the Seminoles fought U.S. Army troops to a bloody stalemate during seven years of warfare. They were never defeated and never moved from their new homeland.

In 1823, Seminole leaders agreed to the Treaty of Moultrie Creek that ceded land and created reservations for the Seminoles. Later, as a result of U.S. removal policies, the Treaty of Payne's Landing of 1832 required all Seminoles to leave

Florida for Indian Territory within three years. According to the treaty, Seminoles with African American blood were to be sold into slavery.

Escaped slaves joined the Seminoles during the Second Seminole War (1835–42), a guerilla war in which the blacks served prominent roles as advisers, spies, and intermediaries. At one point, Gen. Thomas S. Jesup said it was "a Negro and not an Indian War" ("The Black Seminoles," 1998). Jesup eventually promised the former slaves freedom if they would immigrate to the Indian Territory as part of the Seminole Nation.

The war against the Seminoles was one of the most expensive Indian campaigns that the U.S. Army had waged to that time. In addition to the 1,500 soldiers killed (one for every two Seminoles eventually removed to Indian Territory), the government spent an average of $6,500 for each Native person transferred to Indian Territory. At a time when the average job paid less than $1,000 a year, this amount represented a small fortune.

Following the First and Second Seminole Wars (1817–18 and 1835–42), some of the Black Seminoles escaped to the Bahamas. Others were separated from their Native American allies and transported to the Indian Territory (present-day Oklahoma), where they became known as Freedmen. Some of them moved to Mexico, where their descendants, known as *Indios Mascogos* still live. After the Civil War, some Black Seminoles moved to Texas, where, during the 1870s and 1880s, they served with the U.S. Army on the Texas frontier as the Seminole Negro Indian Scouts. Today, members of the Black Seminole community in Texas refer to themselves as Seminoles to set themselves apart from other blacks, to emphasize the pride that they have in their unique history of having escaped slavery.

DEFINING PEQUOT IDENTITY AND ANCESTRY

The Bureau of Indian Affairs (BIA) grants Native American groups recognition, one of the agency's important tasks because it makes groups eligible for several federal-assistance programs. Conferral of recognition also creates a semisovereign national entity, a key prerequisite for gaining immunity from state laws (including those that may prohibit certain types of gambling). In all, 558 Native American tribes and nations had been recognized by the federal government by 2000. Another 200 groups had applied for recognition as of that date, enduring "exhaustive checks by federal genealogists and anthropologists to ascertain that they have legitimate Native American heritage in their specified group.... The BIA requires massive historical documentation supporting Indian groups' claims, and it sometimes takes 15 years or more for the agency's overworked, twelve-member Branch of Acknowledgment and Research to process and verify applications."

The discovery of gambling as an engine of Native American economic development has vastly complicated the process by which Native American nations are officially recognized by the federal government. The Mashantucket, however, were spared this process when they were recognized, by an act of Congress, in 1983. Commented one reporter, "Driven by the lure of billions of dollars in potential casino profits, unrecognized Indian groups across the country have unleashed such an overwhelming and highly contentious barrage of claims for federal tribal recognition that Kevin Gover says his Bureau of Indian Affairs can no longer cope with it" (Claiborne, 2000).

Disputes pertaining to who should be regarded as a Pequot expanded at the turn of the millennium to include two reorganized bands that were seeking the kind of federal recognition that allowed the Mashantuckets to open Foxwoods. The recognition process, if successful, could lead to the opening of two more casinos. One, the Mohegan Sun, already has opened near Foxwoods to tap the lucrative Boston-to-New York City gambling market.

The 600-member Paucatuck (Eastern Pequot) have retained the Lantern Hill Reservation (226 acres) at North Stonington and have applied, without success, for federal recognition (Pequot History, 1997). On December 24, 2000, the Paucatuck Eastern Pequot, one of two Pequot bands seeking the type of federal recognition that allowed the Mashantucket Pequot to open Foxwoods, sent Christmas cards to the 15,000 mainly non-Indian residents of North Stonington, Preston, and Ledyard, Connecticut, pledging never to threaten the holdings of private landowners.

The town councils of the same three towns had spent approximately $1.2 million up to that time fighting expansion of the Mashantucket Pequots' landholdings in court. The towns hired a genealogist to debunk the Pequots' assertions of Native American ancestry. Many of the non-Indian residents agreed with gambling promoter Donald Trump that members of Elizabeth George's family "sure don't look Indian" (Barry, May 14, 2000, B-1). This is the core readership of Jeff Benedict's book. "How do you put it politely?" asked True Miller, a longtime resident of North Stonington who owns a hardware store in central North Stonington. "How much Indian blood does one need to be an Indian?" (Barry, May 14, 2000, B-1)

On April 30, 2001, the U.S. Supreme Court declined to review a challenge by surrounding towns (Ledyard, Preston, and North Stonington) and the state of Connecticut to the proposed addition of 165 acres to the Mashantucket Pequot land base. The court thus defused a suit by Connecticut Attorney General Richard Blumenthal and attorneys for the towns that sought an Interior Department order against the land transfer. In effect, the court let stand the long-established right of Native tribes and nations to petition the Interior Department to take land into trust.

In the meantime, Attorney General Blumenthal and the same towns filed a lawsuit in U.S. district court against the U.S. Department of the Interior and the BIA seeking to block the BIA from issuing final federal recognition to the Eastern Pequot and Pawcatuck Eastern Pequot tribes. The BIA requires submission of detailed history and genealogy of a tribe before it grants federal recognition. The lawsuit contends that the BIA's recognition process in this case has been rife with irregularities. Federal recognition gives recognized Native American nations rights to make land claims, to establish their own law enforcement, and to sustain economic-development projects, most notably casinos.

The town officials who sued the BIA over the recognition process in Connecticut said that Kevin Gover, commissioner of Indian Affairs (who supervised the federal government's recognition process at the time) relaxed BIA standards in approving the petitions, a move that could set the stage for recognition of the Golden Hill Paugussetts, a tribe that Gover once represented as a lawyer. The Paugussetts are seeking to build a casino in Bridgeport, Connecticut. Gover withdrew from the case.

"If the [Mashantucket Pequot] tribe is not a *bona fide* tribe, then they should not be operating a casino," said Ledyard Mayor Wesley Johnson. "We don't expect 13,000 people to be out of work or to see property boarded up ... but something should be done" (Scarponi, September 21, 2000).

Ellen Barry, a reporter at the *Boston Globe,* observed:

> While some are grateful for the job base the casinos have created, many complain about social blights—of children locked in cars in the casino parking lot, of the financial losses of local residents who find they can't stop playing the tables. Most of all they worry about losing more taxable land into the tribe's reservation, where fantastic wealth is building on itself, just out of reach. (Barry, December 12, 2000)

"If they want to stir up trouble, we will meet them on the field of battle. But they are kidding themselves if they think we will abandon [the] Mashantucket," said Gover, a Pawnee. "We tribes believe that if one is defrocked, if you will, then it sets a precedent for all the others. The Mashantuckets are part of the family now, and the tribes will look after them. What's the alternative? To let outsiders decide who is a tribe and who is not? The fear is that my tribe is next" (Barry, December 12, 2000).

After more than two years of trying to reform the trouble-plagued recognition process, Gover concluded that he could not succeed. So, he said, he is willing to give up his power to recognize tribes to a three-member commission that Congress would create under a bill proposed by Senator Ben Nighthorse Campbell. "I know it's unusual for an agency to give up a responsibility like this," Gover said in an interview. "But this one has outgrown us. It needs more expertise and resources than we have available" (Claiborne, 2000).

Looking into the future, Gover said he could not see the recognition process becoming any less politicized. "As more and more money is at stake, I expect it to get nastier still," Gover said (Barry, May 26, 2000, B-1). Processing that all the existing applications for recognition could take the BIA's Branch of Acknowledgement and Research as long as fifty years, Gover said (Barry, May 26, 2000, B-1).

Senator Campbell, whose proposal would create a presidentially appointed Commission on Indian Recognition, said that he proposed the new body partially out of frustration with the slow pace of the Bureau of Indian Affairs recognition process. He told the Associated Press that he was "pleased and surprised" to hear that Gover agreed with him (Barry, May 26, 2000, B-1).

Mark C. Tilden, a staff attorney for the Native American Rights Fund in Boulder, Colorado, said he has been petitioning the BIA on behalf of one tribe since 1980 and for another since 1985. He said the process can cost Indian groups $400,000 to $1 million at a time when "most tribes don't have enough money to pay the light bill, much less legal fees like that" (Claiborne, 2000). Tilden said that politics sometimes causes the delays; when recognition removes land from states' tax rolls, sometimes state governments bring pressure on Capitol Hill, which sifts down to the BIA. "Gover said the meager tribal verification staff and a mountain of other vexing problems that confront the BIA daily—combined with the increasingly frequent lawsuits that surround recognition cases—are to blame for the delays" (Claiborne, 2000).

Benedict's *Without Reservation* prompted a renewed call for a congressional investigation of the Mashantucket Pequots' assertions of identity. Rep. Sam Gejdenson, Democrat of Connecticut, called for the congressional probe. "I believe an open committee review, including a public hearing with witnesses representing all interested parties, is not only appropriate, but essential," he wrote in a June 14, 2000, letter to the chairman of the House Resources Committee (Stockes, 2000). Representative Gejdenson was a member of the committee that reviewed the Mashantucket Pequots' recognition bill in 1983. Although Gejdenson pushed for an investigation, he also said Congress did nothing wrong in 1983 when it approved the settlement act. "As a member of the committee during the period in which legislation was considered, I believe it carried out its responsibility effectively with the information, testimony and evidence made available," Gejdenson wrote (Stockes, 2000).

HISTORICAL IRONIES

As the high-stakes dispute over Pequot genealogy rolled on, the historical irony of their situation seems lost on the Yankees of the towns surrounding the Pequot and Mohegan Sun gambling complexes. European Americans acting as members of an oppressed minority in danger of losing their lands seem ill-suited to stand in the shoes of ancestors who did worse to the Pequots than the Indians ever will do to them. Against this backdrop, a few hours from Foxwoods by automobile, Native Americans gathered in Massachusetts for the thirtieth time, during Thanksgiving 1999, on a hill in Plymouth, near the first Pilgrim landfall. The annual protest was born in 1970, according to Moonanum James, a coleader of United American Indians of New England, "as a direct result of the state's need to keep the Pilgrim mythology alive."

Wamsutta Frank James had been invited to address a gathering of dignitaries commemorating the 350th anniversary of the landing of the Pilgrims. Because his remarks did not fit the mythology, he was told that he could not give the speech he had written. The state was more than willing to write a speech for him that would keep the lies alive. He refused to have words placed in his mouth. Instead of speaking to a group of dignitaries in the warmth of a banquet hall, he and a small group of Native Americans came here to Plymouth, stood in the cold, and declared U.S. Thanksgiving Day a National Day of Mourning. (James, 1999)

The Pilgrims and Puritans knew nothing of the germ theory of disease and had no idea that diseases brought from Europe and spread on their breath had begun killing the native inhabitants before the immigrants even saw the beach. Indians had been dying for years from diseases imported by European fishermen off the coast. Native population in the area, about 80,000 at first contact, dwindled steadily. By 1640, European colonies in New England hosted about 20,000 people, still an island in a Native American sea. By the end of the century, the numbers were reversed.

In 1970, 350 years after a storm-battered ship carrying 102 immigrants landed near a new home they called Plymouth Colony, the descendants of the people who had met them at the beach raised their voices to protest what they regarded to be an officially sanctioned myth. James continued:

> What was it about the speech that got those officials so upset? ... Here is the truth: The reason they talk about the pilgrims and not an earlier English-speaking colony, Jamestown, is that in Jamestown the circumstances were way too ugly to hold up as an effective national myth. For example, the white settlers in Jamestown turned to cannibalism to survive. Not a very nice story to tell the kids in school. The pilgrims did not find an empty land any more than Columbus "discovered" anything. Every inch of this land is Indian land.... Upon first arriving, the pilgrims opened my ancestors' graves and took our corn and bean supplies. Later, from the very harbor we can see from here, the English sold my ancestors as slaves for 220 shillings each. (James, 1999)

The first official Day of Thanksgiving was proclaimed in 1637 by Governor James Winthrop, according to James, to celebrate the safe return of men from Massachusetts who had gone to Mystic, Connecticut, to participate in the massacre of approximately 700 Pequot women, children, and men (James, 1999). Half of the new arrivals at Plymouth Colony died of exposure and scurvy (caused by Vitamin C deficiency) during the first winter, as local Indians introduced them to foods that cured the disease. The Pilgrims, who had arrived at the wrong time of year (late fall) to raise crops to get them through a rough winter in a place they renamed New England, were at first dependent on local Native American peoples for their very survival.

Knowing nothing about how weather behaves, they had expected to find a land warmer than England, because they had been traveling south as well as west. When spring arrived, few of their European seeds germinated in American soil. Finding large areas depopulated at their entry, the Pilgrims (and later the Puritans) thought their God had cleared the land for them. The town of Milford, Connecticut, in 1640 voted a motion saying that the Earth belongs to God and was given to His appointed missionaries, including themselves in that number. This assumption was reinforced by a belief that powered the Protestant reformation: God helps those who help themselves. Thus, the Puritans assumed they had a right to the land because they would make (in the words of modern property-tax assessors) "higher and better" use of it.

Now that the Mashantucket Pequot have taken this to its logical present-day conclusion ("highest and best use" equating to hotels and casinos), many non-Indian New Englanders are upset. This particular application of the Protestant work ethic has become a bit too ironic for their tastes.

FURTHER READING

Associated Press. "Mashantucket Chairman Explains Ancestry on Cable Show." *Danbury News-Times,* May 20, 2000. <http://www.newstimes.com/archive2000/may20/rgf. htm>.

Barry, Ellen. "Agency Willing to Relinquish Power to Recognize Tribes." *Boston Globe,* May 26, 2000: B-1.

Barry, Ellen. "A Question of Ancestry: In Connecticut, Casino Plans Fuel Debate over Tribal Genealogy." *Boston Globe,* May 14, 2000: B-1.

Barry, Ellen. "Recognition Is a Contentious Process: James P. Lynch, Who Debunks Tribes, Says He Was Shocked to Find the Pequots' Proof of Ancestry So Tenuous." *Boston Globe,* December 12, 2000, n.p.

Benedict, Jeff. *Without Reservation: The Making of America's Most Powerful Indian Tribe and Foxwoods, the World's Largest Casino.* New York: HarperCollins, 2000.

"The Black Seminoles' Long March to Freedom." Text for an exhibit displayed in Cohen Library of The City College during Black History Month, February 1998, City College of New York Libraries. <http://www.ccny.cuny.edu/library/News/ seminoles2.html>.

Bourne, Russell. *The Red King's Rebellion: Racial Politics in New England, 1675–1678.* New York: Atheneum, 1990.

Cave, Alfred A. *The Pequot War.* Amherst: University of Massachusetts Press, 1996.

Claiborne, William. "Tribes and Tribulations: BIA Seeks to Lose a Duty." *Washington Post,* June 2, 2000, n.p.

Covey, Cyclone. *The Gentle Radical: A Biography of Roger Williams.* New York: Macmillan, 1966.

Dalla, Nolan. "Tales from the Felt: Sour Grapes Growing in Connecticut." *Cardplayer Magazine.* n.d. <http://www.cardplayer.com/author/cp_magazine/11>.

Dobrzynski, Judith H. "Casino Profits Help Pequot Indian Tribe Reclaim Its History." *The New York Times,* September 1, 1997, n.p.

Eisler, Kim Isaac. *Revenge of the Pequots: How a Small Native American Tribe Created the World's Most Profitable Casino.* New York: Simon and Schuster, 2001.

"Farm Land Sits on Reservation Because of 1983 Congressional Vote." *Gambling Magazine.* n.d. <http://www.gamblingmagazine.com/articles/26/26–368.htm>.

Hauptman, Laurence M. Guest commentary. *Poughkeepsie Journal,* June 2, 2000, n.p.

James, Moonanum. "Speech by Moonanum James, Co-Leader of United American Indians of New England, at 30th National Day of Mourning, Cole's Hill, Plymouth, Mass., Nov. 25, 1999."

Larsen, Kent. "LDS Author Takes on Rich Indian Tribe: Are Pequots Really Pequots?" *Mormon News.* May 25, 2000. <http://www.mormonstoday.com/000528/P2Benedict01. shtml>.

Murphy, Sean P. "Congressmen Seeking Probe of Indian Casinos." *Boston Globe,* December 16, 2000, A-1.

Pequot History. 1997. <http://www.dickshovel.com/peq.html>.

Scarponi, Diane. "Another Document Bolsters the Pequots' Claim of Authenticity." *The New York Times,* September 21, 2000, n.p.

Scarponi, Diane. "Book Questions Ancestry of Connecticut Tribe." Associated Press, Friday May 12, 2000. <http://www.citizensalliance.org/links/pages/news/National%20News/ Connecticut.htm>.

Stockes, Brian. "Controversy Continues over Pequot Recognition." *Indian Country Today,* July 12, 2000. <http://www.indiancountry.com/content.cfm?id=764>.

Sutterlin, Georg. "Handouts behind Them, Pequots Clean Up." *Neue Zurcher Zeitung* (Zurich, Switzerland), January 18, 2001, in *World Press Review,* April, 2001: 32.

CHAPTER 5

◦∿

Names and Games: The Controversy Regarding "Indian" Sports Mascots and Place-Names

Hank Aaron, who hit more home runs than any other player in the history of professional baseball, was invited to throw out the first pitch at the 2000 Major League Baseball All-Star game in Atlanta. Aaron, a black man who received many racist death threats after his home-run total surpassed Babe Ruth's, stepped up to the plate in another way when he arrived in Atlanta for the big game. Aaron, who had worn the Atlanta Braves uniform, told the media that the team's mascot was an unfair stereotype of Native Americans. He is the most prominent athlete to make such a statement. Reporters for various media generally ignored what he said.

Aaron may have lost a battle, but he won a war. Stressing their right to dignity and self-definition of ethnic identity, Native Americans have been bringing increasing pressure on a number of sports teams, from the sandlots to the professionals, to retire stereotypical mascots. "The pace is really picking up," said Cyd Crue, president of the Illinois chapter of the National Coalition on Racism in Sports and the Media. "We're seeing more educators around the country, in middle schools and high schools and at universities, concerned about the racial climate in schools ... dropping these symbols" (Badwin, 2000). Between the early 1970s and 2000, about 1,250 of the 3,000 U.S. elementary schools, high schools, and colleges with American Indian nicknames and mascots dropped them, said Suzan Shown Harjo, president of Washington, DC's, Morningstar Institute (Badwin, 2000). More have fallen since, although no total tally was available.

Political battles over sports' mascot names mirror other debates over names and places, including a lively debate in recent years over the use of the word *squaw*—believed to be degrading to native American women—as well as advertising campaigns for the likes of Crazy Horse Malt Liquor. By 2006, the National Collegiate Athletic Association (NCAA) was denying tournament berths to teams that insisted on retaining their Indian mascots, to fulsome grumbling by some fans who insisted the names celebrated and honored Native Americans.

Scholarly attention to the mascot issue has followed in train with public controversy. Three recently published scholarly books address the controversy (King and Springwood, 2001a, 2001b; Spindel, 2000). The North American Society for the Sociology of Sport in 1999 initiated annual conferences practically in Chief Wahoo's shadow in downtown Cleveland, Ohio. The conference included sessions on the sport mascot issue in the context of Native American rights. Papers included "Escaping the Tyranny of the Majority: A Case Study of Mascot Change" by Laurel Davis and Malvina Rau of Springfield College and "Red, Black, and White: 'Playing Indian' and Racial Hierarchy at Florida State" (where the mascot is a Seminole), presented by Richard King of Drake University.

ORIGINS OF THE MASCOT CONTROVERSY

The mascot issue emerged during the 1960s as the National Congress of American Indians in 1968 launched a campaign to bring an end to the use of Indian sports mascots and other media stereotypes. At about the same time, the American Indian Movement's (AIM's) founding chapter in Minneapolis vigorously complained that calling a team Redskins was as insulting as Niggers, Spics, or Honkies. Because of AIM, some of the first Indian stereotypes fell in the Midwest.

At the University of Nebraska at Omaha (UNO), for example, a chapter of AIM worked with students and faculty to change the school's mascot and team name from Indians to Mavericks, a beef animal with an attitude, in 1971. The change was popular on campus in part because the visual depiction of Owumpie (sometimes spelled Ouampi) the so-called Omaha Indian was so tacky that, by comparison, he made the Cleveland Indians' Chief Wahoo look like a real gentleman.

During spring 1970, UNO began to recruit Native American students, some of whom objected during the school's first home football game the following fall as they watched a white student dressed as Owumpie run around the field in a headdress. The mascot, described as "an angry, dark-red cartoon character with a hooked nose swinging a club and doing a war dance" (Else, 2005, 9-B), thus became an object of protest by the Native students, who joined with non-Indian allies to win support of the student government and the faculty senate. The next stop was the university president, Kirk Naylor Sr., who asked the opinion of the Omaha Nation's government, explaining that he thought the mascot was an honor. The real Omahas (U'ma'has, actually) replied emphatically that they thought Owumpie was an insult, not an honor, so the caricature was retired in May 1971. At UNO, an Indian princess also was retired as homecoming queen (Else, 2005, 9-B). Stanford University changed its mascot from an Indian to a cardinal at about the same time.

In 1980, Choctaw filmmaker Phil Lucas addressed the question on the pages of *Four Winds,* a short-lived glossy magazine devoted to Native American art, history, and culture, by asking how whites would react if a sports team was named the Cleveland Caucasians. What would European Americans think, Lucas asked, if Indians adopted racial names (such as the Window Rock Negroes or the Tahlequah White Boys) for their sports teams (Lucas, 1980, 69–77)?

In 1994, Wisconsin's Education Department issued a directive urging school districts in that state to drop Indian mascots. Los Angeles schools have done the same (Gormley, 2000). Ten public schools in Dallas shed their Indian mascots in 1998, at a time when approximately 50 public high schools, 13 colleges, and three colleges in Texas still used Indian mascots (Doclar, 1998).

In 2003, the Lincoln, Nebraska, *Journal-Star* amended its style to prohibit use of Redskins. The Peoria Chiefs, a minor league affiliate of the Chicago Cubs, retained its name but changed its logo from an American Indian to a Dalmatian fire chief. In June of the same year, The Michigan State Board of Education passed a resolution that strongly recommended elimination of American Indian mascots, nicknames, logos, fight songs, insignias, antics, and team descriptors by all Michigan schools. In September 2005, the American Psychological Association recommended the immediate retirement of American Indian mascots, symbols, images, and personalities by schools, colleges, universities, athletic teams, and other organizations.

Some sports teams, especially the professionals, as private enterprises, have retained their mascots not (by their own testimony) because they make millions of dollars a year peddling the images on ball caps and sweatshirts but (so they say) for Native peoples' own good. Witness the Washington Redskins (a term so offensive to some Native people that they refuse to use it), Cleveland Indians, and Atlanta Braves.

WASHINGTON REDSKINS

Many Native Americans take the word *Redskin* as an outright slur to the point of refusing to say the word in public or print it. Harjo, who is among this number, has sued the Washington Redskins over their use of Indian imagery. The Redskin lawsuit *(Harjo v. Pro-Football, Inc.)* was heard before a three-judge panel of the Trademark Trial and Appeals Board (TTAB), a three-judge panel of trademark judges. In a case heard on May 27, 1998, and decided on April 2, 1999, the board found:

> Although the marks [Redskin logos] were not scandalous, they were disparaging to the relevant segment of the population [i.e., Native Americans] at the time of their registration. As a consequence, the marks had a tendency to bring Native Americans into contempt or disrepute. These findings were based primarily on a survey provided by the Petitioners, and the T.T.A.B. decided to cancel the registration of the word marks at issue, finding that the Petitioners' survey met their burden of proof by preponderance of the evidence. (Harjo, 1999)

The survey in question found that 46.2 percent of Native Americans questioned found the term *Redskin* offensive. The trademark board ruling against the

Washington Redskins was appealed, a legal process that could last for years. The offending imagery was, of course, still very visible.

In December 1996, *Indian Country Today* cartoonist Thom Little Moon presented two football helmets with stereotypical images, one for the Washington Blackskins and the other for the Kansas City Zulu Chiefs, asking, "Would African Americans like being mascots?" The National Coalition against Racism in Sports and the Media fashioned a poster that features pennants for imaginary sports teams—Fighting Jews, Blacks, Latinos, Orientals, and Caucasians—alongside the real pennant of the Washington Redskins (King, 2004, 197).

An online discussion at the right-wing chat room Free Republic (http://freerepublic.com/focus/f-news/993089/posts) discussed the ruling. Many political conservatives did not think that calling a team Redskins demeaned Native Americans:

> Judge Colleen Kollar-Kotelly found the litigant's case to be smelly, so Washington wins. Sing "Hail to the Redskins" and go put some beer in your belly.

> U.S. District Judge Colleen Kollar-Kotelly—where do I mail her a Christmas card?

> Yay! thank God for that too, otherwise the Fighting Irish would be sued by Irish people, and the Falcons would be sued by birdwatchers!

> At least they don't call themselves the "Washington Savages," or the "Washington Firewater Drinkers."

> I guess the Vikings now need not worry about changing their name. I myself would have no problems with a team being named Palefaces. (King, 2004, 189–90)

On September 30, 2003, a U.S. district court in Washington, DC, overturned the TTAB ruling initiated by Harjo's suit that had canceled federal protection of the Washington Redskins' trademarks. Although it found the team's trademarks to be disparaging, bringing Native Americans into contempt or disrepute, the district court decided that the plaintiffs had not met the burden of proof and had failed to file their complaint in a timely fashion (King, 2004, 189). And so the controversy rumbled on.

The connotations of words are socially constructed, and the emotive freight that we vest in them can change over time. One linguistic study asserts, for example, that *Redskins* began its career during the eighteenth century with none of the assumptions of insult it carries today. Smithsonian Institution senior linguist Ives Goddard has concluded that the word *redskin* was first used by Native Americans in the eighteenth century to distinguish themselves from the white others encroaching on their lands and culture. When it first appeared as an English expression in the early 1800s, "it came in the most respectful context and at the highest level," Goddard said in an interview. "These are white people and Indians talking together, with the white people trying to ingratiate themselves" (Gugliotta, 2005, A-3).

Harjo replied to Goddard's case, saying, "I'm very familiar with white men who uphold the judicious speech of white men. . . . Europeans were not using high-minded language. [To them] we were only human when it came to territory, land cessions and whose side you were on." Goddard, who was aware of the lawsuit and Harjo's arguments, replied that "you could believe everything in my article and still oppose current public usage of 'redskin'" (Gugliotta, 2005, A-3).

Likewise, the word *savage* was used in a more neutral tone (from an archaic French term meaning "dweller in the woodland") before Anglo-American aggressions of the nineteenth century turned it into a term of denigration. Benjamin Franklin, for example, wrote an essay that is quite complimentary toward Native Americans that he titled "Remarks Concerning the Savages of North America."

CLEVELAND'S INDIANS

The term *Indians,* on its face, is not overtly defamatory. Sometimes the context, not the name itself, is the problem. In the case of the Cleveland Indians, face value is the clincher—the face, that is, of stupidly grinning, single-feathered Chief Wahoo.

Demian Bulwa opened an essay in the University of California–Berkeley student newspaper following the 1995 World Series between the Atlanta Braves and the Cleveland Indians by describing a purported basketball game between the Philadelphia Amish and the New York Jews. "Do you find this tasteless and degrading?" he asked. "Do you feel as ludicrous reading it as I do writing it? If the answer is 'yes' to either of these questions, then you should feel very uncomfortable about this year's World Series" (Bulwa, 1995).

Cleveland entered professional baseball more than a century ago with a team named the Spiders; in the team's first year, the Spiders lost 134 games. Later, the team was called the Naps. The Cleveland Indian name was adopted by a vote of the fans in 1914. Chief Wahoo was created by a *Cleveland Plain Dealer* columnist during the 1940s. Chief Wahoo was first sewn onto Cleveland Indian uniforms in 1947.

In 1972, in the context of a lawsuit against the Cleveland Indians, Native activist Russell Means openly critiqued the Chief Wahoo image: "That Indian looks like a damn fool, like a clown and we resent being portrayed as either savages or clowns." Means did not content himself with an attack on stereotypes but turned to racial analogy to advance his argument against mascots. "Take the Washington Redskins.... Redskin is a derogatory name ... what if we called them the Washington Niggers, or Washington Rednecks, or Washington Polacks?" (King, 2004, 195).

Until 2000, the Cleveland Indians' official media guide maintained that the Indians name was adopted in honor of Louis Sockalexis, a Penobscot who played for the Spiders between 1897 and 1899. Therefore, many Indians fans boasted that the name was an honor, not an insult. The media guide first mentioned the Sockalexis story in 1968 (just as protests began to roll in from the new American Indian Movement).

Sockalexis was said to have been the first Native American to play in baseball's major leagues. It is unknown whether this is true, or spin control meant to turn a slur into an affirmative-action coup. In 1999, the media guide devoted an entire page to the Sockalexis story, which was coyly declared bogus a year later. In January 2000, the wording of the guide was changed, with the reference to Sockalexis taken as legend. The old version was proved factually inaccurate by Ellen Staurowsky, a professor at Ithaca College in New York, who maintains that the team should drop its Indian moniker. Any change could cost the baseball club a pretty penny, because Chief Wahoo is among the best-selling sports icons on clothing and other merchandise.

Sockalexis began playing baseball at Holy Cross College in Worcester, Massachusetts, less than five years after the 1890 massacre at Wounded Knee. He had grown up on the Indian Island reservation in Old Town, Maine. By 1897, he was playing baseball at Notre Dame, a school from which he was expelled after only a month because of public drunkenness. The Cleveland Spiders signed him for $1,500. At first, Sockalexis experienced something of a hitting streak. By the middle of his first season with the Spiders, he was hitting .335. It has been said that some fans "took to wearing Indian headdresses and screaming war whoops every time Sockalexis came to bat" (Nevard, n.d.). In July 1897, however, Sockalexis got drunk and injured himself. He spent most of the rest of his baseball career on the bench, before being released by the Spiders in 1899. For a decade after that, Sockalexis performed manual labor in Cleveland as he continued to suffer from alcoholism. He died in 1913. A novel based on his life, *The Cleveland Indian: The Legend of King Saturday,* was penned by Luke Salisbury in 1940.

ATLANTA'S BRAVES

Braves, like *Indians,* is not a problem name for many Native Americans. Most Native Americans are not thin-skinned enough to chafe at being called Indians or Braves. Rather, culture-demeaning antics invoked to ramp up team spirit in the name of the Braves, most notably the Tomahawk Chop, have been the rub. Sports legend has it that the Florida State Seminoles originated the Tomahawk Chop. For those who are not familiar with the ritual, the Tomahawk Chop involves the simultaneous lifting of arms (and, sometimes, sticks or ersatz tomahawks) to background music that could perhaps be described as the soundtrack to Henry Wadsworth Longfellow's "Hiawatha" on a bad-hair day.

Before it was called the Atlanta Braves, this major-league baseball team was the Boston Braves. Before that, it was the Boston Red Stockings, the Beaneaters, the Rustlers, and the Doves. In 1912, the name *Braves* was adopted. The Boston Braves baseball club later moved from Boston to Atlanta. Before it adopted the Tomahawk Chop at the behest of Ted Turner, the Atlanta Braves had Chief Noc-a-Homa, who did a stereotypical Indian dance outside his tepee every time the Braves hit a home run. Russell Means, a cofounder of AIM, criticized Noc-a-Homa: "What if they called them the Atlanta Storm Troopers and every time there was a home run a man in a German military uniform came out and knocked a few Jews on the head with a baseball bat? Or Atlanta Negroes, and an old black man came out of a shack and did a soft shoe dance?" (Carley, 1972).

In October 1995, when the Atlanta Braves arrived in Minneapolis for the World Series, they found more than 200 protesters arrayed at the stadium's gates, with placards reading (among other things), "500 Years of Oppression Is Enough." Minneapolis is AIM's home town, and even the mayor had made a statement calling on the Braves to sack their Indian imagery. When the Twins management asked the police to move the demonstrators farther from the Metrodome, they refused, citing the protestors' freedom of speech and assembly.

The Atlanta Braves' emphasis on Indian imagery has spawned a number of mascot wannabes, the best-known of whom is Tomahawk Tom, also known as Tom Sullivan, who previously worked as a management trainee at U-Haul. According to the *Atlanta Journal-Constitution,* Tomahawk Tom arrives at the ballpark "in an Indian headdress, a catcher's mask, and a cape" (Pomerantz, 1995). Tomahawk Tom was not officially sanctioned by the Braves, but he led fans in Tomahawk-chop cheers, signed autographs, and passed out free baseball cards to children. Sullivan also regarded himself as an inventor of an ice-cream treat called The (Tomahawk) Chop Pop.

Tomahawk Tom learned to walk gingerly, however, as protests against the Braves logo and the Tomahawk Chop intensified. In early October 1995, before a Braves playoff game, a Native American protester, Aaron Two Elk, took a swing at Tomahawk Tom, knocking his catcher's mask askew, as he told Tom that he was desecrating Native American cultures. Two Elk, a Cherokee, had become well known for his hand-written placards in a free-speech area near Hank Aaron's statue at the stadium's entrance. A week later, Sullivan called on Atlanta police for an escort into the ballpark. Sullivan henceforth was careful to enter the Braves' ballyard in street clothes, changing into his buckskins in a restroom, to avoid several dozen protestors who frequently gathered in the free-speech area, watched carefully watched by a dozen Atlanta police of the Red Dog squad.

INDIAN MASCOT CONTROVERSIES: A NATIONAL SAMPLER

The struggle over sports mascots can evoke anger and even violence. In the otherwise peaceful burg of West Hurley, New York (in the Catskills), a mascot struggle sparked a battle for control of a local school board. A ban on the use of racial images was enacted in April 2000 by the board governing the 2,300-student Onteora school district. The mascot then became the lead issue in a campaign for control of the school board. In May, supporters of the Indian image won a majority of board seats. In June, the school district's Indian imagery was reinstated.

In fall 2000, opponents of the Indian mascot found their cars vandalized, nails and screws driven into tires, and paint splattered, usually when the cars were parked at school board meetings. Tobe Carey, an opponent of the Indian mascot whose car was damaged, said that a climate of intimidation had made it impossible to speak at public meetings. Citizens working to remove racial stereotypes in the public schools had endured reprisals for 10 months, he said.

Supporters of Onteora's Indian imagery (which includes a tomahawk chop, ersatz totem poles in the school cafeteria, and various pseudo-Indian songs and dances) have been known to bristle at any suggestion that their images degrade Native Americans in any way. Joseph Doan, a member of the school board who voted to reinstate the Indian imagery, said that many white citizens see the Indian image as a symbol of honor and environmental protection. "Our Indian has nothing to do with degrading Indians. It's our symbol and we're proud of it," said Doan (Gormley, 2000). In West Hurley, the proms are called Tomahawk dances. Onteora has used Indian images since the 1950s. Until 1997, no one had formally complained when a student in buckskins led cheers at football games or when songs and dances mimicked Native American religious rituals.

Regarding Chief Illiniwek (an invented name), a many-year-old struggle continues at the University of Illinois–Urbana-Champaign. "The chief is a religious figure for Native American people and he doesn't belong as entertainment for drunk football fans at halftime," said Monica Garreton, a University of Illinois senior and anti-Chief activist. "It's comparable to Little Black Sambo and Amos 'n' Andy" (Badwin, 2000). Every Columbus Day since 1992, opponents of the Illiniwek imagery have held demonstrations on the University of Illinois campus.

In a paper titled "Chief Illiniwek: Dignified or Damaging?" Joseph P. Gone, a Gros Ventre, wrote:

> One primary obstacle to political and economic renewal and self-determination in Indian communities around the country is the appalling ignorance of most American citizens, including policymakers at local, state and federal levels of government, regarding Native American histories and cultures. As multidimensional peoples engaged in complex struggles for autonomy and equality … Indians are virtually invisible to the American consciousness, which gleans any awareness of natives from caricatured Hollywood portrayals, tourist excursions and, yes, popular symbols like Chief Illiniwek. Thus, the continued prevalence of Indian stereotypes fortifies a wall of misunderstanding between our peoples. ("Indian Mascots," 2000)

Marquette University has replaced the team name Warriors in favor of Golden Eagles. Dartmouth changed its Indians to Big Green, and Miami of Ohio changed Redskins to the RedHawks. At Seattle University, the Chieftains have become the Redhawks. In the meantime, producers of Crayola Crayons have done away with the color Indian Red (Badwin, 2000).

Roanoke, Virginia's, Blacksburg High School's faculty voted late in 2000 to retire the school's Indian mascot. Other schools in the Roanoke area also have changed their mascots. The Shawsville High Shawnees became the Colts, for example. A citizen coalition raised the issue in 1999, saying that the names "objectify Indians, teach negative stereotypes and abuse spiritual symbols such as eagle feathers" (Calnan, 2000). The University of California–San Diego retired its Aztec in fall 2000. At about the same time (in late September), Maine's Scarborough School Board voted to drop its Redskins nickname.

THE FIGHTING SIOUX'S BIGGEST FAN: A NAZI AFICIONADO

The battle over the University of North Dakota's (UND's) Fighting Sioux mascot has been notably acute in large part because of the role of Ralph Engelstad, the multimillionaire owner of the Imperial Palace casinos in Las Vegas and Biloxi, Mississippi. He also was the major donor for the $100 million Ralph Engelstad Arena at UND, his alma mater, where he had played hockey on scholarship during the 1950s. Engelstad was an astute investor, having purchased large amounts of land in Las Vegas, Nevada, before the gambling boom. He sold 145 acres to billionaire Howard Hughes that became the North Las Vegas airport. Engelstad, who was born on January 28, 1930, in Thief River Falls, Minnesota, died of cancer on November 26, 2002, in Las Vegas.

Engelstad assembled a collection of Nazi memorabilia in the Imperial Palace, including a painting of himself dressed in a Nazi uniform. On April 20, 1986 and 1988, he hosted birthday parties for Adolph Hitler in a special so-called war room at his casino, where he had parked one of Hitler's parade cars and Heinrich Himmler's Mercedes and hung a life-size portrait of Hitler bearing a faux inscription—"To Ralphie from Adolph"—along with portraits of naked women. The birthday cake was adorned with a swastika and was served with German food and marching music. Bartenders wore shirts that read "Adolph Hitler: European Tour—1939–1945" (LaDuke, 2005, 140–141).

Invoking his public idolatry of Hitler, the Nevada Gaming Commission in 1989 fined Engelstad $1.5 million for actions that damaged the reputation and image of Nevada's gaming industry. When students and faculty at UND complained that the university was taking money from a man with a Hitler fetish, however, the administration mumbled something about bad taste and Engelstad's rather weird sense of humor, then let the matter pass as the money rolled in.

As a condition of building the UND hockey arena, Engelstad required that the Fighting Sioux name be kept indefinitely. If it was not, Engelstad swore that he would leave the arena in an incomplete state. Thousands of Fighting Sioux logos were designed as permanent fixtures throughout the arena to make their future removal very inconvenient and expensive.

Most of the faculty in UND's Teaching and Learning Department petitioned the university's president to change its Fighting Sioux nickname, because, they contended, it dehumanizes Native American people (Benedict, 2000a, 2000b). On October 6, 2000, three UND students were arrested for blocking traffic in protest of the Fighting Sioux nickname. The local newspaper, the *Grand Forks Herald,* reported that these were the first arrests of students engaging in protest at UND since the days of the Vietnam War. The three arrested students, two of whom were Native American, were among a group of about ten who broke ranks with a march of more than a hundred people, a mixture of Native Americans and whites, who were protesting the mascot near UND's student union building.

Although the Fighting Sioux logo is still used, some schools with which North Dakota competes have refused to observe it. St. Cloud State University, for example, refuses to print the name on its tickets, and its game announcers do not use the name (Hofmann, 2005, 161).

THE RABBI AS NAZI SPORTS MASCOT

Perhaps with Engelstad in mind, Massachusetts Institute of Technology linguistics professor Noam Chomsky (who is Jewish) has delivered one of the most searing parodies of American Indian mascots. Chomsky asked what could have happened if Nazi Germany had won World War II and taken a liking for mythical Jews as sports mascots. The sharply acid tone of his satire reflects why many Native Americans believe that stereotypical Native caricatures demean their heritage and culture.

Chomsky imagines that sixty years after the Nazi victory in World War II, a prestigious German state university uses a sports mascot called the Rabbi. In Chomsky's tale, a student from the White Aryan Youth League dresses up in an authentic costume as a Hasidic Rabbi, complete with earlocks and beard. The sports teams call themselves the Fighting Jews; the school's band is called the Marching Jews. Sports fans wear jackets and T-shirts with pictures of the Rabbi stitched onto them. Owners of cars plaster Rabbi stickers on them. Replying to attempts to retire the Rabbi mascot, students and alumni campaign to "Save the Rabbi!" (Boyle, 2005)

This German state university plays soccer matches at the Nuremberg Stadium in front of an audience of about 75,000 White Aryans, almost all of whom are wearing pro-Rabbi images and clothes. "At half-time," writes Chomsky, "the Marching Jews take to the stadium floor and begin playing what they purport to be Jewish sounding music along the lines of Fiddler-on-the-Roof. Then all 75,000 White Aryans rise as one and shout in unison: 'Rabbi, Rabbi, Rabbi, Rabbi' gesticulating wildly and working themselves up into a feeding frenzy" (Boyle, 2005).

Meanwhile, one faculty member protests by shouting "Racist Rabbi!" after which everyone else in the vicinity throws garbage at him, as "the Rabbi runs out onto the arena floor from among the Marching Jews, proceeds to the center of the Nuremberg Stadium, and dances the Hava Nagila while the Marching Jews play on and march into an intricately choreographed maneuver that they all brag about and take special pride in that culminates with the band being organized into a swastika.... By now all 75,000 White Aryans are hysterical, shouting, screaming and yelling: 'Rabbi, Rabbi, Rabbi'" (Boyle, 2005).

This imagined ritual then concludes as nearly everyone joins hands to sing "Deutschland über Alles," with the Rabbi leading. Concluded Chomsky, "Then the Rabbi proceeds to dance the Hava Nagila out of the stadium followed by the Marching Jews. Everyone goes wild, clapping and cheering. This Rabbi ceremony brings tears to the eyes of many drunken alumni and students who had started several hours beforehand getting inebriated on schnapps and good German beer at pre-game tailgate parties" (Boyle, 2005). When it is all over, a visiting law professor from another country asks his host at the soccer match what this spectacle was all about. Without missing a beat the former dean of the law school turns to his guest and says, "We are honoring the Jews" (Boyle, 2005).

Along the same lines, opponents of the Fighting Sioux mascot concocted a fictional team named after Jews in Germany, the Auschwitz Money-Grubbing Jews, with the Lakota as the Fighting Sioux, contrasting the stereotype of greediness with the stereotype of savagery. The contrast clarifies that "both are proud people, minorities forcibly relocated in planned spaces of confinement, who were stereotyped, oppressed, murdered, dehumanized as objects, yet survived as people," even as most in the majority accepted their degradation (King, 2004, 201–2).

MASCOTS: THE RACIAL CONTEXT

Still, after all this, Chief Wahoo endures. The Tomahawk Chop seems to have assumed the kind of historical inevitability that a quarter-century ago was assigned to the Berlin Wall and the federal budget deficit: a rock-solid artifact of imperial popular culture. Ted Turner, who organized the Goodwill Games and gave $1 billion to the United Nations, has been unable, or unwilling, to touch the Tomahawk Chop. Why?

The December 1999 cover of *The Orange and Blue Observer,* a right-wing student newspaper at the University of Illinois–Urbana-Champaign, displayed beneath the publication's masthead a white gunslinger pointing a drawn pistol at an Indian dancer in full regalia, with the caption in large letters reading, "Manifest Destiny: Go! Fight! Win!" (Frueling and King, 2001).

"The U.S. government conducted a strenuous campaign to wipe out American Indian cultures, religions, and languages. American Indian children were forcibly taken from their families to boarding schools where they were physically punished if they spoke their tribal languages or tried to maintain their religious observances," commented Carol Spindel, who teaches writing at the University of Illinois–Urbana-Champaign and has authored *Dancing at Halftime: Sports and the Controversy over American Indian Mascots* (2000). "In a country that prides itself on religious freedom, the First Americans had none until 1934. Before this, Native people faced sanctions even when trying to conduct ceremonies and dances on their own reservations. One of the few historical incidents many of us do know about, the tragic massacre at Wounded Knee, took place because American Indians were gathering to dance at a religious ceremony that the government was determined to suppress. At the same time, Native cultures were being 'preserved' and 'appreciated' via sports mascots" (Spindel, 2005).

After all of this, some non-Indians, most of whom have not been notable for shedding much shoe leather marching for Native American rights under any other circumstances, continue to contend that they support Native American sports mascots because they are honoring the peoples of First Nations. Or, in Spindell's words, "At the same time that we were trying to destroy American Indian cultures, non-Native Americans loved to dress up and play Indian. What could be more American—we've been doing it since the Boston Tea Party. Mascot performances like Chief Illiniwek, a fictional chief who dances at Illinois on the 50-yard line at halftime, or Osceola, who gallops in at Florida State University games carrying a burning lance, trace their origins to the Wild West show, traveling big-tent performances that were part of the American circus tradition" (Spindel, 2005).

Tim Giago, publisher of the *Lakota Journal* and a nationally syndicated newspaper columnist, commented, "Would you paint your face black, wear an afro wig, and prance around a football field trying to imitate your perceptions of black people? Of course not! That would be insulting to Blacks. So why is it OK to do it to Indians?" (Nevard, n.d.).

Carolyn Fiscus, coordinator of Native American Studies at the University of Nebraska–Omaha, said that the continuing use of Native American logos can come down to pure demographic and economic clout. It expresses a power relationship between those who had the land and those who took it. "It's rare in this country that you see a people used like this. It's colonization and commoditization of a people." Native Americans often are too small a group to have much impact with protests, she said. Whereas, said Fiscus, "If every African-American quit going to Florida State, they wouldn't have a football team" (Wegner, 2005, D-2).

At Oklahoma State University, the student newspaper, the *Daily O'Collegian*, reported on September 27, 2005, that students who had scribbled "Scalp the Indians" on local walls defended their prank as an inoffensive expression of school spirit. "Would we dismiss 'Lynch the Negroes,' 'Gas the Jews,' or 'Deport the Latinos' as in the school spirit? What about students of a predominantly non-White school chalking 'Kill Whitey' when playing a predominantly Caucasian school?" asked Cara Cowen and B. J. Boyd in the *O'Collegian*, referring to the school's mascot. Cowen and Boyd, both of whom are Native American, commented that "This stereotypical imagery has become so ingrained in our environment we no longer recognize it for what it is" (Cowen and Boyd, 2005).

Within a few years of the Plains Indian Wars' conclusion in the late 1880s, William Cody (also known as Buffalo Bill) had recruited Sitting Bull, Black Elk, and a number of other Native leaders to appear in his signature acts, such as the Indian attack on the settler cabin, on the circled wagons, and on the stagecoach, all of which survived after the circus era as film and television clichés. Wild West shows were filmed and evolved into Westerns and broadcast around the world (Spindel, 2005). Buffalo Bill had a leg up on Chief Wahoo, however. At least Buffalo Bill used real people.

Spindell pointed out that many Native people enormously resent how superficially colleges appropriate their cultures for entertainment at sports events—ironic for institutions whose main purpose is education. The United States Commission on Civil Rights pointed this out in April 2001 when it urged non-Native colleges to retire American Indian imagery and names in sports.

Such practice does not wash well with other ethnic groups. One parallel symbol, wrote Spindell, "is Aunt Jemima, the slave cook who loved the plantation so much she didn't want to leave when she was freed. She is a white fantasy that denies and betrays the real history of slavery, just like the mascot Osceola. The real Osceola fought against American expansion into Seminole land and was betrayed when he came in good faith to a peace council with American soldiers. But his mascot reincarnation is happy to welcome Florida State fans" (Spindel, 2005).

The National Education Association passed a resolution in 2000, and restated it in 2005 that "rejects the use of names, symbols, caricatures, emblems, logos, and mascots that support ... prejudice" (National Education Association, n.d.). "Indian mascots are used today [as a form of] 'dysconscious racism' and a form of cultural violence. 'Dysconscious racism' ... accepts dominant White norms and privileges. For example, if you have seen these racial antics and negative behaviors portrayed by Indian mascots hundreds of times for most part of your life, you may become absolutely numb to it," said Dr. Cornel Pewewardy, an assistant professor in the School of Education at the University of Kansas ("Indian Mascots," 2000).

Pewewardy, who is Comanche and Kiowa, described how he once rewarded a group of kindergartners and first graders by taking them on a field trip to see the Minnesota Vikings play the Washington Redskins. As they were being escorted through the stadium, a group of adults decked out in fake war bonnets and face paint began taunting them, yelling, "Woo woo woo!" The children began crying in fear.

Pewewardy also recalled his own experience playing sports in high school. Fellow teammates would tease him when the school was about to play another school with an Indian mascot. His coach told him to ignore them and did nothing to stop the hazing. "I didn't know what to do with my feelings at that time.... It becomes a part of shaming," Pewewardy said. "I had no recourse but to suppress my feelings" ("Indian Mascots," 2000).

"So-called Indian mascots reduce hundreds of Indigenous tribes to generic cartoons," Pewewardy wrote in "Why Educators Can't Ignore Indian Mascots" ("Indian Mascots," 2000). Schools, said Pewewardy, "should be places where students come to unlearn the stereotypes such mascots represent."

After a visit by Pewewardy to schools in its circulation area, an editorial in the *Asheville* (North Carolina) *Citizen-Times* wrote:

> What's the big deal, many people, even some American Indians, ask about using Indian mascots for sports teams. They point to teams like the Appalachian State Mountaineers or the Notre Dame Fighting Irish to show that Whites are caricatured as mascots too, or to the Cherokee Braves to how that Indians also use Indian mascots. But there's a fundamental difference. It's one thing for predominantly White schools to caricature themselves, or for Indians to caricature themselves. For one culture to caricature another in such a way is demeaning and disrespectful.... Anyone who knows our history should recognize the racism inherent in these symbols. ("Indian Mascots," 2000)

The American Indian sports mascot issue surfaced in Asheville during the 1997–98 school year when some parents, teachers, and students at Erwin High School objected to the school's use of warrior and squaw mascots. The U.S. Justice

Department opened an investigation into a "racially hostile environment" at Erwin but dropped the probe in 1999 after reaching an agreement with the Buncombe County Board of Education, which agreed to stop using *squaw* to refer to the school's women's sports teams.

The North Carolina Commission of Indian Affairs in 2000 passed a resolution calling for elimination of Indian mascots and logos from all public schools in North Carolina by June 2003. Gov. Jim Hunt endorsed the resolution, pointing to "the impact such negative stereotyping has on the integrity of our public school curriculum" (Morrison, 2000). The resolution opposes the use of American Indian terms for naming mascots and logos because "Sports-team nicknames are considered offensive, disrespectful, demeaning, and they make a mockery of Indian people, their culture, their heritage, and their traditions" (Resolution, 2000).

The commission urged North Carolina's governor "to issue an executive order directing all state government and county agencies, all County Boards or Commissions, and all Boards of Education of each county in the state, to discontinue the use, and remove all references to, American Indian descriptions naming mascots, logos, and sports team nicknames from their policies, publications, instructional materials, signage, etc., by June 30, 2003" (Resolution, 2000).

C. Richard King, an experienced commentator on the mascots issue (King, 2002; King and Springwood, 2001a, 2001b; King, Staurowsky, Baca, Davis, and Pewewardy, 2002) wrote that "No one would think of doing to any other racial or ethnic group what mascots do to American Indians. Pseudo-Indian imagery makes Native Americans exceptional, subject to images that disrespect and dehumanize indigenous peoples in a fashion no longer conceivable, let alone acceptable for others" (King, 2004, 199). Having surveyed mascot opponents' attempts to demonstrate the strength of their case by parodying other ethnic groups, however, King commented, "It is troubling that the critical strategies deployed to demonstrate the inappropriateness and hurtful effects of Native American Mascots pivot around ugly images and ideas about other marginalized groups, often recycling them" (King, 2004, 207).

Commented Tim Wise in *Counterpunch,* "When Notre Dame chose to call themselves the Fightin' Irish, the school was made up overwhelmingly of Irish Catholics. In other words, it was Irish folks choosing that name for themselves. How many Indians do you think were really in on the decision to call themselves 'redskins,' or to be portrayed as screaming warriors on someone else's school clothing?" (Wise, 2005).

Wise recommended that if schools really wanted to honor Native peoples, they could establish Native American studies programs and fund them adequately and increase recruitment of Indian students, staff, and faculty rather than retreating from such efforts in the face of misplaced backlash to affirmative action. Wise said, "They could strip the names off of buildings on their campuses that pay tribute to those who participated in the butchering of Native peoples" (Wise, 2005). Wise suggested, for example, that Nashville, Tennessee, his home town, could begin by renaming, without delay, any building named after Andrew Jackson, who endorsed and enforced the Cherokee Trail of Tears in the face of a ruling by the U.S. Supreme Court. "Perhaps, most importantly," wrote Wise, "we could begin by telling the truth about what was done to the indigenous [peoples] of this land, rather than trying to paper over that truth, minimize the horror, and, once again, change the subject. You know the kind of people I'm speaking of: the ones who refuse to label the elimination of over ninety-five percent of the Native peoples of the Americas 'genocide'" (Wise, 2005).

MANIFESTING DESTINY

Mascots sometimes act as cartoon motifs for the Indian wars. On one occasion at the University of Illinois–Urbana-Champaign, several Fighting Illini boosters responded to American Indian students who were protesting Chief Illiniwek by erecting a sign that read "Kill the Indians, Save the Chief." And in the wake of the North Dakota controversy, faculty members who challenged the Fighting Sioux name have reported that supporters of the institution's symbol have repeatedly threatened those who oppose it (Frueling and King, 2001). The Florida State University Seminoles' football coach, Bobby Bowden, is known to scribble "Scalp 'em" underneath his autograph (Frueling and King, 2001).

In 1999, the *Knoxville News-Sentinel* published a cartoon in a special section commemorating the appearance of the University of Tennessee Volunteers at the Fiesta Bowl in Phoenix, Arizona. At the center of the cartoon, a train driven by a team member in a coonskin cap plows into a buffoonish caricature of a generic Indian, representing the team's opponent, the Florida State Seminoles. As he flies through the air, the Seminole exclaims, "Paleface speak with forked tongue! This land is ours as long as grass grows and river flows. Oof!" The Tennessee player retorts, "I got news, pal. This is a desert. And we're painting it orange!" Below them, parodying the genocide associated with the conquest of North America, Smokey, a canine mascot of the University of Tennessee, and a busty Tennessee fan speed down Interstate 10, dubbed "The New and Improved Trail of Tears." What effect can such a cartoon have on people whose ancestors were victims of the actual Trail of Tears? (Frueling and King, 2001).

THE NATIONAL COLLEGIATE ATHLETIC ASSOCIATION RULES AGAINST INDIAN MASCOTS

The NCAA's Executive Committee during summer 2005 barred from postseason tournaments the teams of 18 universities and colleges with Native American mascots, including three Braves, six Indians, and four specific Native national names (Seminoles, Utes, Chippewas, and Choctaws). In addition, the NCAA listed the Carthage College Redmen, the University of Illinois Fighting Illini and the Southeastern Oklahoma State—let us not bow to political correctness here—Savages.

One could suppose, without witnessing the symbols employed by the school, that *savages* could come from any ethnic group, but attendance at one Southeastern Oklahoma State athletic event would remedy that misconception. Arkansas

State University (Indians) was one of 18 schools with mascots described as "hostile or abusive" by the NCAA, according to an Associated Press report. Sun Belt Conference rival Louisiana-Monroe was also on the list, as were Florida State, Utah, Central Michigan, and Bradley.

The NCAA ruling stated that although the association has no authority to prohibit the use of Indian-theme mascots directly, it can govern the names of teams that take part in its postseason playoffs and other tournaments. Florida State University (FSU; home of the Seminoles) quickly hired an attorney to challenge the NCAA decision.

C. Richard King joked of FSU's reaction to the mascot ban, "Not since the disputed presidential election of 2000 had the leadership of Florida responded with such pronounced urgency to a social or political crisis. Talk of legal action, the convening of emergency meetings among policy makers, and the frenzied pace at which commentators expressed disbelief and disgust were not incited by the failings of public education, the debasement of civil liberties, growing economic inequities, or even the economic and ecological catastrophes associated with rising oil prices" said King (King, 2005). King then asked, "What is the state of democracy in Florida and the nation as a whole, nearly five years after the electoral crisis, when public institutions of higher education like Florida State University refuse teachable moments such as this to reflect upon core concepts such as inclusion, community, dignity, and equality? What will it take for the use of American Indian symbols and names in sports to end, and for indigenous people to be recognized as people?" (King, 2005).

According to Charles Frueling and King, "American Indian mascots directly contradict the ideals that most higher-education institutions seek—those of transcending racial and cultural boundaries and encouraging respectful relations among all people who live and work on their campuses. Colleges and universities bear a moral responsibility to relegate the unreal and unseemly parade of 'team spirits' to history" (Frueling and King, 2001).

Suzan Shown Harjo, director of Washington, DC's, Morningstar Institute, wrote in *Indian Country Today,* "Most of the commentators on this issue lump 'Indian' sports references in with the bears, tigers, banana slugs, geoducks and leprechauns. They don't seem to notice that they are species hopping from humans to creatures and mythical beings, and that only the 'Indians' are based on living people" (Harjo, August 11, 2005). She added, "The NCAA is learning what it's like to be mocked, cartooned, lampooned and vilified—in short, what it's like to be Indian in the world of sports. After only days of this treatment, the NCAA should appreciate even more keenly the importance of [its] decision to the health, safety and emotional well-being of Native and non-Native students, who are and should be their first concern.... It's the rough equivalent of the civil rights movement sending the message that the N-word is not acceptable in polite society. Is this PC? Yes, as someone said long ago, it's Plain Courtesy" (Harjo, August 11, 2005).

"It is shameful," wrote Harjo, "That the mighty Osceola is portrayed as a mascot. He is represented with fakey 'war paint,' which he never wore; on an Appaloosa horse, which he never rode; with a Plains Indian war lance, which he never used; acting the fool, which he never was; and performing for non-Indians—which he never, ever did" (Harjo, August 11, 2005). Florida State University asked the Seminoles (the real ones) to approve of its caricature, to which Harjo suggested that if Florida State University and that state's politicians were so desperate for political cover, the Seminoles should demand that the school change its name to Florida Seminole University. It would not even have to change its initials. While they are at it, FSU could call its team the Floridians and use St. Augustine as its mascot (Harjo, August 11, 2005).

Of the NCAA ruling, Keith Woods of the Poynter Institute, a journalistic think tank based in Florida, wrote:

> So impressed by the indomitable spirit of the Indian were schools like Florida State, we are now to believe, that they appropriated their name (at a time when, surely, they wanted nothing to do with actual Indians), invented a likeness, and now send a horse-borne student galloping across a football field before a tomahawking crowd in the name of honor and respect. The irony takes my breath away.... Here in Florida, where rancorous debate is a redundancy ... no less than the governor [Jeb Bush] has declared the N.C.A.A. policy the work of renegades. He, like the hyperbolic president of Florida State University and the columnists who support them, huff on about the blessing the school has gotten from the Florida tribe and the great Seminole tradition F.S.U. honors. (Woods, 2005)

Former Senator Ben Nighthorse Campbell, who is Cheyenne, called the NCAA's decision "a major step forward" and "a positive, important decision." Campbell said, "A lot of people need help understanding that it's wrong to use any derogatory name for a sports team. When I explain to African-Americans that it would be like a team called the 'Washington Darkies,' they understand. When I ask Hispanics how they would feel about a team called the 'Spics,' they understand" (Harjo, August 11, 2005). Campbell said he had introduced a bill in the U.S. Senate that would have prevented the Washington Redskins from using federal property, including the Robert F. Kennedy Stadium in Washington, DC. Jack Kent Cooke, the team's owner, moved the team to the Virginia suburbs before the bill was passed (Harjo, August 11, 2005).

The NCAA's decision drew a rebuke from the right-wing *National Review*, in which Peter Wood, provost of The King's College in New York City, wrote in an article titled "The Diversity Bowl: No Admittance to the Abusively Named":

> College-sports nicknames and mascots were a natural target for the purveyors of a politics of racial resentment.... In the broader culture wars, the fight over Indian nicknames is a loser for conservatives. The Alcorn State University Braves, the Central Michigan University Chippewas, the Mississippi College Choctaws, and the University of Utah Utes will have to go it alone. I don't believe for a second that these names were adopted with malice; that they are hostile; or that anyone is "abused" by them. They do, however, have the capacity to irritate people, and it is hard to be on the side of chaffing when no really compelling

principle favors it…. A stale conformity will … settle over this aspect of college sports—and America will be just a little bit poorer for the loss of historical reference and cultural exuberance. (Wood, 2005)

Shortly after the NCAA issued its ruling, appeals for exemptions surfaced. Florida State University, for example, was allowed on August 23, 2005, to continue use of the nickname Seminoles because the university had asserted a unique relationship with the Seminole tribe of Florida, which had approved the university's use of the name. The University of Utah and Central Michigan State University also gathered the American Indian support required by the NCAA to retain their mascots. On appeal, the NCAA in May 2006, refused to allow exemptions for the University of North Dakota Fighting Sioux, the University of Illinois Fighting Illini, and the Indiana University of Pennsylvania Indians.

Tim Giago, editor and publisher of the *Lakota Journal,* suggested that if the Seminole Nation so approves of FSU's mascot, "The chairman of the Seminole Nation should attend the next FSU football game and allow the fans to put a collar and leash around his neck and lead him around the 50-yard line at halftime." "If anyone wants to honor Indians," Giago wrote, "honor our treaties" (Giago, 2005, 7-B).

PUTTING THE MOCCASIN ON THE OTHER FOOT: THE FIGHTING WHITIES

A singular moment in the history of the mascot controversy occurred in February 2002, when an intramural basketball team at the University of Northern Colorado composed of Native American, Latino, and European American students collectively decided to change its name from Native Pride to the Fighting Whites. The new name was a purposeful parody of North America's many Native American mascots, most notably nearby Eaton High School's Fighting Reds. It was the first time in popular memory that a multiethnic sports team had decided to adopt a European American stereotype as a mascot. A dozen college students on an intramural basketball team suddenly found themselves playing in the stereotypical big leagues.

The team printed a few T-shirts (their uniform of choice) bearing the team's new name and created a logo—a suited, clean-cut white man with a bland smile on his face—and the slogan "Everythang's Gonna Be All White." Thus ensued a wave of nearly instant, continent-wide publicity that stood the long-standing debate over the decency of Native sports-team mascots on its head. The Fighting Whities (as they came to be called) set thousands of virtual tongues to wagging. Everyone had an opinion on them, from the American Indian Movement to affiliates of the Ku Klux Klan. The reactions provided a flash-frozen image of racial humor in an age of political correctness.

Within weeks, the Fighting Whities had become nearly as well known as established professional monikers such as the Washington Redskins and the Cleveland Indians. A cursory Internet search under "Fighting Whities" (on Google.com) turned up 4,700 hits; "Fighting Whites" provided 2,930 Web-page mentions—something of a media feeding frenzy for a mascot that had not existed three months earlier. The publicity helped sell thousands of T-shirts and other items for a hastily endowed scholarship fund to aid Native American students. By the end of 2002, more than $100,000 had been raised for the fund (Cornelius, 2002).

As the official home page of the Fighting Whites explained, in a statement written by Ryan White (who is Mohawk), John Messner, and Charles Cuny, "We came up with the 'Fighting Whites' logo and slogan to have a little satirical fun and to deliver a simple, sincere, message about ethnic stereotyping. Since March 6 [2002], when our campus newspaper first reported on the Fighting Whites, we have been launched into the national spotlight, propelled by a national debate over stereotyping American Indians in sports symbolism" ("Fighting Whities," 2002).

The Fighting Whites' parody very quickly sprang from the sports pages to the front pages. From the student newspaper, the story spread to the *Greeley Tribune,* then over the state, regional, and national wire services. Some of the stories popped up as far away as the *London Guardian.* The Whities also were contacted by Fox Sports Net and NBC News, among many other electronic media. Soon, the Fighting Whites had developed at least nine T-shirt designs for sale on an Internet site, with receipts fueled by publicity in many major daily newspapers, electronic news outlets, and such other large-audience venues as the *Tonight Show* with Jay Leno. The effect on sales was downright salubrious. Soon the merchandise was available not only on T-shirts but also on sweatshirts, tank tops, baseball jerseys, several styles of caps, a coffee mug, boxer shorts, and mouse pads.

On the court, the Whities confessed that they were hardly championship caliber, but soon their prowess at basketball did not matter. Their reputation soon had very little to do with dribbling, jumping, or shooting and more to do with the incendiary nature of the ongoing debate regarding Native American names for sports teams. Brooks Wade, a member of the Fighting Whites who is a Choctaw and an employee at the University of Northern Colorado Native American Student Services told the *Rocky Mountain News* on March 15, 2002, "It's a huge media rush. It kind of snowballed out of control, really. We started it as more of a protest so we could change things in our little world, and suddenly it's worldwide" (BeDan, 2002, 12-A).

The original protest had been aimed at Eaton High School's Indian mascot, the Fighting Reds, after one of the Fighting Whites' wives resigned a job there in anger over the issue. The protest parody quickly cut a much wider swath. Solomon Little Owl, a Crow, whose wife resigned at Eaton, was director of the University of Northern Colorado Native American Student Services when he joined the team. Kacy Little Owl (who is European American), Little Owl's wife, taught special education at the high school seven miles north of Greeley for two years before leaving at the end of the previous school year (Garner, 2002).

"The message is, let's do something that will let people see the other side of what it's like to be a mascot," said Little Owl ("Fighting Whities," 2002). The Whities had reason to agree with a comment on the *Wampum Chronicles* message board, a Native American Web site: "They'll swamp the country with publicity which has everyone laughing at their opponents, all the while our boys will be laughing all the way to the bank. Way to go, Fighting Whities. Give 'em hell" (Wampum Chronicles, n.d.).

Little Owl said that the couple, as parents of a son who is half European American and half Native, felt uncomfortable mingling with townspeople at school events, especially at ball games where Eaton High School's large-nosed Indian caricature was the prominent team symbol. "It was offensive in its own way," said Little Owl (Garner, 2002).

WHO WAS INSULTING WHOM?

The Eaton Fighting Reds found themselves unwillingly sucked into the tornado of publicity created by the Fighting Whites' parody. The defenders of the Fighting Reds did not take kindly to the notion of basking unwillingly in the reflected glory of the Fighting Whites. According to a report in the *New York Daily News,* "School officials have been unresponsive to the protests of local Native American activists. John Nuspl, the school district superintendent, has said the Indian logo is not offensive but that the Fighting Whities are insulting. Yesterday, a school official would only offer, 'The Eaton school district has no comment, but thank you for your call.'" The inquiring sports writer was then disconnected (Bondy, 2002). A reporter for the Associated Press was told by Nuspl that Eaton's logo is not derogatory. "There's no mockery of Native Americans with this," Nuspl said. As for the Fighting Whites, he said, "Their interpretations are an insult to our patrons and blatantly inaccurate" ("Team Chooses," 2002).

The reaction of Eaton's school superintendent brought to light an unintended irony that dogged the Fighting Whites wherever their newly minted name went: Many people who had no problem with naming a sports team after a Native American image became profoundly offended when the same thing was done, tongue in cheek, with a European American mascot. GOPUSA, a Colorado Web page of "Republican resources," declared the naming of the Whities a case of "Political correctness gone mad!" (GOPUSA, 2002)

Aside from a small number of people in Eaton and one editorial writer in Omaha (described in a later paragraph), most white people harvested a belly laugh or two from the parody. Some commentators went out of their way to show that, as European Americans, they could take a joke. Another virtual commentator had a suggestion for Fighting Whities team colors: "Off-white and Velveeta Cheese yellow!" ("Mr. Cranky," 2002).

Rush Limbaugh, the popular radio commentator, used the controversy to demonstrate his appreciation of all stereotypes: "Now, I think that's great! The team chose a white man as its mascot to raise awareness of stereotypes that some cultures endure. I love this, and it doesn't offend me at all! I'd be proud to be on the team—which is the difference here. There isn't a white person around that's going to be offended by this" (Limbaugh, 2002).

Limbaugh, who called Native Americans "Injuns" in this commentary, aimed perhaps to show that he is as good at taking ethnic stereotypes as he has been at dishing them out. "That's great!" he said. "I had to laugh and laugh on the air" (Limbaugh, 2002). Limbaugh disagreed with Eaton's offended school superintendent: "Now, come on. This is not insulting, Whitie; it's funny" (Limbaugh, 2002). "If these Native Americans had wanted to offend," Limbaugh continued, "They could have come up with something a lot worse than the Fighting Whities.... What's going to happen is you're going to have a bunch of civil-rights groups led by Jesse Jackson saying, 'You can't do that!' Still, it's just too good. The Fighting Whities? It just rolls off the tongue. Who wouldn't want to be on that team?" (Limbaugh, 2002).

The Fighting Whities nearly sent Limbaugh into rhapsody: "In fact, let's rename the 101st Airborne Division the 'Fighting Whities.' I mean, can't you see that painted on some Air Force squadron, on the tail of a bunch of F-16s: the Fighting Whities—and paint the airplanes all white. Oh-ho! I'll guarantee you that this is not going to fly well with the NAACP crowd, folks, because it's good, the Fighting Whities. I really do wish that I had authored this" (Limbaugh, 2002).

Barry Benintende, executive editor of the *La Jolla* (California) *Light,* loved the idea almost as much as Limbaugh. "In this day and age it's tough to come up with a nickname for an athletic department [or] team that won't offend at least some portion of the population," he wrote in the publication's March 2002 edition. "Short of naming every school or pro-sports team 'the Vanillas,' someone is going to have their knickers in a twist over a nickname. Well, speaking of vanilla, let me bring up the name of my favorite sports team of all time, edging out the Banana Slugs of UCSC [University of California–Santa Cruz]—'Fighting Whities.' The slogan they adopted—'Every thang's gonna be all white!'—is pure genius." "Sadly," lamented Benintende, only the most self-conscious whites were offended by the turnabout. "What was intended to turn the tables on insensitivity and support for teams like the Redskins, et al., the reaction shocked the team founders: Caucasians not only loved the name but sent them congratulatory e-mails and requests to buy Fighting Whities jerseys" (Benintende, 2002).

Benintende continued, "I'm a fan of the San Diego Padres, who could be seen as offensive to Catholics. Instead, many of us find the Swinging Friar a lovable guy with whom to identify, much like we would a briefcase-toting Middle-America dad type" (Benintende, 2002). Like many other commentators, Benintende used the Fighting Whities parody to take issue with an April 2001 U.S. Commission on Civil Rights opinion that said Indian-themed sports teams may violate antidiscrimination laws and should be dropped. "Does this commission finding also apply to the Fighting Irish at Notre Dame? The Celtics of Boston? And why limit it to sports teams? Does the name Rabbinical School Dropouts offend Jewish people who do not listen to the Klezmer band?" (Benintende, 2002).

One virtual tongue wagged at *The Geekery: Biased and Unbalanced News:*

> See, this is what I'm talking about. Racial stereotypes got you down? Now you can reverse the stereotypes back on your oppressors and not receive ANY backlash whatsoever. God, I love this country. This is probably the best idea any minority has ever had, next we just need a baseball team, maybe "the Atlanta Trailer Park Trash" or "the Nebraska Rednecks" Hell, let's not stop there. Let's branch off into rugby to and have "the Preppy White Boys from Upper-class Neighborhoods that Look Down upon Every Color they have Only Seen on TV." The possibilities are endless. (Geekery, 2002)

Clarence Page, a syndicated columnist based at the *Chicago Tribune* (who is black) opined, tongue in cheek, "Sometimes offense is the best defense" (Page, 2002). Page remarked that network television, major newspapers, and radio talk shows had made the Fighting Whites the best-covered intramural squad in the nation. The *Greeley Tribune's* Web site crashed when demand for the story soared to 29,000 from the usual 200 hits per day for a high-interest local story (Page, 2002).

Yet, quipped Page, "Caucasians have proved to be remarkably resistant to offense. Many agreed with an e-mailer who saw the new name as an 'honor' to white Americans, who apparently don't get enough credit for their many contributions to history" (Page, 2002). "Help me out here," asked one e-mail to the *Greeley Tribune.* "Why am I supposed to be offended?" (Page, 2002).

In Page's opinion:

> Whether their experiment turned out the way they expected to or not, the Fighting Whites deserve to go to the head of the class for giving us all at least one important lesson in cross-cultural differences: It's not what you slur that counts, it is who is slurring it—and how…. As an African-American who has heard more than my share of slurs, I can tell you: to be truly offensive, it helps for a slur to carry at least a hint of a threat…. Most Redskins fans undoubtedly mean no harm by their passivity about their team's name. If it reminds some Indians of the days when there were bounties on Indian scalps, that's just tough tomahawks, pal. (Page, 2002)

"So," Page concluded, "I give the Fighting Whites credit for keeping their wit about them. Humor often opens doors that battering rams fail to budge. If nothing else, they've stumbled across an unusual way to raise scholarship money. It's like the old saying: If you can't beat 'em, make a few bucks off 'em" (Page, 2002).

The texture and potency of assumed insult soon became the main point of debate for many European Americans. "Some people online were saying that the mascot should be … a fat guy with buckteeth kissing his sister," said Tom Crebbs of Oakland, California, who heard about the idea and started his own Web site selling spin-off shirts, hats, and mugs ("Fighting Whities, n.d.). Michael Gonsalves of New York told the Associated Press: "If you are fighting against a perceived injustice, is the proper recourse to go out and do the very same thing?" ("Fighting Whities," 2002).

Dimitri Vassilaros, a columnist for the *Pittsburgh Tribune-Review,* asserted that no one would give a mascot name to a "business or pet" that carried negative connotations, as other commentators asserted that the notion of making a pet of an ethnic group was derogatory in and of itself. George Junne, a professor in the University of Northern Colorado's Africana Studies Department said that a mascot "is like a pet. People don't want to be pets" (Good, 2002).

Vassilaros, who is a Greek American, wrote that is "just my luck" that "drunken college frat brothers [are called] 'Greeks.'" He asked, "Are there any white men who feel violated whenever they see Fighting Whities mascots such as the Schenley Spartans, Peabody Highlanders, Central Catholic Vikings, North Catholic Trojans, Duquesne Dukes, or even the Quaker Valley Quakers?" In his court of public opinion, Vassilaros found that "The perpetually offended are intellectually bankrupt" (Vassilaros, 2002). A radio station, WOOD Newsradio 1300 in Grand Rapids, Michigan, conducted an on-air poll, asking, "Do you think a basketball team named the 'Fighting Whities' is racially insensitive?" The results: 84.19 percent "no," 15.81 percent "yes" (Newsradio, 2002).

A number of commentators assumed that the members of the Fighting Whites had set out to offend non-Indians, even after a number of newspaper pieces quoted them as saying this was not the case. Usually, such allegations were aired as the commentator strove to display his or her open-mindedness. An example was provided by John Ledbetter, a columnist for the *Destin* (Florida) *Log,* writing under the headline "Cantankerous Caucasian Fights Back," who wrote:

> Offended? I want one of his team's T-shirts. They feature a white dude with a coat and tie and slicked-back hair. He looks like an I.R.S. agent on crack, which isn't a bad name for a team either. But really, if offending us honkies was Owl's criteria for success, he may want a job with the visa department in the I.N.S. [Immigration and Naturalization Service]. It's just not that often that an angle on the Anglos is spun toward something fierce or feisty. Unless you're Scandinavian—Vikings—or from Ireland—Fightin' Irish—there's not a lot of scrappy Caucasians that end up on banners in an auditorium. Of course, if you're Irish you're fighting because you're drunk—and a happy St. Patrick's Day to you too. I'm also part Irish, allegedly, so kiss my blarney if you're offended. And I'm even a lawyer. Now, talk about a maligned group. The San Jose Sharks today rejected a plan to name their team the San Jose Barristers. Ha! (Ledbetter, 2002)

A few commentators criticized the moniker. An editorial in the *Omaha World-Herald* called the Whities parody an ineffective insult. In an editorial titled "'Whities' on the Court; Insult Doesn't Work if Name Doesn't Hurt," the newspaper said, "The lack of deep, personal insult in the term 'white' may reflect the inequality of racial relationships. Because the majority typically has more power—political, economic, social—than minorities, its members are not so likely to feel diminished by words of contempt" ("Whities," 2002).

NOT OFFENSIVE ENOUGH?

The *World-Herald* argued that "The white population is in the majority and lacks the depth of race consciousness needed to make a group sensitive to name-calling. Break whites down into smaller ethnic groups, however—everyone is familiar with the disrespectful names for Jews, Irish, Italians, French-Canadians and so on—and the anger can surface quickly" ("Whities," 2002). By the *World-Herald's* reasoning, perhaps the Fighting Knee-Knocking Norwegians might have been more effective. The editorial continued, "'The Reds' is a generic-enough name that the Greeley high school could easily move from an Indian logo to something less potentially offensive. Neither the Cincinnati Reds nor Nebraska's Big Red refers to ethnicity" ("Whities," 2002).

The *World-Herald's* editorial writer composed this piece without checking how the mascot was being depicted at Eaton High School. Although Big Red is characterized visually by Herbie Husker, definitely a down-home farm boy, the Eaton mascot is a no-bones-about-it American Indian, which was described by Owen S. Good of the *Rocky Mountain News* as "a cross-armed, shovel-nosed, belligerent caricature" (Good, 2002).

The *World-Herald* was too polite to let loose with the names it might use to address the Fighting Whites' asserted lack of racist vigor. Another commentator was not as shy, providing a number of very specific team names meant to insult white people, including "White Slaveowners; Light-Skinned Nigger-Killers; Fighting Crackers; Blue-Eyed Devils; The Rhythm Lackers; The Small Penises; The Non-Dancers; The Big House Massas." The same author commented, "I suggest that, if they really want to get their point across, and they really want to do the equivalent of names like 'Redskins,' I think names like these more accurately represent the negative stereotyping of names like 'Redskins' and the use of images of the 'savage' American Indian" ("T. Rex Essay," 2002).

Some European Americans evidenced severe offense at the use of a white mascot and became very eager to pay back the perceived insult a thousandfold. One militant white nationalist Web page characterized the Fighting Whities parody this way:

> Some redskins on an intramural basketball team up at the University of Northern Colorado got their feathers all in a bunch recently and decided to show white folks—and especially those at nearby Eaton High School, whose motto is "Fightin' Reds," and whose logo is a caricature of an Indian—how insulting it is to have their identity pre-empted this way. Damn, didn't the Sambo's Restaurant chain get into heap big trouble with blackskins and have to change their name because black folks found it offensive to be portrayed as anything less than nuclear physicists? If the blackskins can back whiteskins down so easily, then certainly redskins can do the same thing. (Millard, 2002)

The same site offered links to another site seeking orders for its own European American icon: a T-shirt portraying Knights of the Ku Klux Klan in white sheets burning a cross above lettering reading "The Knight Time's the White Time" (Johansen, 2003).

SERIOUS DEBATES NATIONALLY

Aside from a debate over who was offending whom, the Fighting Whities parody provoked a great deal of serious debate regarding the mascot issue. Student editorialists at the University of Illinois *Daily Illini,* where a controversy has long raged regarding the school's Chief Illiniwek mascot, suggested that the Fighting Whities take its place.

> When University Board of Trustees member Roger Plummer addressed the board about Chief Illiniwek, he said the board has two decisions. Alas, at this prestigious University, we must strive for excellence. That's why Scout was disappointed to see Plummer did not suggest the University adopt The Fighting Whities, the symbol a group of students in Colorado used to make a point. The school could keep "Fighting" on all its merchandise. Just scratch out "Illini." People couldn't call it offensive because it's actually just taking the idea of the Fighting Irish to the next level. ("Campus Scout," 2002)

"In sports," the *Daily Illini* editorial concluded, "There's nothing better than taking it to the next level. In life, there's nothing better than poking a little fun at yourself. The students like 'The Fighting Whities,' too. Scout's received numerous e-mails supporting the suggestion" ("Campus Scout," 2002).

Tanyan Barrientos, a *Philadelphia Inquirer* columnist, took issue with a survey conducted by Harris Research, previously described in the March 4, 2002, edition of *Sports Illustrated,* which asserted that only 32 percent of Indians living on reservations believed Indian names and mascots used by professional sports teams contributed to discrimination against them. Sixty-seven percent said they did not, according to this survey. The same survey stated that the proportion of Native Americans not living on reservations who perceived no discrimination in Indian team names or mascots was even higher, at 83 percent.

"Surprised?" asked Barrientos. "I was."

> Perhaps I should lighten up. But my gut tells me that Chief Wahoo is wrong. He smacks of a Sambo, a lawn jockey, or one of those Mexicans sleeping under a broad-brimmed sombrero. There has to be a good reason why 600 schools, minor-league teams, and other pro-sports franchises have dropped or changed their Indian names and mascots since 1969. (Barrientos, 2002)

Bob DiBiasio, vice president for public relations for the Cleveland Indians, had told Barrientos that Chief Wahoo was never meant to be a racist logo and that "if there is no intent to demean, how can something demean?" "Tell that," he concluded, "to the Fighting Whities" (Barrientos, 2002).

A DEMONSTRATION IN EATON

On Sunday, May 20, 2002, Eaton High School's 450 students found themselves an unwilling audience for a rally against its Fighting Reds mascot. The protest was held one day after the Eaton High School Fighting Reds baseball team had claimed the Class 3-A state championship. The May 20 demonstration also coincided with Eaton High School's graduation ceremony, which was held during the afternoon, after the rally had dispersed.

The Eaton police rehearsed for weeks in anticipation of the event and called in reinforcements from nearby Ault as well as the Weld County Sheriff's Office. "We are prepared to handle this event," said Sgt. Arthur Mueller of the Eaton Police Department. "We don't anticipate problems, but we do have several contingency plans in place" (Ochoa, 2002). These included mounted horse patrols, a K-9 unit, police teams patrolling the perimeter of the demonstration, officers mingling through the crowd, as well as officers posted on nearby rooftops. "We will have zero tolerance when there is an issue of safety for the officers, participants or residents," Mueller said. "And we will have zero tolerance for the destruction of private property or public property" (Ochoa, 2002). Unarmed security guards trained by AIM also planned to provide added security to the rallying group. Dozens of local and county police, on foot and on horseback, as well as private security guards awaited the protesters.

The mile-long Eaton Mascot Education March and Rally started at 9:30 A.M. in eastern Eaton at the intersection of East Fifth and Wall Streets. The marchers strode westward on Fifth Street, turning south on Park Avenue, stopping for a noon rally at Eaton Park, at Third Street and Park Avenue.

As the rally concluded, some 300 marchers promised to return next year, and the year after that, until the mascot image was retired. Coloradans against Ethnic Stereotyping in Colorado Schools wanted nearly forty elementary, middle, and high schools statewide to change American Indian mascots that it believed are hurtful and racist.

"This is our introduction to Eaton on how to live respectfully," said Russell Means, a founder of AIM and a longtime national activist for Native American rights. "If Eaton wants to put up with this every year for their graduation, then so be it" (Migoya, 2002). According to a report in the *Denver Post,* "Protesters marched through town—drums beating, chants rising—on their way to Eaton City Park. There were speeches of heritage and strife, racism and tolerance.... They're upset, saying we ruined their graduation," Means said. "With this [mascot], they ruin every single day of our lives" (Migoya, 2002).

At his home across from Eaton's park, Leslie Smith hung a quiet proclamation of loyalty for the American Indian mascot: computer printouts of the Eaton mascot in red. A red tape surrounded the home. "They have their right to speak and so do we," said Steve Smith, Leslie's son and lifelong Eatonite. "We've listened to what they have to say. Now they can leave" (Migoya, 2002). The protesters included persons from several races from Colorado and several surrounding states. "We're reverencing the Eaton logo. It's an honor to [American Indians]. They're nothing but a bunch of communists and they're invading our territory" Steve Smith said (Darst, 2002).

Newspaper reports suggested that a compromise was being considered. Protesters, led by the organization's founder, Dan Ninham, called for the removal of the mascot image, not the Fighting Reds name, according to Philip Arreola, a member of the U.S. Department of Justice Community Relations Service, who worked with the city and protesters to ensure a peaceful demonstration (Migoya, 2002).

Fred Gibbs, a fifth-generation Eaton High graduate, said he could not understand why some people chose to be offended by a symbol that most people in Eaton (he assumed) considered a respectful honor to American Indians. The mascot was called "a tough little warrior that we're very proud of," by Gibbs, who was watching from his front lawn. "None of us feels like it's a negative portrayal" (Good, 2002).

Means, who is well-known in Denver for demonstrating against the city's Columbus Day parade, said there was nothing even remotely honorable about using American Indian images as sports mascots. "It [comes from] the day when only the fiercest animals were used as team mascots—Lions, Tigers," Means said. "That's what Indians are to these teams, the fiercest of beasts" (Good, 2002). Means suggested that next year's demonstration might confront the school's graduation ceremony directly. "We have a year to convince the school board to dissuade us from attending," Means said (Good, 2002).

EVALUATING THE WHITIES IN IDEOLOGICAL CONTEXT

Internet blogger Bob Maxim wrote on an Internet page devoted to anarchist causes that "Acceptance of racial stereotypes of 'Indians' ... is not only more widespread than any other race, but actually ingrained so steadfastly into the American culture that most people don't see what all the fuss is about" (Maxim, 2002). The proponents of Native American mascots often profess no malice; indeed, they loudly broadcast an admiration of their own stereotyped creations. Sometimes this sense of respect can be taken to absurd lengths, as when some European Americans defend the use of the word *squaw* as a place-name with full knowledge that it originated as a reference to Native women's vaginas. However, wrote Maxim, "The fact is ... [that] disrespect ... is disrespect in the eyes of the offended, not the offender" (Maxim, 2002).

The use of a prototypical European American figure as a mascot for a sports team (even a minor, intramural one) ignited an explosion of debate illustrative of a touchstone issue that has inflamed tempers for years. Maxim proposed that the offensiveness of native stereotypes be tested by using other ethnic caricatures in their places. For example, wrote Maxim:

> Take any name and caricature and change the stereotype and tell me if it seems offensive to your own sensibilities. For example, ask yourself if you would feel

offended if they announced they were changing the Washington Redskins to the Washington "Blackskins," and put a flared-nostrilled caricature of Kunta Kinte on the helmets, or a crazed-eyed Zulu Warrior with a bone in his nose wielding a spear. Do you think folks would argue that they were honoring black people, and their noble fighting spirit?" (Maxim, 2002)

Maxim continued, "How about the Fighting Kikes, or Wops ... or a Boston favorite, The Washington Micks? Imagine the Washington 'Whiteskins,' with a caricature of George W. [Bush] on the helmet" (Maxim, 2002). With a sense of gentle sarcasm, that was the message that the Fighting Whities chose to send. The noise with which the message was received is illustrative of the perceptual power of images.

Why are sponsors of Native American mascots so possessive of their fantasy images? The Fighting Whites (or Whities) spawned intense controversy by doing just that, igniting controversy on a profoundly sensitive issue. Why is the issue so sensitive? In his foreword to *Team Spirits,* Vine Deloria Jr. identifies several reasons: residues of racism, a sense of the Indian as other, and the fact that "Indians represent the American past, and Europeans and Americans have been fleeing from their own past since the days of discovery and settlement" (King and Springwood, 2001b, ix, x). These images are, King and Springwood remark, ideological artifacts reflecting attitudes toward "race, power, and culture" (King and Springwood, 2001b, 1). The defense of Native American mascots by non-Natives can be seen as enforcement of a sense of conquest, of a reminder that European Americans now set the perceptual rules. For all of these reasons, a parody created by an intramural basketball team in a small Colorado college town set off a firestorm of debate.

Two years after creating a firestorm of controversy, the Fighting Whites were still around, set on using humor to bring attention to the use of Indian mascots. The intramural basketball team at the University of Northern Colorado has given $100,000 to the college for the Fighting Whites Minority Endowment Scholarship Fund, but there are indications that the founders of the team may be changing tactics, a change attributed to frustration over the college and the use of mascots in general.

C. Richard King, an experienced commentator on the mascots issue, concluded that the Fighting Whities had worked as an interracial joke but not as a political object lesson. "Although a financial success," he wrote, "the Fighting Whites were a critical failure. The protest voiced in the name change went unheard by most. In many respects, the Fighting Whites was an over-determined project, doomed from its inception. In contrast to comparisons with other oppressed racial groups, such as African Americans or Jews, the analogy with whiteness neither interrupts the workings of racial common sense, nor invokes moral authority through trauma, marginalization, and violence. Judging from the public response, the Fighting Whites seem to confirm, rather than challenge, white-supremacist America—a white-centered, white-identified, and white-dominated society" (King, 2004, 205–6).

MOVING ON MASCOTS IN WISCONSIN

In the meantime, the mascots controversy roiled on. Wisconsin's state schools superintendent Elizabeth Burmaster sent a letter in December 2005, asserting that local officials should scuttle American Indian mascots and logos. School officials in a handful of western Wisconsin communities that display Indian names and images said that they would resist the change, however, asserting that "an Indian name or image is an important part of a school's identity [as] some say they have already worked to remove offensive caricatures from their logos." "It's a huge source of pride, and that's why it's such an issue," said Mike McMartin, principal of Osceola High School, which goes by the Chieftains. "If there was no pride, you wouldn't be talking about it" (Brewer and Harter, 2006). This issue has been raised many times in Wisconsin since the 1960s, as about twenty-five Wisconsin high schools dropped Indian logos and mascots.

The number of Wisconsin schools using Indian mascots is not known, but the Wisconsin Indian Education Association identified 38 schools that it said make offensive use of Indian names or images, including the Osceola Chieftains and Menominee Indians. "We take a lot of pride in Chief Osceola," said district administrator Roger Kumlien. "We teach a unit in fourth-grade classes on Chief Osceola and how our name came into existence" (Brewer and Harter, 2006). Kumlien said that across the nation, 2 mountains, 1 national park, 3 counties, and 20 towns are named after Osceola. "In 1996, [our logo] was more of a headdress. We wondered if it should be this or should it be the actual face of Chief Osceola," Kumlien said. School officials asked the head of the Creek Indian Council about the matter, and Kumlien had a council artist design a new logo for the school. The logo updated the generic headdress by dropping the feathers, updating the profile and adding an arrow and tomahawk. "It's kind of unique," Kumlien said. "We embraced it and put it up everywhere. It's on our sign on the highway, it's on our letterhead, our clothing" (Brewer and Harter, 2006).

David Driscoll, a curator at the Wisconsin Historical Society who has written about the use of Indian mascots in the state, said the fundamental issue for mascot opponents is identity and who controls it. Opponents contend that the use of the names, or racist or cartoonish mascots, is an example of the dominant white culture defining Native culture without Native communities' consent. "Until a deeper understanding of white privilege prevails among the majority of Wisconsin residents, this issue is likely to remain controversial and bitterly contested," Driscoll wrote (Brewer and Harter, 2006).

It has been years since Step-n-Fetchit was sent packing to the racial-stereotype graveyard. It likewise has been a couple of decades since Frito-Lay discarded its Frito Bandito. Yet during the third Christian millennium, we find ourselves arguing over whether professional athletes should wear the likeness of Chief Wahoo and whether fans who generally believe themselves to be decent people should regret doing the Tomahawk Chop.

"SQUAWBLES"

The battle over names was not restricted to the mascots of games, of course. It overflowed into the naming of places and even the labels of liquor bottles. Sometimes, the controversies cross wires. Until 1975, for example, women's sports teams at Bonaventure College in upstate New York were called the Brown Squaws. Men's teams were called the Brown Indians. That year, a Seneca chief and clan mothers visited the college and respectfully requested that the names be changed. Once the faculty, staff, and students learned that *squaw* referred to the vagina, they quickly shed the name. "We almost died of embarrassment," one former Bonaventure woman told Suzan Shown Harjo of *Indian Country Today*. "Of course, we stopped using it immediately" (Harjo, 2005, 170).

In 1995, the state of Minnesota enacted a legal ban on the use of the word *squaw* in geographic place-names for lakes, streams, and points, agreeing with two Chippewa high school students on the Leech Lake Reservation that the word is degrading to Native American women. The state law was overwhelmingly approved by the state legislature and signed by Gov. Arne Carlson. A debate has since developed that the Associated Press, with a straight journalistic face, called a "squawble." The state also was working to ban Indian-themed sports mascots. Fifty school districts at one time had Indian names and mascots in that state, but the remaining schools using such images had fallen to eight by 2006. Of those, three (Mahnomen, Red Lake, and Warroad) have large Indian populations (Brewer and Harter, 2006).

Squaw Lake (St. Louis County, Minnesota) became Nokomis Lake Pond in county and state records; the specific term is Ojibwa for "grandmother," well-known from Longfellow's poem "The Song of Hiawatha" (Bright, n.d.). Squaw Point became Oak Point, and Squaw Creek became Fond-du-lac. Squaw Pond became Scout Camp Pond.

POLITICALLY CORRECT CREEK?

In Minnesota's Lake County, a swatch of forest, streams, and lakes with 10,000 residents that reaches the shores of western Lake Superior near the Canadian border, non-Indian residents suggested that their Squaw Creek and Squaw Bay be changed to Politically Correct Creek and Politically Correct Bay. The state rejected Lake County's proposal, which arrived with a letter from Sharon Hahn, head of the Lake County Board of Commissioners, who wrote, "The term 'squaw' is in common use throughout North America, far beyond its Algonquian origin." "We find nothing derogatory in continued use of this term." Local Indians said that the county's attitude is arrogant and disrespectful; Larry Aitken, a Chippewa tribal historian, says, "It's equivalent to having the New York Mets called the New York Jews" (Bright, n.d.).

Muriel Charwood Litzau, a Native American who is a resident of Squaw Lake as well as the Leech Lake Reservation, loathes the S-word so much that she does not want to tell people where she lives. She says that *Squaw* is a French corruption of an Iroquois (possibly Mohawk) word for "vagina."

Her daughter, Dawn Litzau, and another student, Angelene Losh, began the campaign to illegalize *Squaw* as a geographic place-name in Minnesota as part of a Native American studies class at Cass Lake-Bena High School, a public school within the Leech Lake Reservation. Students of the school's Name Change Committee also met with students at the Pequot Lakes High School in northern Minnesota and persuaded the student body to change its Indian mascot.

County officials in Lake County refused to change names as required by the state, citing standard dictionary definitions that define *squaw* as "Indian woman" (generically) as well as the expense of making the changes on signs and maps. Indeed, the 1983 edition of *Webster's New Universal Unabridged Dictionary* defines *squaw* as (1) an American Indian woman or wife and (2) any woman, chiefly humorous. Some dictionaries attribute the word to *squáas,* in an Algonquian language (Massachuset, Natick, or Narraganset) and add that it is a derogatory word for women of any race or ethnic group. Unabridged dictionaries also sometimes list several derivations, such as *squaw winter,* said to be a spell of unusually cold and stormy weather before Indian summer.

In *Literature of the American Indian* (1973), edited by Thomas E. Sanders and Walter W. Peek, however, *Squaw* is said to be a French corruption of the supposedly Iroquois word *otiska,* referring to female private parts. Which Iroquois language is involved here is not addressed. The phrase was probably carried into the north woods of Minnesota (and the rest of Anglo-American culture) by French fur trappers, later to be anglicized by English-speaking colonists. According to the *Thesaurus of American Slang* (1989), edited by Ester and Albert A. Lewis, the word *squaw* has been used as a synonym for "prostitute." The *Associated Press Stylebook,* the most widely used guide for grammar and style in the newspaper industry, says that *squaw* may be disparaging and should be avoided.

FREEDOM OF NOMENCLATURE

Local residents in the United States may call places anything they wish. Assignment of names to natural features, however, notably specifically federal documents such as topographic maps published by of the U.S. Geological Survey, requires approval by the U.S. Board on Geographic Names. This body has changed words considered offensive; in 1967 it directed that 143 place-names with *Nigger* should be changed to *Negro,* and 26 place-names with the word *Jap* should be switched to *Japanese* (Schmitt, 1996, A-16). The board presently has a policy to consider "squaw" names on a case-by-case basis, as requested by local authorities, such as state naming boards.

According to the Board on Geographic Names, the word *squaw* at one time or another has been affixed to 1,050 geographic names in the United States, most of them in the West and Midwest. In California, for example, a request has been filed with the survey board to change the name Squaw Gulch, in Siskiyou County, to Taritsi Gulch. Also in California, questions are being raised about the name of the Squaw Valley ski resort. Activists in Arizona and Oregon (with about 170 place-names that include *Squaw*) were taking up the refrain, advocating state laws similar to Minnesota's. According to the U.S. Board on Geographic Names, Oregon has more rivers, buttes, meadows, mountains, and gulches named *Squaw* than any other state—170 out of 893 in the United States.

MORE "SQUAWBLES"

By 2005, the movement to erase "squaw" place-names from maps across the northern and western United States was gaining momentum. Following Minnesota's lead, Oregon had enacted a law ordering changes in such names; Wisconsin was considering a similar law. A proposed state law incited debate in Idaho as well. Jack Jackson, a Navajo (Dineh), was frustrated for the better part of a decade in his campaign to change place-names in Arizona. The Arizona State Board on Geographic and Historic Names voted unanimously to refuse a request from American Indian petitioners that a mountain near Phoenix, named Squaw Peak, be renamed Iron Mountain, its name before 1910 (Bright, n.d.). Montana and Maine also passed similar legislation. In Montana, House Bill 412 passed with little debate or opposition, but greater controversy accompanied the ultimately successful efforts of Passamaquoddy Representative Donald Soctomah in Maine (King, 2003, 1).

Jim Fisher, editor of the *Lewiston* (Idaho) *Morning Tribune,* remarked that "Killing a bad name gives birth to many good ones," following calls by Idaho's Indians and others for removal of the name *Squaw* from local place-names (Fisher, 2005, 3-F). Some opponents of the proposed Idaho law argued that swapping *Squaw* for other names would diminish Idaho's cultural richness, erasing historical color for bland political correctness. "Boy, were they ever wrong," wrote Fisher. "That was made clear to me the other day on reading a story from Oregon about that state's enrichment of its place place-names and subsequent maps by replacing 'squaw' with names that are anything but nondescript, and from tribal languages to boot" (Fisher, 2005, 3-F).

Oregon legislators passed a law requiring name changes in 2001, the same year Idaho legislators defeated a similar ban. In October 2005, the Oregon Geographic Names Board voted to change Coos County's Squaw Island to Qochyax Island, which is pronounced "coke-yaw," said Howard Roy, cultural development coordinator for the Confederated Tribes of Coos, Lower Umpqua, and Siuslaw Indians, who first proposed the name Qochyax Women and Children's Island, historically a place to which local women and children fled to avoid being taken as slaves. The name was considered too long, so it was shortened ("Next Stop," 2005).

Squaw Creek was renamed Whychus Creek. The new name is Sahaptin, one of the three languages of the Warm Springs tribes, meaning "the place we cross the river." But it also has a historic precedent as the name for the stream, recorded in an 1855 railroad survey (Fisher, 2005, 3-F). Other names replace *squaw* with *akawa,* the Wasco word for a female badger.

Some opponents of the name changes argue that Native names would be difficult to pronounce. What then, asked Fisher, of the many unique Native place-names that already distinguish towns, cities, and natural features all over the West? Fisher remarked:

> How many of us Northwesterners have tittered while hearing people from other regions wrestle with marvelous Indian names like "Puyallup"? Not all

Indian names are difficult to learn to pronounce, though. In fact, some of the most mellifluous roll off the tongue with delightful ease. Like Skookum-chuck. Klickitat. Issaquah. As a native Washingtonian, I grew up absorbing Indian names as part of my heritage, which of course they are. When my family would visit Mount Rainier National Park (we Tacomans are still pretty steamed about the peak being renamed from the Indian Tahoma), one woodsy stop was Ohanapecosh. The Nisqually River flows into Commencement Bay today as it did then. In our young married years in Seattle [anglicized from Sea'th'l], my wife and I would visit the Stillaguamish River, still one of my favorite names. We would fish the Skykomish, hike up the Suiattle and, on the Olympic Peninsula, the Quinault. At times, our picnic would include Til-lamook cheese.... Amid all these riches, and more on the way from Oregon and elsewhere, who needs "squaw"? Only a few rednecks, I'd say. "Redneck" is an old Saxon word meaning musically deaf, deliberately dumb and histori-cally blind. (Fisher, 2005, 3-F)

In Oregon, the changing of names proved to be complicated. Of approximately 150 "squaw" place-names, only about 10 had been changed by 2005, as required by the state law passed in 2001, according to Lewis L. McArthur, a member of the Oregon Geographic Names Board and author of *Oregon Geographic Names* (Preusch, 2005, B-1). Having passed its bill, Oregon lawmakers set aside no money and appointed no agency or other group to handle it.

As with sports mascots, many non-Indians professed attachment to names that many Native Americans found to be offensive. Perhaps the most prominent name change in Oregon applied to Squaw Creek, originating in the Three Sis-ters Wilderness and flowing through the town of Sisters and a rimrock canyon before merging with the Deschutes River southwest of Madras. The U.S. Forest Service proposed calling the creek Whychus, derived from the Sahaptin language, meaning "the place we cross the water." A government surveyor in 1855 recorded Whychus as the creek's original name (Preusch, 2005, B-1).

In November 2005, the 15,400 residents of White Settlement, Texas (near Fort Worth), defeated by a margin of 9-to-1 a ballot measure to change the name, with about 2,500 voting. With a town seal that features a church, a factory, and a fighter jet (its main industry is defense contracting), most of the town's residents are no friends of nonwhites and like it that way. The town is in decline, however; even the town's Wal-Mart moved away. White Settlement's population was 85 percent European American in the 2000 census (Romero, 2005).

WHAT DOES SQUAW REALLY MEAN?

Having entertained all the aforementioned thunder attending use of the S-word, come now students of language, some of them Native American women, who contend that the whole debate is linguistically beside the point as well as "pro-foundly Eastern Hemisphere, Indo-Germanic, and, I might add, masculine" (Gunn Allen, 2005). Paula Gunn Allen, writing in Barbara A. Mann's *Daughters of Mother Earth* (2006), presents a compelling case that the politics of "squaw" have been socially defined in our time, that the word original incantation meant simply "woman."

At a Women's Studies Conference at Connecticut State University in October 2001, Gunn Allen writes, "the Plenary Session addressed the issue directly. Abenaki (Algonquin) scholar and writer Marge Bruchac made the point that the word has long been a quite respectable word among various Algonquin dialects, and simply meant 'woman.' In her essay, 'Reclaiming the Word 'Squaw' in the Name of the Ancestors' Bruchac instructs us: first, that 'Squaw is not an English word.' In the first subheading, she assures us that 'Squaw means the totality of being female.' Providing linguistic contextualization, she continues:"

> It *is* a phonetic rendering of an Algonkian word, or morpheme, that does *not* translate to mean any particular part of a woman's anatomy. Within the entire Algonkian family of languages, the root or morpheme, variously spelled "squa," "skwa," "esqua," "kwe," "squeh," "kw" etc. is used to indicate "female," not "female reproductive parts." Variants of the word are still in widespread use among northeastern peoples.... Nipmuc and Narragansett elders use the English form "squaw" in telling traditional stories about women's activities or medicinal plants; when Abenaki people sing the "Birth Song," they address "nuncksquassis," the "little woman baby." The Wampanoag people, who are in the midst of an extensive language reclamation project, affirm that there is no insult, and no implication of a definition referring to female anatomy, in any of the original Algonkian forms of the word. (Bruchac, 1999)

Gunn Allen continued, citing Mohegan tribal historian Melissa Fawcett (Tantaquidgeon) in *The Lasting of the Mohegans: The Story of the Wolf People*:

> Red is the color of women and life.... The Mohegan word for woman is "shquaaw" and red is "squayoh." Blood is referred to as "(um)sque" which also has a related "squ' root. [As does] the name of Granny Squannit, leader of the Makiawisug (Little People of the Woodlands). The root of her name describes her very clearly. "Squa" means woman, blood, red, or of the earth. The root "anit" comes from "manit" or "Manitou," often spelled as "Mundu" in Mohegan-Pequot, which means Spirit. Therefore Granny Squannit's name means "Spirit Woman" and implies a connection to the earth and blood.... Quite literally, women are "the bleeders" through whose blood the tribe renews its life. Red is the color of the earth, hence the notion of "Mother Earth." ... A woman Chief is known as a Sunq-Shquaaw, that is to day, the is the "Rock Woman" of the Tribe; since, the word "Sun[q]" means rock in Mohegan Pequot. (Fawcett, 1995, 35)

Definitions of words change over time, of course, and the question of what *Squaw* meant, to whom, and with what effect remains a subject of lively debate.

CRAZY HORSE MALT LIQUOR: A HAPPY ENDING

The one-time makers of Crazy Horse Malt Liquor, Stroh Brewing Company (as owner of G. Heileman Brewing Company), settled with the estate of Crazy Horse and the Rosebud Sioux Tribe in an agreement that included a public apology and payment of 7 racehorses, 32 Pendleton blankets, 32 braids of tobacco, and 32 bundles of sweet grass to compensate for misuse of Crazy Horse's name to market alcoholic beverages. Crazy Horse's estate and the Crazy Horse Defense Project had pursued an apology and damages in the courts for eight years. The 32 Pendleton blankets symbolized the 32 states in which the malt liquor was distributed, and the 7 horses represented the number of breweries Stroh's owned after it acquired G. Heileman. The apology and compensation were delivered on April 26, 2006 during a three-and-a-half hour late-afternoon ceremony at Sinte Gleska University, in Mission, South Dakota, on the Rosebud Reservation. After Eugene Stroh of the brewery's founding family finished reading a formal apology, he handed a Pendleton blanket and a twist of grass to Seth Big Crow, administrator of the Crazy Horse estate. A drum rumbled "and a standing ovation rolled like a slow wave through the crowd," according to a report in the *Sioux Falls Argus-Leader*. Big Crow held high the letter of apology for all to see. "Oh man, it's a beautiful day," he said ("One Brewing Company," n.d.).

Big Crow said that when Stroh offered traditional gifts to honor the Lakota principle of restoring harmony, "I told him today, you have won the hearts of the ... Sioux Nations." After Big Crow had given away the horses and blankets, Crazy Horse's descendants wrapped a star quilt depicting a horse's head with eagle feathers in the mane around Stroh's shoulders.

"This is a historic victory in the battle to protect the name of Crazy Horse and the cultural property of all tribes," said Phyllis Tousey Frederick of the Crazy Horse Defense Project.

"This settlement recognizes the important role of Tribal Customary Law in protecting indigenous intellectual property and sends a strong message that people cannot just take Indian cultural property and use it without permission" ("One Brewing Company," n.d.).

"While this settlement is cause for celebration we remind everyone that the big battle with Hornell Brewing, and Ferolito, Vultaggio & Sons (the makers of AriZona Iced Tea Products) continues and these defendants are liable for both culturally appropriate and monetary damages," said Frederick. "We must continue to put public pressure on these companies to get them to stop making Crazy Horse Malt Liquor and where possible efforts must be intensified" ("One Brewing Company," n.d.).

FURTHER READING

Allen, Paula Gunn. "Does Euro-think Become Us?" in Barbara Alice Mann, *Daughters of Mother Earth*. Westport, CT: Praeger, 2006, 1–28.

Badwin, Don. "Opposition to Indian Mascots Mounts." Associated Press, November 6, 2000 (in LEXIS).

Banks, Dennis, Laurel R. Davis, Synthia Syndnor Slowikowski, and Lawrence A. Wenner. "Tribal Names and Mascots in Sports." *Journal of Sport and Social Issues* 17 (April 1993): 1–33.

Barrientos, T. "A Chief Beef: Some Teams Still Seem Insensitive to Indians." *Philadelphia Inquirer,* March 16, 2002, n.p.

BeDan, M. "International Eye Drawn to 'Fightin' Whities'; Protest of Mascot for Eaton High School 'Has Kind of Snowballed.'" *Rocky Mountain News,* March 15, 2002: 12-A.

Benedict, Michael. "Protesters Block Traffic along University Avenue." *Grand Forks* (North Dakota) *Herald,* October 7, 2000a, n.p.

Benedict. Michael. "UND: Another Voice; Faculty Group Gives Kupchella Petition Urging Nickname Change." *Grand Forks* (North Dakota) *Herald,* November 9, 2000b, n.p.

Benintende, B. "At Least They Didn't Call Themselves the 'Ragin' Caucasians.'" *La Jolla* (California) *Light,* March 2002, n.p.

Bondy, F. "Intramural Name Pales by Comparison." *New York Daily News,* March 14, 2002: 76.

Boyle, Francis. "The Racist Mascot from Urbana-Champaign: Why You Should Boo Illinois." *CounterPunch.* March 30, 2005. <http://www.counterpunch.org/boyle03302005.html>.

Brewer, John, and Kevin Harter. "Indian Mascots Back in Debate; Schools Still Resisting Request for Change." *St. Paul Pioneer Press,* January 16, 2006: n.p.

Bright, William. "The Sociolinguistics of the 'S-Word': 'Squaw' in American Place Names." Unpublished paper. University of Colorado, n.d.

Bruchac. Marge. "Reclaiming the Word 'Squaw' in the Name of the Ancestors." *NativeWeb.* November 1999. <http://www.nativeweb.org/pages/legal/squaw.html>.

Bulwa, Demian. "Tomahawk Chop the Indian Mascots." *Daily Californian* (University of California–Berkeley), October 20, 1995, n.p.

Calnan, Christopher. "Faculty Votes to Retire Mascot." *Roanoke Times,* November 8, 2000, n.p.

"Campus Scout: The Fighting Whities." *Daily Illini* (University of Illinois–Urbana-Champaign), April 2, 2002, n.p.

Carley, William M. "Is Chief Noc-a-Homa Racist? Many Indians Evidently Think He Is." *Wall Street Journal,* January 27, 1972: n.p.

Connolly, Mark R. "What's in a Name? A Historical Look at Native American–Related Nicknames and Symbols at Three U.S. Universities." *Journal of Higher Education* 71, no. 5 (2000): 515–47.

Cornelius, Coleman. "Fightin' Whites Fund Scholarships: T-Shirt Sales Reap $100,000 for Indians." *Denver Post,* December 1, 2002. <http://groups.yahoo.com/group/NatNews/messages/26247>.

Cowen, Cara, and B. J. Boyd. "'Scalp the Indians' from a[n] American Indian Perspective." *Daily O'Collegian* (Oklahoma State University), September 27, 2005. <http://www.ocolly.com/new_ocollycom/new_site/read_story.php?a_id=27966>.

Darst, K. "Protesters Seeing Red." *Longmont* (Colorado) *Daily Times-Call,* May 20, 2002, n.p.

Davis, Laurel. "Protest against the Use of Native American Mascots: A Challenge to Traditional American Identity." *Journal of Sport and Social Issues* 17, no. 1 (1995): 9–22.

Doclar, Mary. "Protests Cause Reassessment of Dallas Schools' Indian Mascots." *Fort Worth Star-Telegram,* December 5, 1998. <www.aistm.org/1998mascot.articles.htm>.

Else, John F. "Indian Mascot Ban Needn't Be Difficult." *Omaha World-Herald,* December 18, 2005: 9-B.

Fawcett, Melissa Jayne. *The Lasting of the Mohegans. Part I: The Story of the Wolf People.* Uncasville, CT: The Mohegan Tribe, 1995.

"Fighting Whities." *The Geekery: Biased and Unbalanced News.* March 11, 2002. <http:// www.gotthegeek.com/newspro/arc-20020311.shtml>.

"'Fighting Whities' Make a Statement; American Indian Students Try to Raise Awareness of Stereotypes." *Philadelphia Daily News,* March 12, 2002. <www.utpjournals.com/ simile/issue9/JohansenX4.html>.

Fisher, Jim. "Killing a Bad Name Gives Birth to Many Good Ones." *Lewiston* (Idaho) *Morning Tribune,* October 23, 2005: 3-F.

Frueling, Charles, and C. Richard King. "'Playing Indian': Why Native American Mascots Must End." *Chronicle of Higher Education,* November 9, 2001. <www.thepeoplespaths. net/Articles2001/ Springwood-King011109Mascots.htm>.

Garner, J. "'Whities' Mascot about Education, not Retaliation; Intramural Basketball Team Takes Shot at Indian Caricature Used by Eaton High School." *Rocky Mountain News,* March 12, 2002. <www.utpjournals.com/simile/issue9/JohansenX4.html>.

Giago, Tim. "NCAA Mandate Shines Spotlight on Demeaning Indian Mascots." *Omaha World-Herald,* August 22, 2005: 7-B

Good, O. S. "School's Nickname Fuels Fury; American Indians March against 'Reds' Moniker." *Rocky Mountain News,* May 20, 2002. <http://jss.sagepub.com/cgi/content/ abstract/28/1/11>.

GOPUSA, Colorado. "Bringing the Conservative Voice to America." 2002. <http://gopusa. com/colorado/>.

Gormley, Michael. "State Commissioner to Take a Stand on Indian Mascots, Names." *Boston Globe On-line,* October 28, 2000. <http://www.boston.com/dailynews >.

Gugliotta, Guy. "A Linguist's Alternative History of 'Redskin'; Term Did Not Begin as Insult, Smithsonian Scholar Says; Activist Not So Sure. *Washington Post,* October 3, 2005: A-3. <http://www.washingtonpost.com/wp-dyn/content/article/2005/10/02/ AR2005100201139_pf.html>.

Harjo v. Pro-Football, Inc. "Citation: 1999 WL 329721. "The Trademark Trial and Appeals Board, U.S. Patent and Trademark Office." April 2, 1999. <caselaw.findlaw.com/ data2/circs/DC/037162A.pdf>.

Harjo, Suzan Shown. "The N.C.A.A. Is Learning What It's Like to Be Indian." *Indian Country Today,* August 11, 2005: n.p.

Harjo, Suzan Shown. "Respect Indian Women—Stop Using the 'S' Word." *America Is Indian Country.* Ed. Jose Barreiro and Tim Johnson. Golden, CO: Fulcrum, 2005. 170–72.

Hofmann, Sudie. "The Elimination of Indigenous Mascots, Logos, and Nicknames: Organizing on College Campuses. *American Indian Quarterly* 29, no. 1–2 (Spring 2005): 156–77.

"Indian Mascots: An Idea Whose Time Has Passed." Editorial. *Asheville* (North Carolina) *Citizen-Times,* September 30, 2000. <http://www.main.nc.us/wncceib/ PeweACT9300editorial.htm>.

Johansen, Bruce E. "Mascots: Honor Be Thy Name." *Native Americas* 18, no. 1 (Spring 2001): 58–61.

Johansen, Bruce E. "Putting the Moccasin on the Other Foot: A Media History of the Fighting Whities." *Studies in Media and Information Literacy Education* 3, no. 1 (2003). <www.utpjournals.com/simile/issue9/JohansenX1.html>.

Johansen, Bruce E. "'Squawbles' in Minnesota." *Native Americas* 13, no. 4 (Winter 1996): 4.

King, C. Richard. "Borrowing Power: Racial Metaphors and Pseudo-Indian Mascots." *The New Centennial Review* 4, no. 1 (Spring 2004): 189–209.

King, C. Richard. "Defensive Dialogues: Native American Mascots, Anti-Indianism, and Educational Institutions." *Studies in Media and Information Literacy Education* 2 (2002). <www.utpjournals.com/simile/issue5/king1.html>.

King, C. Richard. "De/Scribing Squ*w: Indigenous Women and Imperial Idioms in the United States." *American Indian Culture and Research Journal* 27, no. 2 (2003): 1–16.

King. C. Richard. "It's a White Man's Game: Racism, Native American Mascots, and the NCAA." *Popmatters.* September 29, 2005. <http://www.popmatters.com/sports/features/050929-sportsmascots.shtml>.

King, C. Richard, and Charles F. Springwood. *Beyond the Cheers: Race as Spectacle in College Sports.* Albany: State University of New York Press, 2001a.

King, C. Richard, and Charles F. Springwood, eds. *Team Spirits: Essays on the History and Significance of Native American Mascots.* Lincoln: University of Nebraska Press, 2001b.

King, C. Richard, Ellen J. Staurowsky, Lawrence Baca, Laurel Davis, and Cornell Pewewardy. "Of Polls and Race Prejudice: Sports Illustrated's Errant 'Indian Wars.'" *Journal of Sport and Social Issues* 26 (2002): 382–403.

LaDuke, Winona. *Recovering the Sacred: The Power of Naming and Claiming.* Boston: South End Press, 2005.

Lapchick, Richard E. "Hank Aaron Steps Up to the Plate on the Use of Native American Names and Mascots in Sport." Special to the *Sports Business Journal.* Northeastern University Center for Study of Sport in Society. n.d. <www.bus.ucf.edu/sport/cgi-bin/site/ sitew.cgi?page=/news/articles/article_10.htx>.

Ledbetter, J. "Cantankerous Caucasian Fights Back." *Destin* (Florida) *Log,* March 8, 2002, n.p.

Limbaugh, Rush. "The Cutting Edge: Go Whities!!!" March 12, 2002. <www.utpjournals.com/simile/issue9/Johansenfulltext.html>.

Lucas, Phil. "Images of Indians." *Four Winds: The International Forum for Native American Art, Literature, and History,* Autumn 1980: 69–77.

Maxim, B. "Stereotyping of Native Americans: Links and Commentary from My Crypto-Anarcho-Libertarian Perspective." March 17, 2002. <www.utpjournals.com/simile/issue9/JohansenX4.html>.

Migoya, D. "Mascot Foes March into Eaton; Fightin' Reds Protest Given Quiet Response." *Denver Post,* May 20, 2002, n.p.

Millard, H. "Fightin' Whities—Pale Faces Want 'um T-Shirts, Not Blankets." *New Nation News.* 2002. <http://www.newnation.org/Millard/Millard-Fightin-Whities.html>.

Morrison, Clarke. "Education Key to Fighting Negative Ethnic Stereotypes." *Asheville* (North Carolina) *Citizen-Times,* September 26, 2000. <http://www.main.nc.us/wncceib/PeweACT9260.htm>.

"The Motorcycle Company Needed an Indian Sidekick." *Dallas Morning News,* September 26, 1999. <www.indiantrademark.net/t07Media/index.html>.

"Mr. Cranky Rates the Movies: Iris." Comment posted by Mister-Mucus. March 12, 2002. <http://www.mrcranky.com/movies/iris/16/3.html>.

National Education Association. *2000–2001 Resolutions.* n.d. <http://www.racismagainst indians.org/ Resolutions/Resolutions_NEA.htm>.

Nevard, David. "Wahooism in the USA; A Red Socks Journal." n.d. <http://www.utpjournals.com/simile/issue9/JohansenX4.html>.

Newsradio WOOD 1300. "Daily Buzz Results." 2002. <http://www.utpjournals.com/simile/issue9/JohansenX4.html>.

"Next Stop Qochyax Island." Associated Press, October 12, 2005 (in Lexis).

Ochoa, J. "Eaton Calls in Security for Mascot Rally." *Greeley* (Colorado) *Tribune,* May 18, 2002. <http://www.greeleytrib.com/article.php?sid=8641&mode=thread& order=0>.

"One Brewing Company Settles Lawsuit with the Family of Crazy Horse and Rosebud Sioux Tribe." Message from the Estate of T'Sunka Witko. n.d. May 3, 2006. <http:// www.ableza.org/Chorse.html>.

Page, Clarence. "The 'Fighting Whites' Offer Lesson in Cultural Diversity." *Newsday,* March 19, 2002: A-32.

Pomerantz, Gary. "Atlanta Fan's Headdress Ruffles Indian Feathers." *Atlanta Journal-Constitution,* October 21, 1995, n.p.

Preusch, Matthew. "Erasing 'Squaw' from Maps Goes Slowly." NDN News, October 2, 2005, B-1. <http://www.ndnnews.com/October%20NDN%20News.htm>.

Resolution of the North Carolina Commission of Indian Affairs. June 9, 2000. <http:// www.main.nc.us/wncceib/NCCOMMresol.htm>.

Rodriguez, Roberto. "Plotting the Assassination of Little Red Sambo." *Black Issues in Higher Education* 15, no. 8 (1998): 20–24.

Romero, Simon. "A Town with a Provocative Name Says No to Change." *The New York Times,* November 13, 2005. <hnn.us/roundup/entries/18233.html>.

Schmitt, Eric. "Battle Rages over a 5-Letter Four-Letter Word." *The New York Times,* September 4, 1996: A-16.

Spindel, Carol. *Dancing at Halftime: Sports and the Controversy over American Indian Mascots.* New York: New York University Press, 2000.

Spindel, Carol. "Racism and Ignorance." *Inside Higher Education,* August 9, 2005. <http:// www.insidehighered.com/views/2005/08/09/spindle>.

"Team Chooses a White Man as Its Mascot." *Boulder* (Colorado) *Daily Camera,* March 11, 2002, n.p.

"The T. Rex Essay: The Fighting Whities." March 25, 2002. <quinnell.us/sports/essay/ whities.html>.

Vassilaros, D. "Political Correctness Off-base on Mascots." *Pittsburgh Tribune-Review,* March 17, 2002. <http://pittsburghlive.com/x/tribune review/columnists/vassilaros/ s_61645.html>.

Wampum Chronicles Message Board. Fighting Whities. n.d. <www.wampumchronicles. com>.

Wegner, Jonathan. "Honor or Insult?" *Omaha World-Herald,* October 2, 2005: D-1, D-2.

White, R., J. Messner, and C. Cuny. "Fighting Whites: Everythang's Gonna Be All White." *Fighting Whites Home Page.* May 2002. <http://www.cafepress.com/fight-inwhite>.

"'Whities' on the Court; Insult Doesn't Work if Name Doesn't Hurt." Editorial. *Omaha World-Herald,* March 13, 2002: 6-B.

Wise, Tim. "Darken Up, A-Hole: Reflections on Indian Mascots and White Rage." *Counterpunch.* August 10, 2005. <http://www.counterpunch.org/wise08102005. html>.

Wood, Peter. "The Diversity Bowl: No Admittance to the Abusively Named." *National Review,* August 23, 2005. <http://www.nationalreview.com/comment/wood200508230805. asp>.

Woods, Keith. "Nicknames & Mascots: Complicity in Bigotry." *JournalismList.* August 17, 2005.

Comprehensive Index

About the Author

BRUCE E. JOHANSEN is Frederick W. Kayser Research Professor of Communication and Native American Studies at the University of Nebraska at Omaha. He is the author of dozens of books; his publishing efforts are concentrated in Native American studies and in environmental issues.